COMPETITIVE KNOWLEDGE MANAGEMENT

Competitive
KNOWLEDGE MANAGEMENT

Nicholas Bahra

palgrave

First published 2001 by
PALGRAVE
Houndmills, Basingstoke, Hampshire RG21 6XS and
175 Fifth Avenue, New York, N.Y. 10010
Companies and representatives throughout the world

PALGRAVE is the new global academic imprint of
St. Martin's Press LLC Scholarly and Reference Division and
Palgrave Publishers Ltd (formerly Macmillan Press Ltd).

ISBN 0–333–94831–9 hardback

This book is printed on paper suitable for recycling and made from fully managed and sustained forest sources.

A catalogue record for this book is available from the British Library.

Library of Congress Cataloging-in-Publication Data
Bahra, Nicholas.
    Competitive knowledge management / Nicholas Bahra.
        p. cm.
    Includes bibliographical references and index.
    ISBN 0–333–94831–9
        1. Knowledge management. 2. Knowledge management—
    Case studies. I. Title.
HD30.2 .B346 2001
658.4′038—dc21   2001021630

Editing and origination by
Aardvark Editorial, Mendham, Suffolk

10 9 8 7 6 5 4 3 2 1
10 09 08 07 06 05 04 03 02 01

Printed and bound in Great Britain by
Creative Print & Design (Wales), Ebbw Vale

Contents

List of Figures

List of Tables

Acknowledgements

The author has drawn on many sources while writing this book. In particular he and the publishers wish to thank the following for their assistance and permission to quote extensively, or use material adapted, from their works:

CHAPTER 1: Samuel P. Huntingdon, *The Clash of Civilisations and the Remaking of World Order*, Simon & Schuster (1997). Eric Roll, *A History of Economic Thought*, Faber and Faber (1992). CHAPTER 2: Small Business Service, Department of Trade and Industry, UBS Warburg. Alan Burton-Jones, *Knowledge Capitalism* Oxford University Press (1999). Kenichi Ohmae, *The End of the Nation State* HarperCollins (1995). CHAPTER 3: John Knell, *Most Wanted* The Industrial Society (2000). Dr Jim Botkin, *Smart Business*, Simon & Schuster (1999). Laura Empsom, 'Knowledge Management', Mastering Management Series, *Financial Times* (1999). CHAPTER 4: Edward Truch, Henley School of Management. Elliott Masie, The Masie Center. CHAPTER 5: Professor Alexander Kouzmin, Cranfield School of Management. Thomas A. Stewart, *Intellectual Capital*, Doubleday (1997). David J. Skyrme and Debra M. Amidon, *Creating the Knowledge Based Business*, Business Intelligence (1997). Harry Scarbrough and Jackie Swan, *Case Studies in Knowledge Management*, Institute of Personnel and Development (1999). CHAPTER 6: Ikujiro Nonaka and Hirotaka Takeuchi, *The Knowledge Creating Company*, Oxford University Press, (1995). CHAPTER 7: Tom Peters and Robert Waterman, *In Search of Excellence: Lessons from America's Best Run Companies*, (1995). Karin Breu, David Grimshaw and Andrew Myers, *Releasing the Value of Knowledge: A Survey of UK Industry*, (2000). Jean Graef, The Montague Institute (1997). Professor Amin Rajan, *Good Practices in Knowledge Creation and Exchange*, Create (1999). CHAPTER 8: Karin Breu and Geoff Smith, *Selling Knowledge: Making Knowledge Management Mainstream in Today's Connected Enterprise*, *Financial Times*/Cranfield Management Research in Practice Series. CHAPTER 9: Professor Sue Birley, *The Failure of Owner Managed Businesses: The Diagnosis of Accountants and Bankers*, Imperial College, London. Dr Graham Wilson, The Insight Partnership. Chris Argyris, *Teaching Smart People How to Learn*, Harvard Business Review on Knowledge Management (1998). CHAPTER 10: David Barrow at BP Amoco. Dr Karin Breu, 'Europe's Competitive Future in the Knowledge Economy: The Need for a European Contribution to the Emerging Knowledge-based Theory of the Firm', (2001). Professor John Burgoyne, 'What are the implications of the virtualisation of organisations and the emergence of knowledge management for management development'. (2000). CHAPTER 11: Jim Tucker, David Burlison, Mick McLoughlin and Phillip Davidson at KPMG, *Recovery*, the quarterly journal of R3 (the Association of Business Recovery Professionals). CHAPTER 12: David Snowden, 'Storytelling: an old skill in a new context', (2000a). 'The ASHEN model: an enabler of action', (2000b). Thomas A. Stewart, *The Cunning Plots of Leadership*, (1998). CHAPTER 13: Dr Marcus Speh Birkenkrähe at Shell International Finance Limited, *Turtles all the way down and all the way up*, (2001). CHAPTER 14: Professor Prabhu Guptara, *Relationship Marketing*, (1998). Hannah Brown, Managing Director, Kendal Tarrant Worldwide and Karen Hand, Independent Consultant, *Staying Power*, (2001). CHAPTER 15: Seija Kulkki and Mikko Kosonen, *How Tacit Knowledge Explains Organisational Renewal and Growth: The Case of Nokia*, Sage (2001). Steve Kerr at General Electric, Professor Kesav V. Nori at Tata Consultancy Services, Debbie Carlton at The Online Courseware Factory Limited. The Indian Society for Training and Development, *The Brahman (Soul) in Training*, M.B. Athreya (1994).

The author has also received support and assistance from the following organisations, which are also featured in this book as case studies:

- PricewaterHouseCoopers
- Hay Group
- Arthur Andersen
- Firefly Communications
- Department of Trade and Industry
- Chartered Institute of Personnel and Development
- Wolff-Olins
- Intellectual Capital Services
- Pearn Kandola
- McKinsey & Company
- Cable & Wireless
- BBC
- Ernst & Young
- Burson-Marsteller

In addition the author would like to thank Aardvark Editorial for their services, Stephen Rutt, publishing director at Palgrave, Professor Eric Frank for suggesting this project, plus his family and friends for their support, encouragement and patience.

Introduction

Something is happening in the world of business. This event has been developing for the last 25 years and has gathered momentum during the last nine. This activity has managed to influence governments, international business professionals, consultants, academics and respected writers. This event is real, it is happening now and it is not going to go away. It is the knowledge economy.

As you read this book, you will encounter original case studies from leading experts at Shell International, McKinsey & Company and the BBC. You will read accounts and testimonies from specialists working for the largest professional services firm in the world (PricewaterhouseCoopers) and from BP Amoco, the number one company on the UK stock market.

You will read about Nokia, the company that *Fortune* magazine lists as number eight in their all-star global most admired list, and gain a real insight into how this success was not achieved by chance, but by a deliberate set of business interventions and processes. After you have read about how companies have succeeded, you will read about how their success has been acknowledged from an academic viewpoint and substantiated by leading experts.

As your interest grows in this subject, you will realize that the hype surrounding it is not just a sales pitch, but a real and genuine concept that is set to change the way business is conducted. These changes will affect you, your family and your friends. The chances of your life not being affected by what this book has to say are negligible. This means that you will probably need to read this book to understand how the world of business and management is developing if you have any intention of pursuing a professional career in the future. If you choose not to read this book, be aware that the smart individual who sits next to you in your office (you know, the ambitious one) yes, she has read it. And guess what, she has also understood it.

If you think this introduction is a hard sell, you are wrong. This is only the beginning. From now on, every business school in Europe and every company that takes itself seriously will be teaching, promoting, lecturing and developing some level of expertise in this subject, if they have not already done so. This subject is called knowledge management. It is about knowledge and it is about management.

1

Why is knowledge management on the lips of every professional today?

The first reason is because it makes money. There is also documented proof that it saves money. The sums of money are significant, perhaps tens or hundreds of millions of pounds, dollars or euros per year.

The second reason why there has been such an increase in interest surrounding this subject is that it puts technology into perspective. It allows individuals and organizations to develop systems and processes that are meaningful and relevant.

The third and most significant reason that knowledge management is establishing itself as the management discipline of the decade is because it is about people. What is unique about knowledge management is that employees benefit from this business process. They enjoy their work more, they contribute more, they learn more and they understand more.

These are the three reasons you need to read this book. It is about people, it is about money and it is about computers. Economics, information technology, human resource management, plus a dash of marketing management – these are must knows, if you are a business professional, consultant, trainer, director or manager. If you are a student, you will need to read this book, plus about a dozen others that will be recommended throughout this book. Although the knowledge management journey is not an easy one, it will probably be the wisest career investment you have ever made.

Why trust my word as an author? To be honest, I had to research this more thoroughly than anything else I have written. The reason was that I had doubts at first. I had doubts because I thought that knowledge management was just a smart way to sell computers. Then I thought that the message was so unclear that it was as if someone had invented a concept and thought, 'If we say it often enough, then people will buy it'. Then I realized what was happening.

Business schools and management theorists often develop fashionable buzzwords to assist in selling their concepts and courses in a competitive market. Consultancy firms sell expensive solutions and sometimes need to brand these solutions to differentiate services within their portfolio. Let us be clear. There is without doubt an element of this happening within the knowledge management movement, but we need to be clearer than that when there is so much at stake.

Who says that knowledge management is important?

In 1987, the *Harvard Business Review on Knowledge Management* featured essays from some of the most highly respected (and paid) professors, theorists, consultants and business professionals including Ikujiro Nonaka, Peter Drucker, Chris Argyris and John Seely Brown.

In 1995, Ikujiro Nonaka and Hirotaka Takeuchi, both distinguished professors at Hitotsubashi University, Tokyo, wrote *The Knowledge-Creating Company*. In 1997, Johan Roos, Goran Roos, Nicola Carlo Dragonetti and Lief Edvinsson (who pioneered his theories at Skandia, the Swedish insurance company) wrote *Intellectual Capital – Navigating the New Business Landscape*. During the same year, Thomas A. Stewart, the editor at *Fortune* magazine, a respected American business title, produced a book with a similar title, *Intellectual Capital – The New Wealth of Organisations*. This became a best seller.

Today, we are at the point where knowledge management and intellectual capital meet. They are two sides of the same coin and as Robert Reich said, 'In a knowledge-based economy, the new coin of the realm is learning' (quoted in Von Krogh et al., 2000, p. 3). This complex interplay between subjects as diverse as personnel and training, finance and economics, information technology and telecommunications, marketing and brand management is the basis for a new business discipline. It also includes research and development, innovation, trademarks and patents and intellectual ownership. E-commerce and the Internet are also involved, yet they are only a part of the puzzle.

Knowledge management is a puzzle. You take a piece and you connect it to another. You string five pieces together and then you cannot find the piece that fits. Then after careful deliberation, a little persistence, a discussion with half a dozen people you trust, you find it. The entire picture is in front of you – it is a map; it is a piece of beautiful scenery. It is the way business is conducted at the most sophisticated of levels and the way forward for years to come.

How do we know that this is the way forward?

Investment has been high and is set to increase. Ovum was founded in 1985 in the UK and has expanded to a global company with sales of over $30 million. They provide independent analysis and consulting, offering expert advice on IT, telecoms and e-commerce from their offices in

London, Boston, Melbourne and Buenos Aires to over 10,000 senior executives worldwide.

In November 1999, Ovum published a White Paper, 'Knowledge Management: Building the Collaborative Enterprise', written by Madan Sheina. Here is an extract:

> Knowledge management is not a passing fad. Knowledge management addresses important business issues facing modern organisations – issues that concern both their internal adaptation and their relationships to the external world. Leading organisations across a range of vertical sectors recognise that in a 'knowledge-based economy', intellectual capital is now their prime asset. Knowledge management will inevitably be linked with, and will generate, new concepts and technologies. Some will be hailed as superseding knowledge management but, in fact, will represent sub-movements within the broader wave of change covered by that term. (p. 2)

The Ovum White Paper made the following predictions:

> The knowledge management market is evolving rapidly and will continue to gather momentum over the next five years as it becomes a core element of corporate IT strategies. The market for knowledge management software will grow from $515 million in 1999 to $3.5 billion in 2004. In the same period, the knowledge management services market will grow from $2.6 billion to just over $8.8 billion. (p. 2)

This figure of $8.8 billion represents only the IT and services element of knowledge management. In fact, there will be a range of other developments in knowledge management that will not be so easily estimated financially. These relate to personnel, legal, consulting, training and support services, which are vital to the knowledge management market. If these market predictions are correct and we have few reasons to doubt them, can you afford to ignore this subject? As I mentioned before, the person behind you probably will have chosen to learn. Learning will become her or his competitive advantage. In fact, the only real competitive advantage you have in the world of the knowledge economy is to learn more quickly than your competitors.

The style, structure and research method of this book

This is a book about knowledge management written for people at various levels of understanding about this developing subject area. During my research, I interviewed numerous experts at consulting firms, international organizations and academic specialists. All these people were extremely helpful and willing to share their information and knowledge.

Most of the people interviewed, and the papers, books and journals that I read, commented how, in the future, the knowledge worker and the knowledge-based economy will supersede the industrial age. This has been understood for many years, yet it is only now that we are witnessing this evolution on a daily basis.

Therefore, I thought it would be useful in Chapter 1 to outline the old economy and how it has developed into the new economy in Chapter 2. Chapter 3 describes the new work models and notes such issues as work/life balance and shifting patterns of employment. Chapter 4 questions where knowledge management belongs in an organisation. Is it owned by finance, IT, HR or marketing? Chapter 5 develops arguments surrounding the differences between knowledge management and intellectual capital along with the relationship of these concepts to the learning organization.

Chapter 6 explores the work of Nonaka and Takeuchi and knowledge creation and sharing. It also provides a description of tacit and explicit knowledge and how different modes within an organization can facilitate these processes. Chapter 7 is about management and measurement. It provides examples from a study conducted at Cranfield School of Management depicting achieved versus potential business benefits and also a self-assessment toolkit to measure systems, values and behaviours, supplied by Professor Amin Rajan.

Chapter 8 helps you to recognize success. It mentions the role of 360 degree appraisals and benchmarking best practice in knowledge creation. Chapter 9 provides guidance on how to avoid failure. One of the examples used is Boo.com; however, Professor Sue Birley's study depicting owner-manager failures is equally relevant. The role of innovation is covered, with examples from 3M.

Chapter 10 gives guidance on how to maintain market position with BP Amoco (the largest industrial merger in corporate history) being the first example. There is also a description of the work of Professor John Burgoyne from Lancaster University and how he introduces possibly the most important concept – wisdom. Also Dr Karin Breu, from Cranfield

School of Management, puts forward an argument for European-level knowledge management research.

Chapter 11 provides advice relating to crisis management and advice from KPMG's e-structuring team. They describe how insolvency is usually different within a new economy firm and describe strategies to employ should it all go wrong.

Chapter 12 explores the area of storytelling. This concept is useful for leaders and managers and a description of the ASHEN model used by IBM is featured. Chapter 13 looks at the future of knowledge management and features input from Dr Marcus Speh Birkenkrähe at Shell International. Chapter 14 features an insight from Professor Prahbu Guptara at UBS Warburg and also some observations from Kendall Tarrant Worldwide. Chapter 15 features the work of Mikko Kasonen at Nokia and information relating to corporate universities.

At the end of each chapter, there are one or two case studies. These case studies are edited transcripts of one-to-one interviews held at the offices of the interviewee during the summer of 2000. The interviewer was myself, Nicholas Bahra. There were also numerous other telephone interviews and discussions with people from various European countries and America.

1 The Old Economy

As you commence your journey of discovery into the world of knowledge management, there are a few principles that I wish to establish. First, I do not purport to understand or promote any particular religious belief or science. Second, if this sounds like a disclaimer, you are correct. Writing this book has reinforced my belief that no one person has absolute knowledge and to suggest that there is a superior knowledge is complex and difficult to prove.

Every civilization develops people to become knowledgeable, however, how this knowledge is used is important. Nitin Sawhney, winner of the Mercury Music Prize in 1999, writes on the back of his 1999 CD *Naked Skin:*

> This is an album with a time span that runs backwards – it begins with the Indian Prime Minister – Vajpayee – proudly announcing the testing of 3 nuclear bombs on Indian soil. Vajpayee is the leader of the BJP – the 'Hindu fundamentalist' party. These tests first took place in 1998. In 1945, two years before the independence of India, Oppenheimer, creator of the atomic bomb, witnessed the first test of his creation. Afterwards he quoted from the *Bhagavad Gita* – the Hindu 'Bible' – in condemnation of his own creation. His quote ends the album. He quotes Vishnu saying 'Now I am become death, the destroyer of worlds' as he breaks down in tears.

President Bush had a little bad luck prior to his election victory in 2000. In a television interview, he could not remember the name of the prime minister of India, a country with a population of over 900 million, around three times the size of America, a country where size matters. Are the souls of the Indians equal in value to the souls of the Americans, or the Chinese or the Russians, or even Englishmen and women?

As globalization has established itself in the dialogue of business and politics, I feel it is important to point out the obvious. If you speak with your professional colleagues, some of them would agree that politicians have lost some of their political power to corporations. Some international businesses have a turnover larger than some countries. 'America Online, one of the world's largest Internet companies merged with Time Warner, the media group, yesterday to create a business worth an estimated \$350 billion [£220 billion] – the biggest deal in the world by three times', wrote Chris Ayres and Adam Jones in *The Times* (2000). At the time, \$350 billion (US) was the equivalent to the GDP (gross domestic product) of India (\$357.4 billion), the fifteenth highest in the world. It was more than the combined GDPs of Hungary, Ukraine, the Czech Republic, New Zealand, Peru and Pakistan.

If you ask your local king, queen or emperor, my impertinent guess is that they might agree with the following statement: 'You cannot have authority without responsibility'. Half the world's wealth moves around the top 500 corporations. I have nothing against wealth. I believe that all forms of richness, be they monetary, intellectual or health, can be positive. Let me explain why you need to read this book.

Thomas A. Stewart, the editor at *Fortune* magazine, wrote the best-selling book, *Intellectual Capital* (1997). In it he writes:

> Information and knowledge are the thermonuclear competitive weapons of our time. Knowledge is more valuable and more powerful than natural resources, big factories or fat bankrolls. (p. ix)

If you are an ambitious professional, you will need to understand the world wherein you work, which means, at the very least, an appreciation of international politics and business. If you are not ambitious and would like to keep your job or stay employed, you will need to know how to serve your ambitious boss to the best of your ability. Those who learn will gain competitive advantage. It is the one area that could make a difference between staying in business or not.

I have great respect for the German people and understand that they must be extremely bored with the following example, but please bear with me for a moment. An American medical doctor, Fritz Redlich (2000), has put up a pretty convincing case that Adolf Hitler was insane. The classic line we remember about Hitler's staff is that 'they were only following orders'.

If you are an employee, my contention is that you must take some social responsibility for what you and your employers do. Whether the issue is the environment, biological warfare, food safety standards or the psychological health of your co-workers, to ignore these in the future will probably be considered as you reneging on your responsibilities as a corporate citizen.

I am not arguing for the third way. I believe that no individual has all the answers but raw capitalism is not good enough for this planet and neither is extreme communism. If people die from market failure, the media glosses over it and tries to put an acceptable face on our actions. This is dishonest and protects us from learning about our mistakes. It breeds denial. If people decide not to behave as the majority, supporting their co-workers and friends in a spirit of solidarity, this is considered to be disloyal. This can be peer pressure at its worst and covertly manipulates people's individual freedom of thought.

My solution is that balance is needed. Balance between sensitive and intelligent state intervention when necessary, with a private sector that flourishes and provides excitement, interest and progress, along with freedom of intellectual thought, ideals and behaviour to the degree that a society can reasonably tolerate.

We know that utopia is probably elusive, however, if we give up trying to create it we are letting down ourselves and future generations. Responsible knowledge management is a corporate issue, a governmental issue and an individual issue. To understand how we are arriving at the new economy we need to explore the old.

Samuel P. Huntingdon, in his book *The Clash of Civilisations and the Remaking of World Order* (1997), describes 'The World of Civilisations – Post 1990'. He divides the world into the following groups:

- Western
- Latin American
- African
- Islamic
- Sinic
- Hindu
- Orthodox
- Buddhist
- Japanese.

He notes that during the 1970s and 80s 'over thirty countries shifted from authoritarian to democratic political systems' (p. 26). He believes that, 'economic development was undoubtedly the major underlying factor generating these political changes'. Huntingdon also noted the changes in world gross economic product during a 42-year period (Table 1.1).

As the business world develops into a more global environment, there are some important questions to be addressed relating to international education and training. Although I do not have the time or space in this volume to answer many of these questions, I hope that my work in the future will allow me to answer them in more than a superficial fashion.

Competitive Knowledge Management

Table 1.1 Civilization shares of world gross economic product, 1950–92

Year	Western	African	Sinic	Hindu	Islamic	Japanese	Latin American	Orthodox	Other
1950	64.1	0.2	3.3	3.8	2.9	3.1	5.6	16.0	1.0
1970	53.4	1.7	4.8	3.0	4.6	7.8	6.2	17.4	1.1
1980	48.6	2.0	6.4	2.7	6.3	8.5	7.7	16.4	1.4
1992	48.9	2.1	10.0	3.5	11.0	8.0	8.3	6.2	2.0

Note: The Orthodox estimate for 1992 includes the former USSR and the former Yugoslavia. Other includes other civilizations and rounding error.

Source: Huntingdon, S.P. (1997) *The Clash of Civilisations and the Remaking of World Order*, London, Simon & Schuster

Some of these questions have been raised and perhaps answered by others. Kevin Barham and Claudia Heimer, authors of *ABB, The Dancing Giant* (1998) note that this company is 'going with the shift in the world's economic centre of gravity', that is, towards Asia.

Kenichi Ohmae, author of *The Invisible Continent* (2000) notes the 'Rise of the Region-State' and how 'economic boundaries drift and change far more rapidly than national boundaries'. Questions of nationalism and economic prosperity are being considered also by the European Union (EU) as it looks towards possible enlargement.

Critical to these questions are education and training. In November 2000, Juhani Lonnroth, the European Commission's Director of Employment said: 'In the US, 34 per cent of adults between 25 and 64 years of age participated in training at the workplace during the year, whereas the figure for Europe was only 19 per cent.' He added: 'We know that, within ten years, 80 per cent of the technology in use today will be outdated. At the same time, only 20 per cent of the labour force will possess the degree of knowledge and skills required to master the new technology if nothing is done to upgrade these skills' (quoted in Taylor, 2000).

Ageism is also on the agenda. Anna Diamantopoulou, the European Commissioner for Employment and Social Affairs, commented in November 2000 that older employees have a significant role to play in the workplace. 'There is a continuing tendency for men and women over the age of 55 to take early retirement, despite the clear demographic evidence that much greater use will need to be made of older workers – we face a reduction of about 12 million potential workers in the 20–40 age group over the next few years' (quoted in Taylor, 2000).

One theme that recurs throughout this book and was mentioned by virtually everyone that I interviewed or discussed the topic of knowledge management with is culture. Many people use this term in an organizational sense, however, for some its meaning is broader and certainly it could be necessary for us to understand what this means at a much deeper level than is currently the case.

There has been interesting cross-cultural research published by Hofstede, Hall, Hampden-Turner and Trompenaars, yet, for some reason, I believe we have only scratched the surface of what is an extremely deep and complex subject. Wendy Lord, an Oxford-based chartered psychologist, is currently investigating research into this area. For a few years I have been planning to write on this subject area and my working theme has been 'The psychological processes of intercultural sensitivity in a working environment', or, put more succinctly, 'How international teams succeed'.

On an individual level, the question of identity will become more important as this century unfolds. Social exclusion and identity are already on the agenda at the EU and there are interesting predictions as to how many languages and people will disappear during the next 50 years. There are also interesting predictions relating to population change and one estimate by the United Nations suggests that about one third of the population of Eastern Europe will disappear during the next five decades. This will be due to a low fertility rate and an exodus from the territory due to a lack of economic prospects (Doole, 2000).

Questions that must be answered soon are whether and when the Indian rupee and the Chinese yuan will become convertible and tradable in world economic markets. Will we develop new currencies such as the cyberdollar?

In the autumn of 2000, *The Money Programme*, a BBC television production, put forward compelling arguments from leading experts suggesting that after 2005 the world supply of oil will rapidly diminish. The predictions from some of those interviewed were astounding. Expert geologists and scientists, who had over 30 years' experience with multinational oil companies, were predicting international dispute, war, famine and drought causing world chaos, as a result of an impending world energy crisis. Is knowledge management about managing the knowledge we have about future predictions and devising strategies to avoid such disasters? Problem avoidance is preferable, as prevention is better than cure.

We are constantly reminded that history repeats itself. Before examining the present, or attempting to look into the future, we need to look at the past – the old economy.

A brief history of economic thought

Of everything which we possess there are two uses: both belonging to the thing as such, but not in the same manner, for one is the proper, and the other is the improper or secondary use of it. For example, a shoe is used for wear, and it is used for exchange; both are uses of the shoe. (Aristotle, quoted in Roll, 1992, p. 21)

So, there are two uses for a sandal: you can wear it, or you can barter with it.

Plato's most famous student was writing at a time when Greece was experiencing change. He was not of aristocratic origin and he developed theories associated with finance and human resource management. According to Eric Roll (1992, p. 21), 'his analytical ideas can be summarised under three headings:

a   The definition of the scope of economics

b   The analysis of exchange

c   The theory of money.'

In terms of human resource management thinking, he was fairly straightforward. Roll suggested that Aristotle retained both reason and benevolence as he thought the state was divided into rulers and the ruled. The rulers were:

■ The military class
■ The statesmen
■ The magistrates
■ The priesthoods.

Age, for Aristotle, was the determinate in terms of job specification; men were soldiers when young and strong, statesmen in the prime of life and priests in old age. The ruled were the 'farmers, craftsmen and labourers' (p. 21). Trade was an unnatural occupation and although Aristotle was prepared to tolerate trade to some extent, he also thought that some people were slaves by nature and that slaves should be recruited from non-Hellenic origin.

For Aristotle, the economy proper was the science of household management and the other component of economy was the science of supply. This was concerned with the art of acquisition. 'The science of supply' was the term used for what we now consider to be capitalism.

Various thoughts of both Aristotle and his teacher Plato have been researched and refined over many years. One contribution to the economic debate from Aristotle is that of a real analysis of exchange value. His work was concerned with how to value commodities that were exchanged, for example how many shoes was a house worth. Presumably, he had to work out how many labourers toiled night and day to create a house and how many to create the shoes.

Later, the Roman Empire developed from a number of small agricultural communities, with 'a rigid division of social classes' (p. 25), to a different style of economy. Initially it had very little trade and then a wealth of natural resources (along with favourable geographical conditions) assisted the Romans through the process of colonization to solve the problem of impoverished farmers. Naturally, the social structure was becoming more complex and, although growth and transition of this empire was less turbulent than Greece, it was not without its conflicts. According to Roll (1992, p. 25): 'The wars and conquests which extended the power of Rome were accompanied by serious economic dislocation and an intensified opposition of interests between poor and rich.'

The small farmer endured increased tax burdens. These taxes benefited the large landowners, moneylenders and merchants. This created a new wealthy class of people. They could profit from the economic activity of war and the inevitable consequence of reconstruction. As Roll (p. 25) puts it: 'Soon, however, the establishment of the empire and the consequent consolidation of administration and finance led to a period of prosperity which made it possible to lighten the tax burden and to quieten discontent by bread and circuses.'

The Greeks and the Romans had some fundamental differences in their beliefs, values and attitudes. During these times there were important developments in perception and also attitudes to the concept of slavery. Greek philosophers tended to justify slavery repeatedly. The Romans suggested that slavery was an uneconomical form of labour. The other significant difference seems to be the way that Aristotle viewed property. His ethical thinking wanted to limit the rights of property. The Roman view was unrestricted individualism. Aristotle became *the* philosopher of the Middle Ages and one of the sources of canon law, but it is Roman law that serves as an important basis for the legal doctrines and institutions of capitalism.

In medieval times, the early fathers developed the theory of the 'just price'. Yet it was not until the eighteenth century that a positive theory of value was developed in the Western world. For some writers and commentators, mercantilist theories appeared in a crude form towards the end of the fourteenth and fifteenth centuries. Some writers suggest that a distinction must be drawn between bullionism, which existed during the later part of the Middle Ages, and mercantilism itself, which appeared during the seventeenth century.

Schmoller identified mercantilism with state making (Roll, 1992, p. 49). Heckscher regarded mercantilism as '"a phase in the history of economic policy" which contains a number of economic measures designed to secure political unification and national power' (quoted in Roll, 1992, p. 49). 'The building-up of nation-states is put in the forefront, and monetary, protectionist, and other economic devices are regarded merely as instruments to this end. State intervention was an essential part of mercantilist doctrine' (p. 49).

Whatever the academic debates surrounding mercantilism, it is conceded by most that 'mercantilist capitalism preceded and prepared the ground for modern industrial capitalism' (p. 51). Industrial capitalism viewed the state and its intervention as a 'serious hindrance to its own development' (p. 51). The Middle Ages in England are generally considered to be a period of around 1000 years starting from the fall of the Roman Empire. Its span is acknowledged as this period: 450–1450 AD. For some, the Middle Ages was a period of economic stagnation. This was possibly set in the context that later economic progress was dynamic by comparison and looking backwards events looked a little slow, if not stationary.

The decline of the Roman Empire also coincided with changes in the distribution of land ownership. There was an increasing tendency to place administrative power in the hands of landlords, which led to the development of new estates and economic and political units. According to Roll (p. 31), there were two underlying principles that unified medieval society. First, the 'principle of division' was deemed to be the very foundation of society. This meant that the 'worldly inequality of men' (p. 31) was accepted without question. Second, the individual's place and position in society was regulated 'according to status'. This included his (and presumably her) place in society, the individual's duties and the privileges enjoyed by that person. These duties were clearly defined in association with the state and its political features.

Prior to this, there was an understanding of the organic community of the tribe, which operated with a spirit of cooperation and equality. It seems from a number of historical perspectives that this tribal community was replaced by a much more brutal regime. Eric Roll again comments upon group loyalties and suggests that later they 'were merely more numerous and more variegated and were exacted by means of brutal coercion' (p. 32). There was also a second, but by no means less important, socially unifying principle and that is the role of the Church, which is clearly related geographically within a European context.

The increasing institutionalization of the Church occurred after the fall of Rome. This had a direct effect upon the material and spiritual power of the Church. The Church was, in the Middle Ages, one of the most important pillars of the economic structure. This had a great impact upon feudal society, which at this point enjoyed a harmony with the Church as a consequence of the combination of secular and spiritual power. As Roll writes (1992, p. 32): 'It is this harmony which explains why the Church could claim to order the whole of human relations and conduct on the earth as well as to provide the precepts which would lead to spiritual salvation.'

Naturally, there were competing views and opinions and Saint Augustine's view that trade turned men from the search for God was also supported by the views of Tertullian who argued that to 'remove covetousness was to remove the reason for gain and, therefore, the need for trade' (Roll, 1992, p. 33).

As towns prospered and grew in economic activity, the Church could not impose its views upon the populace so easily and one of the most widely respected and well-known theologians, Saint Thomas Aquinas, was purported to have 'a distinct tendency to reconcile theological dogma with the existing conditions of economic life' (Roll, 1992, p. 33).

As there was a direct linkage between Christian teachings and morality, ethics and economic principles, it also was the case that the medieval world found it difficult to separate its ethics from its *raison d'être*. Therefore it combined teachings of the Gospels and the early Christian Fathers with those of Aristotle. Aristotle 'had tempered his realistic views of the economic process with ethical postulates' (Roll, 1992, p. 32). The canonists accepted the distinction put forward by Aristotle that there was a natural economy within the household and also an unnatural form or science of supply which was money making. To them the concept of economics represented a body of laws, not in the scientific sense, but rather in the context of 'moral precepts' which were specifically 'designed to ensure the good administration of economic activity' (Roll, 1992, p. 32).

Therefore, according to Roll, the part of economics, which was in practice very much akin to that laid down by Aristotle, rested on a foundation of Christian theology. So it appears totally connected – money, politics and religion.

We also know that the 'Gospels and the Fathers leave an impression which is clear and precise relating to the opposition of worldly goods. Christ often condemned the search for riches' (p. 32).

Another contemporaneous area of debate during the Middle Ages was the notion of the 'just price'. Early economic thought suggested that profit derived from trade was simply a reward for labour. To actually justify trade later was partly dependent upon whether the exchange itself was just. Was what was given and actually received of equal value? In Saint Augustine's example of the honest buyer, he says that 'although the vendor was ignorant of the value of the manuscript he sold, the buyer paid the just price' (Roll, 1992, p. 34).

For Alburtus Magnus, Saint Thomas Aquinas and many others, the cost of production was determined on the principle of justice. Above all, it was designed to prevent enrichment by means of trade. Civil law, with its Roman foundations and the natural instincts of man, seemed to encourage men to sell goods for more than they were worth. Saint Thomas argued that this practice of selling goods for more than they were worth was against divine law. In his opinion, divine law was superior to man-made law – 'the common instinct of man often led to vice. Trade, therefore, could only be justified if it was designed to further the common weal; it must ensure an equal advantage to both parties' (p. 34).

Trade in medieval times was rather haphazard due to the constraints of transportation and problems relating to communications; therefore to ensure that a steady supply of goods and services would be available, it was necessary to enforce rules. These 'rules against forestalling, regrating, engrossing and the fixing of maximum prices were common features of legislation and guild regulation' (p. 35). As the amount of trade increased, an interesting change was noted within the Church, that of a gradual retreat, suggesting that profit from trade was unacceptable. This position always had some degree of flexibility surrounding it and 'Saint Thomas had permitted oscillations round the "just price" according to some market fluctuations' (p. 35). For example, he had justified the taking of a higher price where the seller could have incurred a loss.

Roll also mentions that later writers introduced various rules and qualifications. 'The cost of transporting goods to market, miscalculation, and differences in the status of the participants in exchange become valid reasons for departing from the "just price". In time, even variations of supply and demand were allowed to affect the market prices'.

Later, according to Roll, in the fifteenth century, Saint Antonio introduced numerous qualifications into the marketplace. This eventually diminished the principle of the just price being established as a direct result of objective force and thus laid the foundations of a more complex process and a beginning was made with the 'recognition of the impersonal forces of the market' (quoted in Roll, 1992, p. 35). With canon dogma in decline, the entire question surrounding the development of economics and the principles that related to usury were in contention. The teachings of Christ on this point, according to Eric Roll, are quite unmistakable.

Although there seem to be various interpretations of the Gospels, they do say that enrichment through the lending of money at interest was then regarded as the very worst form of the pursuit of gain. 'Hebrew law had also prohibited the taking of interest' (p. 35) .

During the Middle Ages, the Church and its prohibition policy only applied to the members of the clergy and this did not have a great effect upon the economy, as there was no developed economy for people to make great investments into and therefore profits to be reaped. The Church received large sums of money as a result of feudal dues paid by lords and kings in kind. Money lending appeared to needy persons to be for the purposes of consumption and the notion of imposing interest was considered to be 'exploitation and oppression of the weak' (p. 36).

So there we have it – the old economy. This style of thinking laid the foundations for the economy that we all know and work with in the West. It developed through the period of industrialization to the end of the millennium. This stage in economic history started in the 1600s and ended 400 years later. The various issues of interest during this journey were the struggle between commercial and industrial capital. The struggle between bullionists and mercantilists was its theoretical expression.

Adam Smith began his celebrated critique of mercantilism (*The Wealth of Nations*) with an attack on the popular notion 'that wealth consists in money, or in gold and silver' (quoted in Roll, 1992, p. 51). Commercial capitalism was a fresh approach, with the circulation of goods as the essence of economic activity.

In 1621, Thomas Mun wrote *A Discourse of Trade from England into the East Indies*. Mun had become a Director of the East India Company in 1615 and the company enjoyed the privilege of exporting £30,000 of bullion on each voyage. This was granted with the understanding that the same amount must be reimported within six months. His book put forward the argument that the East India Company's trade brought in more treasure than all the other trades put together and that he had made it cheap by cutting out the middleman, in this case, Turkey.

So here in this old economy Thomas Mun writes of the importance of trade and how too much wealth in an economy is against the interests of capitalism and the balance of trade. In Mun's words (quoted in Roll, 1992, pp. 65–6):

> For all men do consent that plenty of mony in a Kingdom doth make the natife commodities dearer, which as it is to the profit of some private men in their revenues, so is it directly against the benefit of the Publique in the quantity of the trade; for as plenty of mony makes

wares dearer, so dear wares decline their use and consumption ... And although this is a very hard lesson for some great landed men to learn, yet I am sure it is a true lesson for all the land to observe, lest when wee have gained some store of money by trade wee lose it again by not trading with our money.

So with one Englishman employing 10 men in one of the colonies, for example a West Indian plantation, this would provide work for 4 Englishmen back home to support the 11. New England was a different story. It was not a useful colony as it did not provide work for people in England. Therefore, the value of colonies was linked to their ability to act as exclusive markets for the manufacturers of the mother country. It was their ability to supply raw materials and produce which would normally have to be sourced from other foreign countries. This formed a reservoir of cheap labour.

During the late seventeenth century and early eighteenth century, the foundations of modern industry were being laid. Governments were practising state regulation and all-round protection. Tariffs were created, embargoes were enforced and skilled craftsmen and their tools were prohibited from leaving their countries of origin. Governments actively encouraged the importation of raw materials and the production of these materials domestically. The Navigation Acts strengthened the King's Navy and increased the profit of the mercantilists. The 100 years prior to Adam Smith writing *The Wealth of Nations* (1776) saw the rise of industrial capitalism on a national scale. The mercantilists had served a purpose.

Strong nation states emerged as medieval restrictions were dismantled. These nation states were powerful forces and instruments that fostered and encouraged trade in the new era of industrial capitalism. These new powerful states achieved economic supremacy that could compete with any others in terms of military might and financial power. These forces were centred around two nations – England and France.

The foundations of the new economy are deeply rooted in the old economy and to have some real understanding of its philosophical under-pinning, it might be useful to explore a little more about one of its founding fathers.

Adam Smith was born in 1723, the son of a Scottish advocate and comptroller of customs. Educated at Glasgow and Oxford, he become professor of logic and later professor of moral philosophy at Glasgow. Although he is known for his work, *The Wealth of Nations*, which took many years to complete, his earlier work, *The Theory of Moral Sentiments*

(1759), established his thinking in the 'problems of human conduct'. Smith was apparently influenced by his tutor, Francis Hutcheson, who helped him to develop 'his faith in the "natural order"'.

This philosophical economic underpinning may be traced back to the traditions of the Greek Stoics and Epicureans. According to Roll, 'The naturalist school of philosophy to which he had belonged had an unbroken tradition from the later Greek Stoics and Epicureans onwards. It reappeared in the works of Roman Stoics like Cicero, Seneca, and Epictetus, received an enormous stimulus in the Renaissance and Reformation, showed itself again in a modified form in Bacon, Hobbes, and Locke, and came to full flower in the writings of Smith, the physiocrats, and the later radicals' (quoted in Roll, 1992, p. 126).

This belief system may be interpreted as a single thread of understanding and thought. According to Roll (1992, p. 126): 'It implies a belief in the existence of an inherent natural order (however that may be defined) which is superior to any order artificially created by mankind.'

Human conduct, according to Adam Smith, was 'naturally actuated by six motives'. These were:

1. Self-love
2. Sympathy
3. The desire to be free
4. A sense of propriety
5. A habit of labour and
6. The propensity to truck, barter, and exchange one thing for another (quoted in Roll, 1992, p. 129).

Smith thought that, 'Given these springs of conduct, each man was naturally the best judge of his own interest and should therefore be left free to pursue it in his own way. If left to himself, he would not only attain his best advantage, but would also further the common good' (p. 129).

Smith believed that everyone was obliged to bring the results of their own efforts 'into a common stock, where every man may purchase whatever part of the produce of the other man's talents he has occasion for' (quoted in Roll, p. 131). He also believed in laissez-faire international policies, favouring no barriers to trade, as they could reduce the common profit. If goods could be bought more cheaply overseas than they could be made at home, then the prudent individual would purchase the cheaper. Capital should be allowed to find its way naturally to industries that required it and not encouraged into areas to favour one industry over another, for example agriculture over industry.

This was the underpinning thinking that allowed Adam Smith to influence so many economists, politicians and industrialists into believing that, as each individual pursued his own advantage, they were 'led by an invisible hand to promote an end which was no part of his intention' (quoted in Roll, p. 129).

So, capitalism was clearly a spiritual concept less than 300 years ago in Scotland.

SUMMARY

- Aristotle described two uses for a sandal: you can wear it, or you can barter with it

- Aristotle defined economy proper as the science of household management and the other component of economy was the science of supply

- 'The science of supply' was the term used for capitalism

- Mercantilist capitalism preceded and prepared the ground for modern industrial capitalism

- Industrial capitalism viewed the state and its intervention as a serious hindrance to its development

- The Church in the Middle Ages was one of the most important pillars of economic structure

- Saint Thomas Aquinas and many other thought that trade could only be justified if it was designed to further the common weal; it must ensure an equal advantage to both parties

- According to Adam Smith, human conduct was naturally motivated by self-love, sympathy, the desire to be free, a sense of propriety, a habit of labour, and the propensity to truck, barter and exchange one thing for another

- Smith believed that everyone was obliged to bring the results of their own efforts 'into a common stock, where every man may purchase whatever produce of the other man's talents he has occasion for' (quoted in Roll, p. 131).

Case Study

PricewaterhouseCoopers

TISH ANDREWARTHA *Global Knowledge Director*

Q: What do you do in terms of knowledge management?

A: Three things mainly, the first is based on the need to create new and dynamic e-business platform models for clients.

The second is that as one of the world's largest employers we are recognizing that there is a new model for the way employees work and a lot of that has to do with increasing flexibility, trying to adapt lifestyle changes into the workplace to benefit the employer and employee. Knowledge management systems can be extraordinarily helpful in achieving that, if you think about extracting knowledge or case history information for work assignments and so on that can all be done at home, or while travelling or someplace else outside the office, providing you have the right equipment, the storage systems and the dissemination systems that allow you to do that.

The third, most difficult and least definable key area of knowledge management is the whole area of culture change, figuring out how you reward and stimulate communities to exchange knowledge in an environment where, up until the last couple of years (particularly in management consultancy but also in most of our lines of service), your value as an employee was based on your knowledge, therefore to share that knowledge decreased your value as an employee. We try to change the model to show that if you share your knowledge and empower other people to do things faster and better for clients then that actually makes you a more valuable employee and therefore we have ways to reward you for doing that.

Q: Aren't there cynics that are scared by this sort of approach?

A: There's a great cynicism and it's not only the cynicism that we need to overcome. It's an enormous task to change a culture and remuneration system that is not designed to deal with this. For example, how do you track how much someone's knowledge sharing has increased revenue? We're looking at ways to do this, we have teams trying to find quantifiable ways to measure this. One of our practices spends a lot of time tracking changes through the knowledge repository system we have. If you take the time and effort to create a document on this system and that document is then used by someone else for another piece of client business, we can actually track through all the individuals that touch that piece of knowledge. At the end of the year we can see who has put a lot of information into the system, who has contributed to the knowledge enterprise and then maybe increase that person's bonus or reward them in another way. This is very time consuming but it really is new territory we are covering.

We are very dependent on the available technology and it's not all there yet. Making things even more difficult is the fact that, while this is going on, the world and the working environment are constantly changing so you are having to adapt while still trying to put structures in place.

Q: *So understanding what knowledge is still useful is essential?*

A: This falls partially under the area of content management. Good content management systems, practices and risk-management practices can guard against stale knowledge being used. We've got some very good technical systems and we are now looking at management and people systems to find out how often we need to refresh the knowledge that is there and how to set schedules to remove content. For example, if a document is written three or four times, can we now get rid of the original, is it now in effect a new document, a new piece of knowledge?

Q: *So people can make decisions about individual pieces of knowledge but people can make mistakes. In seven or eight years time you might go back to the knowledge pool and find something was binned that you need, so you have to rely on an employee's memory; we've come full circle?*

A: What you need to guard against this are very good, relevant validation systems for new information depending on the content type, for example an intranet bulletin board has very different content rules than a business repository that looks at case history solutions to particular client problems. There are different vetting procedures for publishing the information and also for the review and removal of the information.

Q: *So this still remains fairly internal judging from the examples you've given?*

A: Well it does and it doesn't. A lot of the content we publish goes out on extranets to clients and we need to have portability of that content depending on whether it is internal or external. Content managers set a number of rules and regulations for all information, internal or external.

Q: *Is knowledge management making an impact here at PWC (PricewaterhouseCoopers)?*

A: Definitely, new knowledge management systems are improving work lifestyle conditions, making it less essential that people sit in an office from nine to five.

Q: *So if knowledge management is making a positive difference to you internally and hopefully to some of your clients, then we can hope that this cascades out and changes the behavioural patterns of other clients?*

A: Absolutely, for example we hope that if we place someone in a client site then through a dial-up portal they can have access to all the systems they would have had if they'd been sitting at their desk at Pricewaterhouse-Coopers. They can be more effective on a local site but with access to all our knowledge.

Q: *Is your knowledge management department everything it claims to be?*

A: I hope so. We have many technological systems but have also undergone a fundamental change in looking at people as knowledge workers and that part of their job is not just doing it but extracting the lessons learnt and the knowledge from a particular assignment and sharing that within the organization.

Q: *That implies that at the end of a job a consultant needs to pause and reflect?*

A: At the end certainly, but also as an ongoing process as part of a review of an assignment. In the future for every assignment undertaken there will be a knowledge worker allocated to it. It is their job to ensure that all the information is harvested – there are systems in place that allow them to do that – and that it is vetted for confidentiality and so on. This gained knowledge is then available all over the world.

Q: *That is very much dependant on people being motivated to access this information. What methods are there to ensure that people are motivated enough to use all this stuff?*

A: Well, in terms of control mechanisms there are none, but there are plenty of reward mechanisms, from peer recognition through to financial, throughout our practices.

Q: *So it's based on trust?*

A: It's ensuring that people know they have to deliver. It's also about setting goals and plans. So far, there has been no problem getting people to do their job. For the most part, people have recognized that they have been able to extract information quicker and faster and that this is a two-way street, if they don't put information in you can't get anything out.

Q: How would PricewaterhouseCoopers use knowledge management to solve some of the problems experienced recently by Marks & Spencer?

A: It's hard to say from a generic perspective. We can look at particular issues and have worked with retailers around the globe solving problems and learning lessons. Consultants can check knowledge repositories to see if similar problems have been faced and solved elsewhere and can then talk to the consultants who have already found solutions. The principle questions asked of knowledge systems are of the type, 'Is there an expert in transfer-taxes in Singapore and how do I find them?' A good knowledge management system should be able not only to answer that but also deliver any documents or material relevant to the question.

Q: That is a big leap forward!

A: It certainly is and requires a lot of the mundane system-building groundwork to get it running. It also requires a lot of content management to ensure that the knowledge is useful. Classification and data structure are critical to being able to pinpoint what you require.

Q: In human resource terms, I think this sort of quantifiable knowledge pool and measurement of who's doing the work is a great guide to promotion and rewards, do you agree?

A: Yes, good knowledge management should enable any employee with the same skill set to be more effective in their work within Pricewaterhouse-Coopers because there is a knowledge structure that surrounds you and makes you better than you could be alone. The same individual in a different company would not be as effective because the knowledge management just isn't there.

Q: There is a school of thought that the smaller niche consultants are gaining the market now, the big six consultants having had their day. Does knowledge management offer a tool against this swing in the market?

A: Yes, knowledge management offers extra support and knowledge at people's fingertips. Even things like multi-language searches increase our effectiveness.

Q: *So there could be more international multi-company support type roles appearing?*

A: Maybe, although things like that can damage intellectual property, which is something we all guard very closely, sharing within a company can be easy (providing there is also sharing in economic interest), it becomes harder between companies.

Q: *Will specialist knowledge managers be more in demand in the future?*

A: I think it would be a lot easier if the term knowledge management disappeared forever.

Q: *Why's that?*

A: Because people don't understand it, they think it's an additional layer of bureaucracy with no cost benefit. There's nothing to my mind that hasn't existed for years before knowledge management, it's just that the technology of the Internet and electronic delivery of product has changed the speed at which we do these things. The concept of lessons learned from other experiences was all done except that it was transferred differently, in training sessions and so on.

Q: *Have you found in the UK that being a woman has worked against you in the male-dominated world of the city?*

A: Not at all, you couldn't pay me enough to go to work in the USA, it's a different story over there, but here I think that men have much less of a problem accepting women as their intellectual equals. There are probably thousands of cases where genuine sexual discrimination has occurred, but I must be lucky, maybe a generation younger and so have missed all that.

2 The New Economy

Figure 2.1 shows a virtual map of the new economy. You can see a similar map of the market updated daily at Smartmoney.com, a site for the private Internet investor. Darkness corresponds to growth in shareholder value and the size corresponds to market capitalization. Note that large parts of the old economy energy and manufacturing companies are lagging behind software and telecommunications new economy companies.

The map can be reordered by introducing two axes (Figure 2.2). These are asset intensity and speed of change. According to Dr Marcus Speh at Shell International: 'The winners of the current economy are those whose assets lie mainly in the area of digital networks, and who constantly operate at a high speed of change.' To really understand the new economy, how we have arrived at this point and what sensible predictions we can make to guide us into the future, we need some idea of recent international historical events in terms of the world's economic development. Therefore, this chapter will focus on some of the economic and social changes that developed between 1850 and 2000 across different continents. Key questions emerge when exploring the concept of knowledge management or intellectual capital in relation to world economies. To place knowledge management into a contemporary context it is useful to establish some general developments in economic history. A report published by the World Bank, 'Workers in an integrating economy', noted one estimate that the average income per head of the richest countries had soared from 11 times that of the poorest in 1870 to 52 times in 1985.

Another report from the United Nations notes that in 1820 the difference between the richest and the poorest countries was a ratio of about three to one. Britain's GDP per capita in that year was around $1,765 (1990 dollars). China in 1820 was one of the world's poorest countries with a GDP per capita of $523. In 1992 things had changed. The USA was the world's richest economy and enjoyed a GDP per capita of $21,558; by contrast Ethiopia's GDP per capita was among the poorest on the planet at $300. A comparison of the ratios is shown in Table 2.1.

Nicholas Bahra is grateful to the DTI Small Business Service for assistance. Some of the material in this chapter is adapted from information supplied by them. Also to The Industrial Society for some of the material adapted from John Knell's report, 'Most Wanted – Quiet Birth of the Free Worker'.

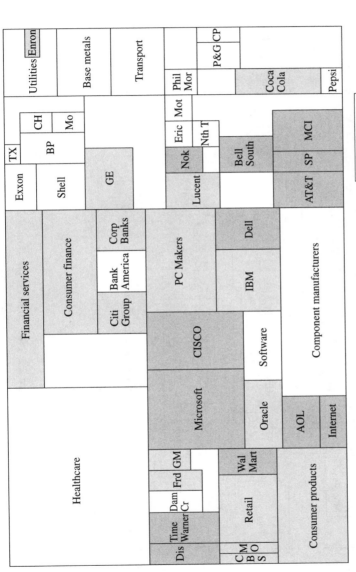

Figure 2.1 A virtual map of the new economy – 2000

Source: Smartmoney.com

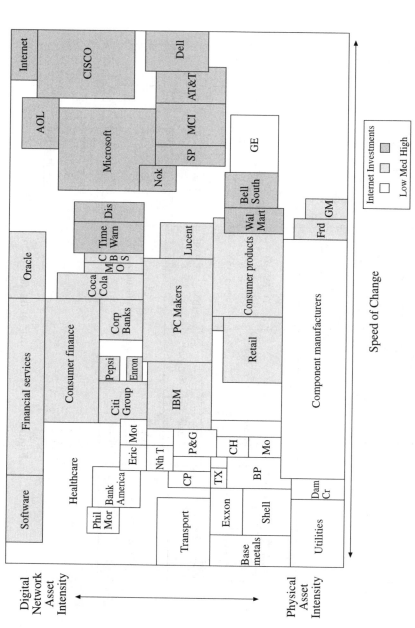

Figure 2.2 New strategic positions – 2000
Source: Smartmoney.com

Table 2.1 Comparison of GDP per capita

	Richest	*Poorest*	*Ratio*
1820	$ 1,765	$523	3:1
1992	$21,558	$300	72:1

Source: United Nations Human Development Report

This trend shows no sign of reversing itself. In a *Financial Times* 'World Economy Report' (2000), Martin Dickson mentions that the number of people in absolute poverty, that is, living on less than a dollar a day, seems set to increase over the next two decades. Dickson writes, 'the question, "is global inequality getting worse or better?", is simple, but the answer is complicated as it really depends upon the definition of "inequality" and the statistics used to measure it'. The measurement commonly used is GDP which, in the opinion of Dickson, is inadequate as it does not take into account 'non-market measures of well being'.

This whole notion of well-being is subjective and, although there are ways in which this has been measured by some recent reports, I believe that this area of consideration will become much more important in the future. For example, it is only in the last few decades that psychologists and other commentators have noted the importance of emotional intelligence and its impact on human behaviour. If we take the definition of the 'new economy', as proposed by Ed Crooks of the *Financial Times*, which mentions 'globalization, liberalization and information technology', it seems probable that how diverse cultures work and mix together will be of critical importance to the success of corporations and economies. This suggests that the research and work of occupational psychologists will become more important. The more we understand, learn and know about the complexities of international human behaviour, the better we are able to plan and develop strategies and processes to succeed in the new economy.

There were an estimated 3.7 million businesses active in the UK at the start of 1999 (Table 2.2). This figure has risen since 1980 when there were 2.4 million. Most of the growth in the business population between 1998 and 1999 has been in the 1–4 employee category. Of the 3.7 million businesses in 1999, over 2.3 million were size class zero business, that is, those made up of sole traders or partners without employees. The number

Table 2.2 Number of businesses, employment and
turnover by size of enterprise, January 1999

Size (number of employees)	Number of businesses	Employment (000s)	Turnover (£m ex VAT)	Business %	Employment %	Turnover %
None	2,324,340	2,708	90,463	63.2	12.5	4.7
1–4	963,615	2,395	221,986	26.2	11.0	11.4
5–9	201,835	1,459	123,029	5.5	6.7	6.3
10–19	109,280	1,533	149,451	3.0	7.1	7.7
20–49	46,955	1,462	147,505	1.3	6.7	7.6
50–99	14,450	1,011	102,860	0.4	4.7	5.3
100–199	8,165	1,131	116,638	0.2	5.2	6.0
200–249	1,570	349	38,633	–	1.6	2.0
250–499	3,220	1,121	149,275	0.1	5.2	7.7
500+	3,515	8,576	804,039	0.1	39.4	41.4
All	3,676,940	21,746	1,943,880	100.0	100.0	100.0
All with employees	1,352,600	19,038	1,853,417	36.8	87.5	95.3

Source: DTI (2000) *Small and Medium Enterprise Statistics for the UK, 1999,* Small Business Service

of size class zero businesses has fallen since the start of 1998, especially in the agriculture, construction and wholesale/retail sectors.

Of the entire business population of 3.7 million, only 24,000 were medium sized (50 to 249 employees) and less than 7,000 were large (250 or more employees). Small businesses, including those without employees, accounted for over 99% of business, 45% of non-government employment and (excluding the financial sector) 38% of turnover. In contrast, the 7,000 largest businesses accounted for 45% of non-government employment and 49% of turnover.

The European Commission has for some years been promoting the importance of small and medium-sized enterprises, in terms of growth and employment. The figures are similar, as small and medium-sized businesses make up 99% of all businesses across Europe and provide two-thirds of all jobs in the EU. In 1995 there were about 18 million businesses in the EU, with the largest presence in construction, trade, hotels and restaurants.

Of the total businesses, only 36,000 belong to the category of large enterprises (250 employees or more) and their economic significance is high. They account for about 34% of total employment and 45% of total turnover. Together they employed more than 110 million people out of a total of 150 million and generated ecu 17,000 billion. (These figures are the most recent official numbers available at the time of writing and relate to 1995 – European Commission, 1998.)

The new economy has been with us for a while. The *Financial Times* and *The Economist* have mentioned it literally hundreds of times in the last two years. Yet during the research phase of this book, I interviewed numerous people who worked in international finance and investment banking who could not provide a clear definition. So, to clarify matters, here are two current definitions of the new economy. The first is from Ed Crooks, economics editor at the *Financial Times*.

> It is the idea that an interrelated series of factors including globalisation, deregulation and above all information technology have brought about a fundamental change in economic relationships. (Crooks, 2000, personal communication)

Andrew Cates is a Senior International Economist at UBS Warburg and says that the economic conditions prevailing today are unusual. 'We haven't had a positive supply shock for a century.' His definition of the new economy is:

> The new economy concerns the exploitation of information technology and the degree to which this fosters a shift in the productivity performance of the world economy. (Cates, 2000, personal communication)

In simple economic parlance, the supply curve has shifted to the right. According to Cates (2000, p. 1), 'the opportunities afforded by new technology are the crux of what is often referred to as the New Economy'. He suggests that there is a general expectation that the current surge of investment 'will create economies that are more productive with growth being led by supply-side improvements rather than cyclical fluctuations in demand'

(p. 1). The UBS argument is that the majority of information and communications technology (ICT) investment is indirect. This means that is impacts the total factor productivity, which is the way to assess efficiency that labour and capital combine to produce the economy's value added. Real-time information and knowledge, according to Cates, allows firms to allocate their resources more efficiently. This brings cheaper and easier exchange, and greater outreach in both the supply chain and the distribution channel. This makes labour more productive and reduces the amount of physical fixed and short-term assets needed to support a company's level of sales.

The transmission of knowledge and information is crucial to the theoretical argument and according to Cates (2000, p. 1):

> it is the ability to transmit information and knowledge more quickly and more efficiently to a wider global audience that lies at the root of the New Economy's productivity potential. The reason why the potential is so great is because knowledge displays the property of infinite potential. One person's intake of information, for example, does not detract or prevent anyone else from gaining the same, if not more, from this information. Extra copies of research, for example, can be more or less freely made, used and consumed without drawing down the physical functionality of the original. Indeed, unlike most goods or services, information is unique to an economy because it is not scarce. The seller of a car, for example, no longer possesses the car. The seller of information still possesses the information.

E-commerce still represents only a tiny fraction of overall economic activity. The prediction made in a recent report from Forrester Research is that the collective e-commerce activity from all countries will be significant, amounting to US$7 trillion in 2004. This represents 8.6% of the global sales of goods and services.

According to the Industrial Society, 'The new economy is not the internet economy, it is the intangibles economy'. In their recent publication, *Most Wanted – The Quiet Birth of the Free Worker*, (Knell, 2000, p. 1) they write:

> Governments are urging businesses to become more competitive by exploiting the distinctive capabilities of knowledge, skills and creativity. The capital markets have been transfigured, with a soaring valuation of 'new economy' companies on world stock markets, leading

to the controversial restructuring of the listings that comprise the FTSE 100 index.

Intangible assets, especially human capital assets – which five years ago would not have been considered significant enough to measure – now account for up to 80 per cent of the value of large companies, according to a 500-corporation study. When IBM acquired Lotus for $3.2 billion, it estimated the R&D, mainly ideas in people's heads, to be worth $1.84 billion.

There have been numerous theories of a post-industrial society during the last few decades and many writers have commented on this emerging trend. Peter Drucker has mentioned the rise of the 'knowledge worker' and the general theory according to Alan Burton-Jones (1999, p. 4, quoting Touraine, 1969) is as follows:

The production of goods would decline in favour of services, knowledge would become the basis of economic growth and productivity, and occupational growth would occur mainly in white-collar managerial and professional jobs.

The definition of services has always posed problems, although some definitions have suggested that a service is something that is consumed as it is produced, for example a taxi ride or a haircut. One definition commonly used by economic journalists is 'anything sold in trade that could not be dropped on your foot'.

Most trends have been relatively consistent with these predictions, however, there is now a shift in thinking and definitions, as many goods and services are, without doubt, knowledge and information intensive. The change that has occurred in this new economy is that knowledge has become the primary and defining feature of most economic activity instead of goods or services.

As this book progresses, it will illustrate how, by necessity, accounting practices have needed to adapt in order to capture and illustrate this change and reflect its impact on the balance sheet.

Knowledge is now the most important factor of production for many companies and individuals. It is not always understood, yet its importance is not to be underestimated. Some confuse knowledge with information or data. One way to depict how they relate to each other is shown in Figure

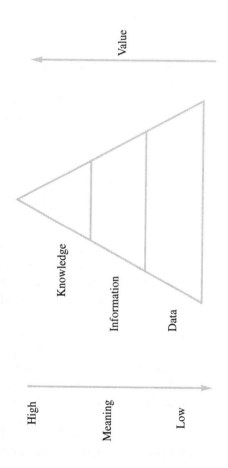

Figure 2.3 Data information and knowledge

Source: Burton-Jones, A. (1999) *Knowledge Capitalism*, Oxford University Press

2.3. The traditional economic view of knowledge and information saw them as being one and the same. In practice, they are very different concepts which complement each other.

Learning may be termed as 'knowledge acquisition' and creation as 'invention or innovation'. According to Burton-Jones (1999, p. 6): 'Knowledge acquisition (learning) and creation (invention, innovation) can only occur to any significant degree in the human brain'. But knowledge itself is reflected in other ways. A firm may identify its knowledge capital in its workforce. This may also be termed as its 'intellectual capital' or 'intellectual assets'. The same firm may term its customers' demands and preferences as its 'customer capital'. Its 'structural capital' will be defined as its systems, products, processes and capabilities (Burton-Jones, 1999, p. 6).

Innovation also connects to the economy. It was Joseph Schumpeter in the 1930s who is credited to have recognized the impact of technological innovation on an economy. Burton-Jones (1999, p. 16) notes that for Schumpeter:

> innovation lay at the centre of economic change causing 'gales of creative destruction'. He proposed a taxonomy of technological change based on three stages: invention, innovation and diffusion.

Burton-Jones also notes the S-shaped curve of growth, which shows how successful innovations of all types will grow slowly for a while, enter a period of rapid growth, and then flatten out. He describes five long waves that have occurred since 1750, water power, steam transport, steel and electricity, Fordist production techniques and, most recently, information technology and biotechnology (p. 17).

Weiner and Brown (1997, p. 7) describe the US experience of the layering of economies/reformation of societies and write of these four eras. The agricultural economy led to the agricultural society prior to the eighteenth century. This was followed by the industrial economy which led to the industrial society that lasted between 1800 and 1970. Then followed the post-industrial economy which began around 1950 and will continue until about 2005. They predict the next age will be the emotile economy which will lead to the emotile society. This began in 1992 and will rise to dominance around 2005.

Competitive Knowledge Management

Table 2.3 Optimal operating unit changes as we move
from the industrial to the information age

	Old game	*Rise of*	*New game*
	Industrial age	*the region*	*Information age*
Timing	*19th–20th century*	*state*	*Late 20th–21st century*
Description	Driven by nation state governments		Driven by private capital and information
	National sovereignty		Citizen sovereignty
	Strong control by centralized forces		Autonomous networks of interdependent private enterprises and regional entities
	Sensitive to borders		Inherently borderless
	Favours domestic capital and protects domestic companies		Welcomes foreign capital and world class companies/expertise, creating high quality jobs
	Aims for one-state prosperity through development of export-led, manufacturing driven economic growth		Aims for harmonious regional prosperity based on interdependent, network-centric companies creating information-intensive services to capture value from customers
	Government initiatives		Entrepreneurial initiatives
	Good government strengthens priority industries		Good government nurtures regional development, not focused in specific industry
	Change occurs gradually over decades		Change occurs suddenly in months to years
Winners	Germany		Hong Kong/Shenzhen
	Japan/'New Japans'		Singapore/Jahor/Batam
	United Kingdom		Taiwan/Fujian
	United States		Southern China (Pearl River Delta)
			Southern India (for example Bangalore)
			North Mexico/Southwestern USA
			Silicon Valley
			New Zealand
			Lombardia
			Pacific Northwest of the United States

Note: Region state is defined as an area (often cross-border) developed around a regional economic centre with a population of a few million to 10–20 million.

Source: Ohmae, K. (1995) *The End of the Nation State*, HarperCollins, London, p. 143

Historical context

Jevons wrote in 1865:

> The plains of North America and Russia are our cornfields; Chicago and Odessa our granaries; Canada and the Baltic are our timber forests; Australasia contains our sheep farms, and in Argentina and on the western prairies of North America are our herds of oxen; Peru sends her silver, and the gold of South Africa and Australia flows into London; the Hindus and the Chinese grow tea for us, and our coffee, sugar and spice plantations are all in the Indies. Spain and France are our vineyards and the Mediterranean our fruit garden, and our cotton grounds, which for long have occupied the Southern United States, are now being extended everywhere in the warm regions of the earth.

During the last couple of centuries, economies have clearly changed and developed. The most salient change in Western-style economies has been from an agrarian to an information economy. Ohmae (1995) writes that the developed world is making the transition from the industrial age to the information age. He writes of 'primary forces shaping the global economy' and that the chief and irreversible effects of technology are influencing changes to the 'structure of business processes and on the values, judgements, and preferences of citizens and consumers in all parts of the world' (p. vii).

For Ohmae, global information is akin to a genie out of a bottle and cannot be put back. He does not believe that any 'entrenched form of organization can stand untouched or changed'. Ohmae takes the view that there is an 'old' game, (the industrial age) and a 'new' game, (the information age) (p. vii).

The patterns of human migration seem to be changing as knowledge workers appear to be more in demand than ever before. During the past few decades, the UK, France and Germany invited unskilled workers from former colonies and lesser developed economies such as Turkey, Africa, India and the Caribbean to fill vacancies that their indigenous populations did not wish to accept. Currently knowledge workers are being invited from India to both Germany and the UK. These are software engineers with specialist skills who are interested to fill various vacancies in Europe that the local populations are unable to fill through skill shortages.

According to a recent report by the London Chamber of Commerce and Industry reviewed by Oldfield in the *Sunday Times* (2000), it was found that 'two out of three firms were struggling to find the right workers, especially at professional and managerial level'. In response, the Education Minister David Blunkett is planning a national skills task force, plus the introduction of a system to speed up the flow of skilled overseas people into the UK by an easier work permit administration.

The demographics of Central and Eastern Europe are changing, according to a report from the United Nations, which predicts that population levels will fall (in the former Communist countries) by one third during the next 50 years (Doole, 2000). This is due to a dramatic fall in the birth rate. The transition economies have the lowest fertility rate in the world as they struggle with the transition to a market economy.

The triad economies

The impact of this changing economy is noticed in three primary economic areas, the USA, Japan and Europe. These are commonly known as the triad economies.

Van Wolferen (1993) writes that due to its lack of absolute leadership, Japan is unable to deal effectively with the rest of the world. This is also the reason the rest of the world has difficulty in dealing with Japan. The assumption that Van Wolferen makes is that Japan has consciously created a system within which to live. Dobbs-Higginson (1994, p. 27) refutes this argument and suggests that the Japanese have:

> never made a specific, conscious decision to live as they do ... The goal of ensuring the survival of their self-contained system remains their only constant.

In order to do this Dobbs-Higginson believes that Japan will find its place in the world 'only with the support of Asia Pacific' and that many countries in this region have already agreed that they need Japan's support. The argument is that Japan's defence is to maintain the growth of free trade and international cooperation, to open its borders in terms of its economy and its culture. Dobbs-Higginson (p. 81) argues that Japan needs to 'develop multi-dimensional leadership skills and individual accountability'.

Table 2.4 World economic trading blocs

ANZERTA	Australia and New Zealand
ASEAN	Association of South East Asian Nations – Brunei, Indonesia, Laos, Malaysia, Philippines, Singapore, Thailand, Vietnam
CIS	Commonwealth of Independent States – Armenia, Azerbaijan, Belarus, Georgia, Kazakhstan, Kyrgyzstan, Moldova, Russia, Tajikistan, Turkmenistan, Ukraine, Uzbekistan
EU	Currently 15 member states possibly rising to 21 by 2010
MERCOSUR	Southern Cone Common Market – Argentina, Brazil, Paraguay, Uruguay, Bolivia, Chile
NAFTA	North American Free Trade Agreement – Argentina, Brazil, Canada, Mexico, North America, Paraguay, Uruguay
PRC	People's Republic of China, 30 provinces
SADC	South African Development Community – Angola, Botswana, Congo, Lesotho, Malawi, Mauritius, Mozambique, Namibia, Seychelles, Swaziland
SAPTA	South Asia Preferential Trade Agreement – Bangladesh, Kingdom of Bhutan, Republic of India, Republic of Maldives, Kingdom of Nepal, Islamic Republic of Pakistan, DSR Sri Lanka
Japan	Membership of APEC. Includes China, US plus 18 other countries

Since World War Two, the world experienced a process of constant repositioning into political, economic and social groupings. During the latter part of the twentieth century and the beginning of the twenty-first, there has been much speculation of the triad economies, that is, the dollar, euro and the yen. Ohmae's contention is that 'there has been a fundamental change in the environment within which those managers work' (1995, p. 27). He believes that information technology is at the heart of a series of related developments. Many international trading agreements have been negotiated and some fall into geopolitical boundaries (Table 2.4).

These geopolitical boundaries were developed for numerous reasons and prior to this, in 1947, there were a number of organizations established to assist the world economies. These were: GATT – General Agreement on Tariffs and Trade; The IMF – The International Monetary Fund; and IBRD – International Bank for Reconstruction and Development. The IBRD became the World Bank and the IMF is controlled by the G7. The G7 was formed in 1985 and includes USA, Japan, Germany, France, UK, Italy and Canada.

There have been significant changes in the way that international business is conducted, primarily in the use of technology. Funds may travel across continents in seconds rather than minutes or days and as Ohmae (1995) mentions, the new economy is private capital and information led.

The subject of knowledge management and intellectual capital has raised serious interest at the most senior levels of organizations such as the Organisation for Economic Cooperation and Development (OECD).

> Knowledge is now a crucial factor underpinning economic growth. Producing goods and services with high value-added is at the core of improving economic performance and international competitiveness ... Increasing intangible investment, which is difficult to measure, ... has become a major issue for enterprises and governments. (Jean-Claude Paye, former Secretary General, OECD, quoted in Amidon and Skyrme, 1997, p. 1)

Questions must be raised as to whether European firms and governments are sufficiently conscious of this subject area as a business discipline and if they are able to harness knowledge management to compete effectively in world markets.

Trompenaars and Hampden-Turner (1993, p. 26) write of 'excessive universalism' and one conclusion to draw from their writing is that only the richer northern economies will benefit in the information age and particularist cultural styles will falter due to knowledge management being alien to their culture. The work of Nonaka and Takeuchi would refute this argument, however, questions need to be raised in relation to the rise and fall of the tiger economies and how both China and India will cope with globalization.

Kenichi Ohmae writes of the 'Rise of the Region-State' in *The Invisible Continent* (2000). He notes that Singapore is a good example of an 'emerging region state' (2000, p. 129) and that there are many more examples including: Ireland (call centres), Finland (telecoms), Trinidad and Tobago (chemicals and fertilizers) and New Zealand.

SUMMARY

- Between 1850 and 2000, there have been significant changes to the structure of the world's economy

- These changes have tended to favour the richer northern economies, for example, the USA, UK, Scandinavia, France and Germany

- These changes have led economies from the 'old game' of agrarian economies to the 'new game' of information-led economies

- The skills required to be successful in the new economy are different

- There has been an emergence of the triad economies (dollar, yen and euro)

- New trading blocs have emerged to assist smaller developing economies

- An information-led economy could benefit many cultures and nations, irrespective of their global positioning, through the effective use of knowledge management

Case Study

Hay Group

VICKY WRIGHT *Managing Director, Knowledge Management and Integration*

Q: *How has Hay Group changed itself in terms of its organizational structure during the last couple of years?*

A: We were very country centric in the past and we decided that we would move to a 'matrix' organization. The group chief executive appointed me to the one global role in the first instance and that would be 'knowledge management and integration'. It was really to start acting as a change agent to develop cross-country knowledge sharing.

Q: *There must have been a fair amount of discussion about this?*

A: Yes there was. There was quite a lot of ambiguity when I took it on. This was a first cross cutting global role and it went against the grain in terms of the general behaviour of the firm. It was built around some very basic propositions that I think most professional service firms are dealing with; in addition we are a 'content rich' consultancy. We have tools and methodologies that are special to Hay. The real issue for us is; are we leveraging those?

We needed to rapidly develop the abilities of some of our remoter far-flung parts and give them access to tools and methods, which actually allows them to fight beyond their size. So, to take an example of that, you look at Hay offices globally and the US and the UK between them account for a large proportion of our revenues. Hay UK has 160 consultants and out in Norway there are only a handful. The issue for us is that if you have 160 consultants you have the full 'Hay' range of offerings and the full 'Hay' range of skills. What you know in Norway is that they are not going to have the full range of skills, but they have to be able to relate to clients across the full range, and know how to use resources from elsewhere. To achieve this, they need to know what's going on in Hay to be able to do that.

We are also driven by the needs of our global clients. I've seen a big change in clients in the last three or four years. The model of the multinational does not apply to a lot of our clients, they are now truly global in HR. There is a great demand for Hay to be global too.

Q: *How far is your knowledge management role about taking the leading edge forward compared to dealing with basic knowledge dissemination?*

A: This comes back to Hay being a 'content expert' consultancy. Making the choice as to how far I should concentrate on the 'leading edge' or universalising existing knowledge is difficult given limited resources.

One of the consequences that has happened, is that I have become one of the most 'networked' people there is in Hay. I get e-mails every day from all over the globe saying, 'we don't know who knows this but we know that you must know someone who does'. Part of that is very interesting because increasingly there is a need to develop 'knowledge centres'. We have spent a lot of time trying to get people to use the knowledge databases that we have developed and also to actually demonstrate some of the behaviours about knowledge sharing. In addition to this role of knowledge and integration, I am also the Managing Director for 'Reward Consulting' worldwide which represents about half of our revenues. Recently, I have become head of the global business streams. That has meant that I have spent less time in knowledge management and integration but that's meant that the person who works underneath me has become a very critical person. Really, I have become the sponsor and breaking things down and dealing with it at a higher level. The person underneath me, Jackie Cotter, has really grown into that job. I think she is now considered the knowledge management person worldwide. She now spends a lot of time in the US.

There are a lot of good things currently happening in organizations linked to knowledge management. Both Shell and BP Amoco are good examples. I think the interesting thing for me though is that there is a big difference between each company. Each takes it's own view of knowledge management but one of the things here, being in a professional services firm, is that knowledge management is almost your livelihood. What I have discovered about knowledge management, is that in a professional services firm it has a different feel to it to a certain extent, there are parallels – let me be absolutely clear about that – and certainly some of the best practice in BP Amoco and Shell I've been very interested in. But the truth of the matter is, I think there's a certain sub-set of knowledge management about the professional service firm that has taken on a slightly different feel.

It's about opening up all sorts of opportunities because at the other end of my interests are the exploitation of knowledge through e-commerce, because that is really taking some of our consulting knowledge and putting it into a different context. There's a big debate there as to how much of our intellectual capital should be put out free or for small amounts of money.

For us when we come in to knowledge management there's something about creating new economies. The interesting point in Hay is how to harvest, disseminate and leverage intellectual property and really the intellectual capital in Hay as well. One of the things that has come to the fore, certainly in the three years I've been doing this, is the importance of client information as part of our intellectual capital. What our consultants know about our clients is very important as well as trying to link that back into working with other clients. The relationship management process has become much more important, that comes back to the global account process.

It's very interesting because if you said are you a chief knowledge officer, well no I'm not really, but what I've become is someone who is involved in the development of the firm. That's because the development of the firm and knowledge management are inextricably linked. Also it's about business issues that are particular to a professional service firm. Let me give you an example.

We have a diagnostic tool around the 'work culture' in companies. Suppose I said copyright and various other things protected this tool we invented as we have invested in it over the last few years. In its original form it was a series of Post-it notes and now you just click on a screen and it is an 'expert system'.

It's probably used 270 times a year by consultants worldwide and when it's embedded in a project the actual fee for just doing that little bit is $20,000 for one client as there is a lot of consultants' time in there. Supposing I then go and sell it on the Internet as a business-to-business process and sell it direct to companies. There's no need for consultant intervention as it is sold as an expert system.

Q: *Are we going to see changes that are going to be necessary for consultants for them to continue being consultants?*

A: The issue for us is really what drives consultancies and these are two things. One is, you've got to innovate all the time. I have to say that Hay is probably one of the luckiest consultancies because we had Hay guide charts (job evaluation guide charts) that were invented in the 1940s, copyrighted in the 1950s and are still in use today, having only marginally changed from that copyrighted position. I have to say when I look around at those guide charts you could never imagine them to last that long or have had that profit stream attached to them. Most consulting ideas don't have that kind of life span.

Incidentally, the parallel I would put is with the 'balanced scorecard'. The 'Kaplan and Norton Balanced Scorecard', despite several attempts to protect it's copyright, has possibly made more money outside of the Kaplan and Norton Enterprises than there has been within.

Most fundamental ideas have got a lesser shelf life than they used to have because the ability to copy them is so much easier. Take EVA as another example. The general principle is being widely used by everybody now. I think the McKinsey argument is interesting because it forces you to innovate your next real 'value added' to the client and that comes back to my view. Which is, in some of these debates, it is the consultants that have got to be adding far much more value than they used to be to clients. As ideas get easily copied your ability to make super normal profits out of your ideas goes down. That would be in favour of the McKinsey argument.

The ability to protect some of these ideas that consultants have is very low. Also, basically the whole consultant ethos must be about maximum value added to clients. You must be constantly going up the value-added chain; you can't make money from old rope. Old ideas get old faster than they used to because of the amount of stuff that goes out onto the Internet. It may not be an abuse of your intellectual property, it may just be someone with the same idea.

Q: *Clearly, there may be a slightly different ethos around today in terms of the way consulting tools are shared?*

A: That comes back to the economic model of the firm. The question it is raising for me is that you have to look at the value margin that various levels of people create. Hay has always been top heavy on senior people, part of that is there is a lot of tacit knowledge in our consulting. There are elements of process facilitation, there are elements of how to coach individuals, there is an element of creative thinking about something like design that you can only do by craft skill, and a lot of tacit knowledge, which we find difficult to capture. What we do in bringing new consultants in is trying to get them up the learning curve and into this high tacit knowledge area as fast as we can. We do this not only because it makes money but it is also the only way of adding value to clients because the real value added in our firm is through that tacit knowledge area. If we can capture and change that tacit knowledge into explicit knowledge numerous other people will be able to do it too. The argument would be that the last thing you want to do is rely on that tacit knowledge when somebody has already made it explicit.

What you are constantly doing is going up that value-added curve, that innovation curve, and that tacit knowledge curve. What you cannot make money out of now is direct intermediation of explicit knowledge.

Q: Many people would say it's impossible to measure knowledge.

A: I have some very clear scorecard dimensions – increased rate of innovation, increased revenues, increased mergers, improved client satisfaction, improved employer satisfaction.

Q: History and identity are important in terms of a company's culture. How important are your historical roots at Hay?

A: The whole success of Hay was formed on a very basic triangle of offerings. They took the intervention of job evaluation at Hay and they linked that to salary management, which basically said there is a rational way of managing pay, and the creation of an information business. This allowed you to compare your pay with someone else on the market. From that we've managed to create a business, which includes a range of offerings including: leadership and organizational change.

Hay is now a leader in the 'people consulting' sponsor businesses.

At Hay our tag line is 'People before Strategy'.

Human Factors International

Business Psychologists

Where teams are finding it difficult to function effectively together, it is important to assess the source of such problems as the critical first stage towards achieving maximum performance. At Human Factors International we often find that external difficulties are imagined rather than real, and the main problems are in fact individual team members' behaviours. To assist our work with teams, we have developed a measure called Teametric which focuses on the behavioural dynamics within the team, as perceived by team members. This provides diagnostic feedback to team members on the strengths and limitations both of themselves individually, of the team, and also of the team's behavioural style. This information forms part of a three step process of diagnosing the current state of the team, building acceptance and ownership of the results, and action planning to better exploit strengths and overcome weaknesses at both the team and individual levels.

To provide more detail, Teametric assesses both individual team members and the team on eight key areas of team work: support, team spirit, communication, openness, giving recognition, building relationships, can-do attitude, and team vitality. These form four underlying factors of behavioural style shown here:

- activeness: proactive ↔ responding
- openness: traditional ↔ inquiring
- socially-oriented: independent ↔ social
- sharing: local ↔ global

Teametric has been used to resolve various team dysfunctions, yet a key theme throughout these has been knowledge management – how can team members optimise the use and sharing of their individual knowledge skills and capabilities and, in effect, work as a 'team'.

The key issue is behavioural style which is evaluated along the four areas already shown. Team members are provided with a series of graphs showing their individual style as well as those of their colleagues in the team. Each of these graphs compares two of the four factors. An example of one of these graphs is shown below, comparing activeness and sharing for a fictitious John Smith. John's behavioural style on these two factors is shown as a darker spot while other team members are indicated as the paler spots. Looking first at activeness, John's graph shows that he balances proactive and responsive behaviours in his interactions and participation with colleagues. Relative to his team, it can be seen that most team members are more responsive than John and he is likely to be viewed as relatively proactive.

For the second factor of sharing information with team members, John commonly shows a local orientation indicating that he exchanges information and helps the team build knowledge principally with neighbouring team members rather than those who are more distant either geographically or functionally. This is typical of the team overall.

This assessment raises the team's awareness of their strengths and development needs both as a team and for the individual members. The next step is to work together to plan actions that will improve the team's performance in key areas such as proactive information seeking and knowledge sharing.

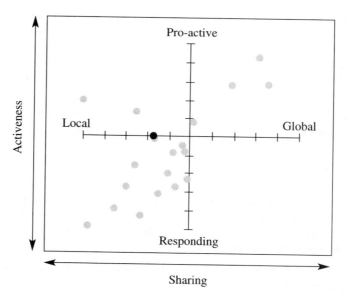

Figure 2.4 John Smith's behavioural style
in relation to other team members

3 The New Work Models

It is all about life/work balance, according to the Industrial Society. Note the life part comes before work. People's skills, knowledge and creativity, generally now described as human capital, undisputedly have become increasingly important in the creation of economic value. As these intangible assets have increased in importance, the raw materials within a product have become less significant.

The World Bank has noted the rise of the knowledge-based economies:

> The balance between knowledge and resources has shifted so far towards the former that knowledge has become perhaps the most important factor determining the standard of living ... Today's most technologically advanced economies are truly knowledge based. (World Bank, 1998)

'The costs of attracting and keeping talent are also on the agenda. For many companies, it is not the lack of finance or consumer demand that is limiting their growth, but the absence of quality people that is the issue' (Burton-Jones quoted in Knell, 2000). According to Ware and Fern, one particular company in California's Silicon Valley estimates that it costs them an average of $125,000 every time an employee leaves. Bill Gates has also commented that if 20 of Microsoft's key people were to leave, his company would risk bankruptcy.

This change in the relationship between employee and employer, with the balance of power shifting in favour of the talented, creative individual has also coincided with the changes in working practices in terms of job security. In 1995, Professor Norbert Walter, Chief Economist at Deutsche Bank, noted that job security was a thing of the past. He commented: 'Three career moves and eight job changes will be the norm in the future.' So lets look at the current evidence.

America's biggest employer is not General Motors or IBM, but Manpower, the temporary employment agency. According to the Industrial Society's *Most Wanted* report:

- The average 32-year-old American has worked for nine different firms

- 65 per cent of US workers say employers are less loyal to them than five years ago

- 78 per cent of US middle managers say employees are less loyal to them than five years ago

- A recent poll by Shell in the US revealed that the youngest American workers already have had more employers (an average of five) than today's retirees had in a lifetime. (Knell, 2000)

Loyalty, commitment and trust are also in question:

- Only 14 per cent of employees are proud of their organisation

- Only 30 per cent feel loyal to their organisation

- Only 28 per cent are sufficiently attached to their organisation to say that they would turn down another job if it offered higher pay. (Knell, 2000)

The same report also points out that the majority of managers (93 per cent) have no faith in their employers' willingness to advance their career interests.

Just as smart investors have realized that it is unwise to hold all their eggs in one basket, the free worker has realized that investing all their human capital in one employer is also unwise. The old corporate promise is not a good, or even a safe, bet.

The underpinning philosophy of the free worker is to 'enhance their intellectual, social and reputational capital ... not through a long-term association with one employer; but by developing a network of contracting arrangements and passing relatively quickly through high value relationships with a wide variety of contracting agents' (Knell, 2000).

This report highlights the simple fact that jobs that were in the past owned by firms are being replaced progressively by careers owned by individuals. Other facts highlighted by this report mention:

- 16% of the workforce in the USA are self-employed, independent contractors, or temporary workers

- This amounts to 25 million free agents in the USA, who move from project to project and work on their own, sometimes for months, sometimes for days

- This trend is heading eastwards to the UK and the rest of Europe

- 10% of the workforce in the UK are independent and associated with such industries as design, fashion, broadcasting and the Internet

- These workers generate £50 billion per annum, rising to £80 billion during the next decade, representing 6% of the UK's economic output

- One third of self-employed Britons are working in business, education or the health service. This figure was only 16% in 1984

- Half of all self-employed people are currently in managerial or professional occupations

- In 1992, one in ten professional employees were on temporary contracts, in 1996, the figure was one in seven

- Between 1979 and 1998, the proportion of managerial and professional workers who were self-employed grew by almost 300%

- Self-employment is growing much faster than small business growth (Knell, 2000).

As the demographic patterns suggest, this situation is not going to reverse itself, but is the beginning of an increasing trend. As fewer workers will be entering the job market than are leaving, there will be an increasing demand for the free worker. Many of these new employees have parents who have experienced problems with redundancy and are possibly less likely to trust company hierarchies.

The importance of networks is critical to the knowledge worker. Those who have developed numerous quality networks are likely to be able to manipulate the job market to work for them. They can command the highest fees from organizations that will recognize and respect their talent and allow them to learn and earn and develop their skill base. What better way to do this than by acquiring experience fast with numerous high quality firms.

One prediction made by Davis and Meyer (quoted in Knell, 2000, p. 15) notes, "'the day will come when we will put our fifty-two week trading range on our resumes", capturing the high and low points of the market value of our skills and knowledge'.

The implications for recruitment are clearly not to be underestimated. In the USA, recruitment is a $17 billion per annum industry and Forrester Research predicts that online recruitment will represent around ten per cent ($1.7 billion) by 2003. In 1998 it was a mere $105 million.

Knowledge workers and knowledge leaders

Much of the management development activities during the 1980s evolved around the business plan and tried to link people development activities to the strategy of the organization. This by definition suggested that management development activities were planned and systematic. The differences in approach with knowledge management appear to be that organizational structures are much more fluid and take a more individualistic approach to people development.

Later during the 1990s, companies were undergoing such rapid change that most people development policies often became unworkable as organizations downsized or rightsized and the shift was toward self-managed learning. Chawla and Murphy (1995, p. 95) write of 'generative coaching' which they describe as 'self-correcting' and 'self-generating'. They write: 'These goals apply to commitment as well as to competence.'

Some of the ideas that made a real impact on people and corporations were the introduction of mission statements and identifying the core competencies necessary to the firm along with its value system or culture. Boyatzis (1982), Argyris (1993) and Schein (1997a) pioneered the foundations of the competency approach. There are numerous writers and contributors associated with competency assessment of leaders, for example, Moss Kanter (2001), Adair (1993) and Belbin (1996).

Leadership is one of the key themes emerging in knowledge management. Botkin (1999) examines key leadership traits that appear to be critical to success in a knowledge-based community. Botkin asks the significant question:

> How do you lead a knowledge community, and, what is different about knowledge in contrast to capital, or about community in contrast to teams, that influences what traits are needed to lead a knowledge community? (p. 177)

According to Botkin (1999), the three Ls are fundamental: the leader as listener, learner and linker:

> *Leader as Listener:* Jan Lapidoth, founder of the Customer Focus Institute in Stockholm, advises his clients to listen to their customers. He cites the lessons from Moments of Truth and suggests that you have 10–15 seconds to hear a customer in distress and win his or her confidence that you want to help. Many people have their ears open, but few

know how to listen to hear clearly what others are saying, especially when it is negative. You've got precious few moments to win them over psychologically so that they feel you're on their side.

Listening, an important life skill anywhere, is doubly important in knowledge communities, because you're constantly dealing with new subject matter and with often conflicting views from multiple members. It's the skill we wish more political leaders exhibited; it's the trait we value most highly in good doctors when they check symptoms. Good leaders spend a lot of their time listening, especially listening to negative feedback, strong resistance, and doubt as well as genuine disagreement.

Leader as Learner: Gary High is responsible for learning at Saturn. Recently, his assignment was extended to education and training for all small car employees of GM North America. He makes a distinction between 'knowing leaders' and 'learning leaders'. In the past, automobile executives came across as knowing leaders. They always had an answer for everything. Not having an answer was seen as a sign of weakness.

At Saturn, we wanted to develop learning leaders rather than knowing leaders. That is, leaders who can learn how to operate in a new environment rather than leaders who project yesterday's rules of the game into tomorrow's completely different game. (p. 177)

Botkin then explains that learner leadership is not an easy trait to develop and represents a major personal transition for many current high-level executives. He believes (p. 177) that someone who 'has thought a lot about how to guide this transition' is Mark Schleicher, Director of Knowledge Management for Motorola University. For Schleicher, there are three groups: 'first-time line managers and other new hires; experienced middle managers; and expert senior managers' (p. 177). The first require 'basic architecture' training courses. The second require 'interactive coaching' supported by knowledge banks. The third need a 'knowledge nugget' focus with peers. Botkin writes 'His [Schleicher's] goal is to develop leaders as learners' (p. 178).

Leader as linker: This, according to Botkin, is where the community is used as an exercise in networking. Botkin recommends (1999, p. 178):

to start building knowledge communities, put a first rate networker in charge. Forging alliances, building partnerships, creating working groups, connecting visionaries with pragmatists and conservatives with early adopters. Those are the traits of the knowledge community leader. As Sullivan puts it, 'Leadership is a team sport'.

Botkin then suggests that people sometimes assume that companies that avoid conflict are the most successful, but he says this is not always the case, and that, in fact, most successful companies are those that use conflict as a learning opportunity. The parallels drawn by Botkin are interesting and include theories of 'creative destruction' in capitalism, how 'new paradigms' destroy 'old ones' and the 'progression of science being caused by ideas clashing'. He makes the suggestion that successful communities welcome conflict as learning but 'preserve the passion of the dissenter'. For Botkin, successful communities are 'hard on ideas and soft on people' (p. 178).

There is a fourth L for leaders, provided by Karin Bartow of the Forum Corporation's Experience Centre. Bartow says that a leader may perform as the illuminator or 'lighter' (p. 178). This means that good leaders of knowledge communities illuminate the problem or opportunity areas for a group to focus its attention. Comparisons may then be drawn from the thoughts of scientists and researchers who ask which are the domains to concentrate their attention?

Clearly, the role of leadership is fundamental to the creation of knowledge management and one of the most significant contributions for any leader to make in an organizational context is to create 'specialist knowledge workers'. This term has been used for a number of years and Borghoff (1998) writes about characterizing knowledge work and the study of knowledge workers. Borghoff explores how there exists a strong emphasis on how the human issues make or break new methods and tools at work. The history of interactive computing validates this theory and suggests that, for the designers of new technology to be successful, they must think deeply about how they propose to develop systems within organizations.

Knowledge work must also be distinguished from procedural work. Kidd (1994 quoted in Berghoff, 1998) has proposed several features which distinguish the differences between the two:

■ Knowledge workers are changed by the information in their environment, and they in turn seek to change others through information. Information, according to Kidd, is to be consumed and once digested is often of little further value. Information which may have a long-term use, such as drawings on white boards, is often left visible and uncategorized

■ Diversity and ad hoc behaviour patterns are common in knowledge work. New information is sought out, reused and passed on in opportunistic ways, dependent on the changing context and interleaving of the worker's activities. In contrast, consistency of method and output is important in procedural work

■ Communication networks are highly variable, with different patterns and use of media. Teams form and disband within the space of a day. The structure and job titles on an organisation chart are even less representative of what people do.

Proactive knowledge analysts, technical storytelling among staff and document-centred discourse are three ways in which knowledge is shared within organisations. Media that are now emerging within many organizations to support these processes are Web intranets integrated with agents and broadcast media, desktop audio/visual recording tools and document discussion environments.

Other key personnel in the knowledge management mix include consultants. The increasing interest in knowledge management or intellectual capital has inevitably led to an increase in the providers of knowledge management consultants. According to research conducted by Huseman and Goodman (quoted in Empson, 1999): 'No fewer than 78 per cent of major US companies in a recent survey claimed to be "moving towards becoming" knowledge based.' There are two fundamental reasons for this at the practical level, according to Empson (1999). First, during the 1990s capital and labour intensive industries in developed economies have continued to decline, while the relative importance of technology and information intensive industries has increased. Second, the use of technology has simultaneously liberated companies to promote the development of sophisticated systems to capture, disseminate and exploit new information more effectively. Empson then writes (1999):

At a theoretical level, two concurrent developments have contributed to an increased emphasis on knowledge in the strategic management literature. The first is the popularity of the resource based view of the company. This clearly identified knowledge as potentially the primary source of sustainable competitive advantage. The second is the development of post-modern perspectives on organisations which have challenged fundamental assumptions about the nature and meaning of knowledge within companies, industries and societies as a whole.

Empson then notes how many of the traditional models related to strategy have tended to focus on the external environment surrounding the organization, a typical example being Michael Porter's 'Five Forces Model'. This model does not explore the internal aspect of an organization. In contrast to this the resource-based perspective examines the need for a fit between the external market context in which a company operates and its internal capabilities. Empson then suggests that:

A company's competitive advantage, according to this view, derives from its ability to assemble and exploit an appropriate combination of resources. Sustainable competitive advantage is achieved by continuously developing existing resources and creating new resources in response to new market conditions.

Naturally there are contrasting views to this theory, notably Frank Blacker who argues that 'knowledge does not – and cannot – exist in any absolute or objective sense' (quoted in Empson, 1999). This challenges the notion that knowledge may be stored, measured and moved around the organization much like any other asset. Much of this thinking is based upon what we recognize as legitimate knowledge and how we choose to interpret and apply that knowledge. If knowledge is a social construct, then the prevailing conditions in the organization will directly influence how employees react to knowledge itself. Also, as a social construct, it would follow that it cannot be formally managed and Empson recommends caution when purchasing advice from consultants who will install a knowledge management system for a substantial fee.

This is where the crucial and most important challenge will be for organizations who want to develop into knowledge-based companies in the future. The most significant problem that they will face is creating the right culture and climate within the organization and developing the people to adapt and embrace this new way of thinking, acting and working.

What sort of behaviours should we expect from the key players in the organization and why are these behaviours important?

One major reason why there has traditionally been a resistance to sharing knowledge is the fact that knowledge represents a source of power for an individual. People worry about losing personal worth or value to their organization if they share their knowledge. Davenport and Prusak (quoted in Empson, 1999) are two proponents of knowledge sharing and have argued that there are three main conditions that will assist you to share your knowledge with your colleagues:

1. *Reciprocity.* Time and energy are finite and you are only likely to spend time to help a colleague if you think you will receive valuable knowledge in return, either now or in the future.

2. *Repute.* It is in your interest to be viewed as an expert in your company. With no reputation you have no power. It is very much in your interest to ensure that your colleagues respect you and acknowledge your expertise, giving you full credit wherever possible.

3. *Altruism.* According to Davenport and Prusak, this is also similar to self-gratification. There are some subjects we find interesting and fascinating and feel the need to talk to others about them.

These three fundamental conditions have led Davenport and Prusak to argue that an internal market for knowledge exists within an organization and that knowledge may be exchanged between buyers and sellers. The payment and reward systems are reciprocity, repute and altruism. Trust is clearly the essential lubricant for the smooth functioning of this market and examples of this have been shown to work in organizations where hoarding and refusing to share information have led to people being disciplined.

How do we encourage and support the key players in an organization to agree to promote and contribute to developing a knowledge-based culture which recognizes and rewards good knowledge sharing practice and discourages people from hiding and hoarding their expertise? According to Nonaka and Takeuchi (1995), there are five key conditions that must prevail if successful knowledge creation is to take place.

1. Senior management must be committed to accumulating, exploiting and renewing the knowledge base within the organization and be able to create management systems that will facilitate this process

2. Autonomy must exist. As it is individuals who develop new and innovative ideas, they must be allowed to explore the opportunities which present themselves and be given maximum scope to follow their own initiatives

3. The process of exploration can lead to creative chaos where flux and crises cause a reconsideration of established principles at a fundamental level

4. Redundancy means that knowledge should not be hoarded or rationed and that good practice in knowledge sharing, including that between totally unrelated individuals in an organization, must be rewarded

5. The final condition is known as 'requisite variety'. This means that an organization must be able to respond to the outside world and that the company's internal diversity must match the complexity of the external environment in which it is operating.

The reality in many organizations will be far removed from this model in some cases, as chaos and crises may stifle creativity and only serve to promote anxiety and insecurity. The lessons drawn from the era of business process re-engineering show us that the management of change and other recent fads have been used to disguise and cover up the hidden agenda of senior management to streamline and downsize.

Probably one of the most significant concepts to clarify in the minds of the key players within the organization is whether they are dealing with knowledge management or information management, that is, information management is often mistakenly rebranded as knowledge management. Empson writes (1999):

> problems arise because we are trying to incorporate the inherently ambiguous, fluid and abstract concept of knowledge into mental models, which have been shaped by highly structured, static and systemised forms of organisations.

This leads to the education of the key personnel within the organization and their personal training and development. By now it will now be clear and established that senior management within an organization has to genuinely and sincerely understand the real benefits of promoting knowledge management as a positive process within their organization. This may be much more difficult to achieve than it will first appear. The internal political climate will dictate and influence people's behaviour and attitudes towards the concept and eventual successful implementation of knowledge management.

Botkin (1999) maintains that knowledge management is critical to business success and his writing closely follows Drucker, who he quotes:

> To make knowledge work productive is the great management task of this century, just as to make manual work productive was the great management task of the last century.

SUMMARY

- There has been the emergence of knowledge workers and knowledge leaders

- Knowledge workers are changed by their environment, and they in turn seek to change others through information

- The most significant problem is to create the right culture and climate within the organization and to develop the people to adapt and embrace a new way of acting and thinking

- Reciprocity, repute and altruism are key to knowledge sharing

- The reality is that many organizations will be far removed from promoting knowledge management

- Recent fads such as the management of change have been used to cover up the hidden agendas of downsizing and rightsizing

- Senior management within an organization has to genuinely and sincerely understand the real benefits of promoting knowledge management as a positive process.

Arthur Andersen

TERRY FINERTY *Partner*

Q: *So what is Knowledge Management all about?*

A: Knowledge Management for me is about learning and making the most of what you learn. Knowledge is the sum total of three different approaches. It is something that is bought, something that is generated through thought and something that is gained through experience and learning, you need all of these ideas to paint a successful picture of knowledge. Tools such as best-practice databases are important, but that's not all, you still need people to learn new things, you have to learn about new technologies and what your targets are. It's a constant cycle of questioning yourself. You must create intellectual space to allow learning and to facilitate success.

Q: *And what other factors contribute to success?*

A: It's important to keep things in perspective with the workplace. If people do not enjoy what they actually do then this doesn't create a good environment to learn in, there is little curiosity or innovation. If you are a manager of a bunch of people who simply don't care what they are doing then no amount of technological systems can make them effective learners or very cooperative. This is a very important element. I also think that a sense of community, some common objectives must be present to generate success. Trust is another important factor, although I stress that this alone doesn't guarantee success. There must be no conflicts of interest.

Q: But in terms of benefits, in my experience, people invariably work to benefit themselves, how can you ensure that staff can remain interested in their work even when they gain no benefits for completing it?

A: This is the challenge, to keep a workforce motivated. I can remember a case of a small company that turned itself around by empowering the staff and removing high levels of control thus making everyone responsible. Within two years the dirty little factory full of a disloyal, de-motivated workforce began to thrive. Careful selection processes can help to recruit staff that actually want to work and be happy.

Q: If we strip off all the technical management models and theories are you saying that to be a successful business the emphasis rests largely on teambuilding?

A: No, however, it's an important factor so, for example, I could build a team together that are very good at performing their tasks, but they may not be able to see the future, to drive forward. If they can't see a move in the market you may have an effective team but they may not learn at a pace quick enough to be competitive, they may not be adaptive enough.

Q: So do you think that 'The Learning Organisation' as a concept is a prelude to Knowledge Management or is it the same?

A: I think it's the same, the early stuff all resonates very well with modern Knowledge Management. Productive conversation is important, the old factors of honesty and truth are still vital. To be honest enough to tell the truth and not skirt around issues is the best way to learn. There must always be space for reflection, to decide what you would have done differently and to see what must be done next, that's also a key factor in learning. If you have those things in place, what I think of as traditional Learning Organisation, then you can have groups of people collaborating and learning, creating new intellectual capital and explicit knowledge. The next step is to think of what kind of mechanisms I can use to leverage that learning and get the most out of it.

Q: What do you mean by leverage?

A: To make the most of what you are doing, particularly in the context of a large organisation. For example, our methodology database contains knowledge that can be used by consultants in unfamiliar roles. Where there is a gap in their personal knowledge the database can fill-in or put them in contact with someone more experienced in his area. It is constantly updated and creates all sorts of opportunities for learning. The database alone isn't enough, there needs to be the right community, technology and organisational space to use it.

Q: *Can technology form barriers, particularly if there is limited time to work?*

A: Yes sure, sometimes all that is required is a list of people to call up for help, sometimes the process of knowledge sharing is heavily technology dependent but in other cases it may well not be. Not just the ease of use but also the cost of technology and accessibility can be a hindrance. Again there needs to be an organisational mindset to allow knowledge sharing for it to be advantageous.

Q: *Do you think that specialist Knowledge Managers will become increasingly sought after in the New Economy?*

A: I don't know how it will shape out. Certainly the role of what we call now Knowledge Managers will continue to be important although they may not still be called Knowledge Managers. People will have to think about how do I create the conditions for innovation and how do I make the most of it?

Q: *That's a leadership role within an organisation, surely part of leadership is to encourage innovation?*

A: Yes that's true, I think all companies would agree with that but I don't think many are particularly good at it! Many companies have such rigid structures they inhibit innovation regardless of what they say about being innovative. There is much reflection going on, the agenda is to keep doing well and to do what is proven to work. Also sometimes it can be very hard to get your head up and look to the future and then even when that is done it can be very difficult to make the required change. There's a theory called 'Organisational Inertia' that basically says that although a company may look up and see the oncoming problems it may find it impossible to stop doing what has been successful for them historically. Therefore it's not the recognition of future pitfalls that is cause of problems but it's the incapability to react to them.

Q: *So resistance to change is a problem faced by many Organisations, how can this be overcome?*

A: Well a crisis is not the best way to do it, the best way is to get everyone pulling for an exciting future vision. Leadership is a big part of the solution.

Q: *Is that what the New Economy is really going to be about, change or suffer?*

A: It could be. The models we use for the New Economy is that historically we think of a business as it's assets that have been accrued over time, valuable physical and financial assets. But there are really a whole bunch of assets we don't currently think of as adding value. Things such as brand value, customer relationships, reputation and networks of supply, organisational assets such as intellectual capital and process knowledge. For example Microsoft are worth a lot of money because of the capabilities of their employees, their intellectual property, the lines to suppliers and the relationship with all their customers. The New Economy and successful management in it require an understanding and control over all these functions. This is where Knowledge Management can help. An example of poor management of these skills is Marks and Spencer plc. They have gradually eroded their relationships with suppliers and have lost track of the whole product development process, they no longer respond to consumers and customers. Five years ago you would have said that M & S had one of the strongest brand loyalties with their customers, now they don't. I wonder what management tools they've had to control this. I don't think the problems have arisen through mismanagement of their physical retail network or because of financial mismanagement but probably through supply agreements and customer awareness.

When I look at what's happening in the New Economy the explosion of technology facilitated by the low cost and trend to Globalisation has created a different mix when thinking of the worth of a business and importance of each individual function.

Q: *Can you elaborate, any examples?*

A: Sure, look at Dell, they have very few physical assets. Most things are outsourced, the factories, call centres, suppliers and manufacturers and so on. What Dell does is design the PC's and then manage the brand. Michael Dell used the telephone as a tool, located where the value is and then completely unseated people like Compaq and IBM. Cisco use new ways to recruit people in order to build up intellectual capital. It's done from their web-page and by e-mail where once you've expressed an interest you gain a buddy there who tells you what it's really like to work here and assesses you. In the New Economy the ubiquitous explosion of technology has allowed us to think of new ways to do things and get results.

4 The New Work Theories

Is knowledge management 'owned' by IT, HR, finance or marketing?

Reason (1994, p. 40) describes how a paradigm is taken as:

> a primarily intellectual structure; it is a set of agreed ideas and practices to which members of the scientific community conform.

Reason (p. 41) writes of Kuhn (1962) and his research into 'paradigm cases', and how the:

> methodologies of human enquiry can be seen as disciplines which can train the individual and develop the community towards a consciousness for future participation.

The literature covering both subjects of knowledge management and intellectual capital is interdisciplinary and wide ranging. During the literature review of this subject, knowledge management is written about in the context of human resource management, culture, the learning organization, management training and intellectual capital. Subject areas covered include financial benchmarking and information technology. Its roots are difficult to determine, however, it is clear that during the 1990s both subjects enjoyed popularity in various areas. I believe that from knowledge management and intellectual capital it is possible to identify a new management discipline or paradigm. I call this simply competitive knowledge management, hence the title of this book. Figure 4.1 depicts how knowledge management is the paradigm created after linking numerous other disciplines in a theoretical model.

Edward Truch is the Director of the Knowledge Management Forum at the Henley School of Management, which, at the time of writing, has over 40 corporate members. Truch agrees that a new academic and business discipline is developing in the area of knowledge management and that the crossover between information technology and human resource management is the challenge ahead. Truch argues that there are not enough people

Knowledge management   **Intellectual capital**

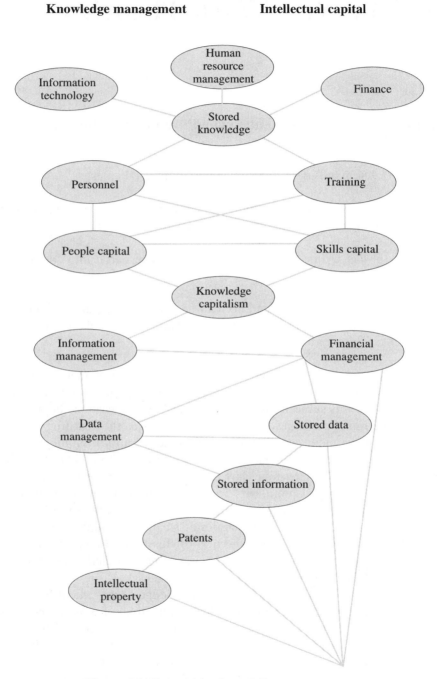

Figure 4.1 Competitive knowledge management

who really understand both these areas well enough and suggests the following reasons for the rise in popularity of knowledge management.

1. Knowledge management allows us to leverage the human potential and enables people to be far more effective, which benefits them at a personal level and the organization for whom they are working

2. As the proportion of intellectual assets increase in companies, there is greater pressure to demonstrate what value these assets represent

3. Investors, when looking at the potential of companies to shareholder value, are looking at precisely this type of measure

4. It is the enormous divide between the human resource and the information technology communities that needs to be bridged. (Truch, E., 2000, personal communication)

Many experts are quoting the new economy and the information age and it is the contention of many writers, including Burton-Jones (1999, p. 4), Roos et al. (1997, p. 10) and Stewart (1997, p. 12), that the information age defines knowledge as a factor of production, which suggests a different style of accounting practice to cope with this new business paradigm. As a new paradigm forms, it is usual for the underlying theory underpinning the new paradigm to draw on established theoretical frameworks from many disciplines. For example, brand management as a marketing discipline will include an element of knowledge management within its philosophy. This will be linked to the ownership, protection and leverage of a brand.

With new business paradigms, it is often the case that there are businesses or companies that push forward the ideology and demonstrate some form of leadership. Porter (1985, p. 181) discusses the differences in technological leadership and technological followership. Porter then examines differences in style between companies that decide to 'be the first down the learning curve' and those that 'adapt the product or delivery system more closely to buyer needs by learning from the leader's experience'.

Scarbrough et al. recognized the need to define knowledge management, its ideology, meaning and purpose and assess the impact it was making on people issues. Scarbrough et al. (1999, p. vii) noted that:

knowledge management tends to be treated mainly as an issue for information systems experts. The schemes they introduce are predominantly on the supply side, focusing on data and communications systems and the processes for making people's tacit knowledge explicit and available to the rest of their organisation. As a result, knowledge is treated as a commodity and often confused with data.

Similarly, Empson (1999) also tries to define knowledge and make clear the distinction between data and information. She considers it important to decide what is not knowledge, and writes:

It is not data and is not information. Data are objective facts, presented without any judgement or context. Data becomes information when it is categorised, analysed, summarised, and placed in context. Information therefore is data endowed with relevance and purpose. Information develops into knowledge when it is used to make comparisons, assess consequences, establish connections and engage in a dialogue. Knowledge can therefore be seen as information that comes laden with experience, judgement, intuition and values.

Masie (1999) notes the increasing popularity of the concept of knowledge management and how it is, 'on the lips of the Big Six audit and consulting companies'. Masie defines it as:

The systematic process of finding, selecting, organising, distilling and presenting information in a way that improves an employee's comprehension in a specific area of interest. Knowledge management helps an organisation to gain insight and understanding from its own experience. Specific knowledge management activities help focus the organisation on acquiring, storing and utilising knowledge for such things as problem solving, dynamic learning, strategic planning and decision making. It also protects intellectual assets from decay, adds to firm intelligence and provides increased flexibility. (http://www.masie.com/articles/knowl.htm)

Masie also writes of the impact of knowledge management on the technology training market and predicts that it will be significant. The following six areas will be affected:

1. Growing role of the big six and business consulting groups in organization-wide decisions about training and skilling

2. Growth of the big six and training management firms as outsource partners for all training

3. Opportunities and market pressure to serve as a supply chain for outsource partners

4. Need to integrate training management systems into core knowledge management and human resource management systems

5. Growth of new classification systems for training content, which will need to be integrated into offerings

6. Increased demand for ROI (return on investment) and assessment information.

SUMMARY

- Knowledge management is interdisciplinary

- Knowledge management includes subject areas such as information technology, human resource management, financial management, data and information management, training and development and intellectual property

- All these areas combined may be termed as 'knowledge management'

- A new business paradigm is being created and formed and is therefore evolutionary

- Knowledge leadership is a key factor in its development and progress

- The professional areas that will benefit in the immediate term are consulting and training services.

Case Study

Firefly

CLAIRE WALKER
Managing Director

Q: *How long have you been involved with knowledge management programmes?*

A: Since the company was formed in 1988, we have had a culture of continuous learning and sharing. This is as important to us today as it was 12 years ago. We have also been running PR campaigns raising the aware-ness and benefits of effective knowledge management for our clients for many years.

Q: *How seriously is knowledge management taken by senior management?*

A: Any successful and fast growth company should have knowledge manage-ment programmes in place. If they don't then it's a real threat for them and their growth will be limited. People can only remember a limited amount and a corporate memory can give people the information when they need it, in whatever form they need. You can measure the loss of knowledge by the amount of time it takes a new joiner to fill the gap of someone who's left.

At Firefly we take it very seriously. Not just the senior management, but everyone in the company is very aware of the importance of sharing. We know only too well that up-to-date information about developments in the media, shared amongst one another, can create previously unknown oppor-tunities and breathe extra life into a PR campaign. Our 100+ client-facing consultants spend on average one third of their day liaising with the media, one third liaising with clients and one third planning, researching, preparing and generating materials. Some of what you've learnt needs to be shared with colleagues. In Firefly we all need to know about changes, movements and upcoming stories/issues in the media, but one journalist can't personally keep in touch with 100+ consultants from Firefly.

Internally knowledge management has always been a challenge and a crit-ical factor in contributing to continued growth. From our experience with other companies, we know that the bigger you are the less able you are to share information as effectively. We have 125 people in the company and more than 100 of those are client-facing consultants. We are a people busi-ness. We have to have an effective knowledge management policy and sharing culture, so all our people can operate most efficiently and we can deliver excellent results for our clients because we understand their busi-nesses and we understand the media. When so much knowledge and value is in people's heads, without a knowledge management policy or a sharing culture, when people leave, are out of the office or on holiday they take that vital piece of information or their accumulated knowledge with them. So our focus is primarily on retention of people to keep building know-ledge within, and to encourage and reward sharing information when appropriate amongst ourselves, and finally by building a corporate memory via our intranet for everyone to benefit from.

Q: *Is it really possible to have a sharing environment?*

A: Yes, but it has to be worked on every day.

Our natural instinct as human beings is to achieve and be successful but not necessarily to share everything we have, and some selfish or ruthlessly ambitious people still may think 'information is power' – a hackneyed 80's saying. We come across them from time to time, and call them hippies (hoarders of information for political purposes) but within Firefly we discourage any such selfish behaviour, albeit in a positive way.

We instil in our people a sharing culture, and encourage and reward people for sharing relevant and timely information. We have around 70 client-facing teams all working in a cross-lattice environment, working on various projects and campaigns within the company. Most of these teams have been selected and networked together to share information and use or develop specific skills. With so many people working on so many clients, one team could be working on a campaign that is groundbreaking and national news and yet another team at the other end of the office has absolutely no idea what they are working on or why. Now in some situations that's how it should be because it is confidential campaign and that's fine, but in many situations what you would want to do is share the experience and share that knowledge accumulated with other people in the company.

Within Firefly we hold day-long off-sites twice a year to share information, we run monthly company meetings, frequent swapshops to share knowledge and expertise, hold smaller pow-wows to either brief everyone on company developments and to receive feedback on company matters and initiatives. We have regular Directors Question Time for all employees to ask unfiltered questions live, bulletin boards to enable online discussion forums, and a very comprehensive induction process to bring new joiners up to speed as quickly as possible. We also have mentoring schemes and new joiner events to encourage fast mixing into the organization.

Fireflies have an internal employee café area, and enjoy declared 'chill hour' on a Friday night to encourage people to talk to one another and share experiences from the past week. The senior executives run many internal training courses, always drawing on experiences from within the agency to tell 'war stories'. We have regular awards for excellence across the company for all levels and for all functions, whereby a manager will verbally declare to the entire company why a person has won an award and what precisely they did to win it.

Q: *How do you monitor or assess whether knowledge management is happening?*

A: You can't really measure precisely how successful it is, but you can witness it happening to some degree. You can measure team satisfaction in terms of knowledge that is communicated and shared, you can measure good leadership, coaching and the depth of understanding.

A testament to our knowledge management success from an external perspective is an overall highly positive rating from our clients in understanding their business and their markets and also our business. The evidence shines through in the independent client survey that we conduct each year. Further proof is provided by our positive rating on knowledge and understanding of the media, as researched in our independent annual survey of the media contacts we deal with daily. More evidence would be a drop off in internal e-mails at Firefly asking 'where can I find x?', or 'how do I do this?'

Q: *After 15 years of working, researching and reading in the area of human resource management, I feel that there can be a fair degree of cynicism within organizations. Do you think there is a low level of cynicism in this organization?*

A: I think there is a healthy level of cynicism here. But people are constructive in the way that they give feedback. When we get negative feedback, initially it might not taste so great, but we always take it to heart and respond. We solicit and get a lot of input into how the business is run, and what improvements can be made. If we didn't take on board people's suggestions, they wouldn't bother making any. There are many things that we get right and we get a lot of praise in our culture audits, and there are always some things that are not as right as they could be but no one hesitates to give us feedback. Two of our core values are to be inventive, and to evolve.

Q: *Sometimes employers find out when people leave the company what the problems really were.*

A: Sometimes it's not until you lose someone that you appreciate all the knowledge they have, and realize how difficult and slow it is to replace that knowledge. We always give exit interviews to outgoing staff and clients to find out where they have had problems, and how we can improve. That information is fed back constructively to individuals, or to managers or to teams.

Q: *Why do you think knowledge management is easier now than ever before?*

A: The technology boom over the past two decades has made a big difference and given us the resources that were previously incalculable and a conduit for good knowledge management to happen. It is now possible to share almost any type of file, and to store vast quantities of information that could be vital to any person at the right time. Technology searching capabilities are so sophisticated that you can search for word in a particular context so that the data recovery is not only superbly fast but almost 100% relevant or accurate.

However, whilst the technology capabilities can drill down to almost unimaginable depths, people still need to know what question to ask, value the source of the answer and know how to apply it. Now that's good knowledge management.

5 Is There a Difference between Knowledge Management and Intellectual Capital?

Knowledge management has become increasingly popular as a concept in business and management circles as the following quotes illustrate:

> Knowledge Management is an integrated, systematic approach to identifying, managing, and sharing all of an enterprise's assets, including databases, documents, policies, and procedures, as well as previously unarticulated expertise and experience held by individual workers. (Barron, 2000)

> Knowledge Management is a generic description of the culture, processes, infrastructure and technology within an organisation which maintains, grows, and optimises the use of its intellectual capital to deliver the strategic goals of an organisation with measurable financial results in the market place. (Handley, 2000, personal communication)

> Knowledge Management is the expropriation and process of professional knowledge in the hands of professionals who have traditionally used their knowledge to barter power, prestige and autonomy from management. It represents the last battleground between management and intellectual labour. (Kouzmin, 2000, personal communication)

> Knowledge Management caters to the critical issues of organizational adaption, survival and competence in face of increasingly discontinuous environmental change ... Essentially, it embodies organizational processes that seek synergistic combination of data and information processing capacity of information technologies, and the creative and innovative capacity of human beings. (*Journal for Quality & Participation*, 1998)

According to Thomas Stewart (1997, p. x):

Intellectual Capital is intellectual material – knowledge, information, intellectual property, experience – that can be put to use to create wealth. It is collective brainpower. It's hard to identify and harder still to deploy effectively.

Stewart also describes the time we live in as the 'new era' (p. x) and writes, 'wealth is the product of knowledge'. Stewart then describes some changes in international accounting practices. For example, the book price of a company, which appears on its balance sheet, and its market capitalization price may be two very different figures. A firm may be valued at £10,000,000 on its balance sheet, yet be worth £100,000,000 on the London Stock Exchange. So how does the £90,000,000 appear? The answer, according to Stewart, is in its intellectual capital.

Stewart's argument is based on his perception and understanding of the information age. He writes (1997, p. ix):

Information and Knowledge are the thermonuclear competitive weapons of our time. Knowledge is more important and more powerful than natural resources, big factories, or fat bank rolls.

He notes that Wal-Mart, Microsoft and Toyota were not richer than Sears, IBM and General Motors, but owned something for more valuable than physical or financial assets – their intellectual capital. He then suggests that numerous companies do not manage their corporate brainpower, which is the most important asset they have, and this represents a loss of billions of dollars in revenue and profit.

Other writers on this subject seem to follow a different theme. Roos et al. (1997, p. v) believe that intellectual capital is:

a language for thinking, talking and doing something about the drivers of companies' future earnings. Intellectual capital comprises relationships with customers and partners, innovation efforts, company infrastructure and the knowledge and skills of organizational members. As a concept, intellectual capital comes with a set of techniques that enable managers to manage better.

The perspective taken by Roos et al. is that the definition of intellectual capital must be clear in order to understand it and it must be measurable, that is, in order to manage intellectual capital it must be measured. For Roos et al., intellectual capital is essentially a strategic organizational

Table 5.1 Perceived value of a chief knowledge officer

	Not at all/not very valuable	*Very or extremely*
North America	48.8%	21.1%
Europe	32.5%	33.3%

Source: Amidon, D.M. and Skyrme, D.J. (1997) *Creating the Knowledge-based Business*, Business Intelligence, London, p. 59

issue, and the philosophy underpinning intellectual capital has a human resource management focus.

For Amidon and Skyrme (quoted in Bock, 1998, p. 7), the key personnel involved in developing and promoting intellectual capital are chief knowledge officers, who tend to be strategic thinkers with influence at board level at the respective organizations that they serve. These chief knowledge officers 'track the flow of knowledge from its source to its destination'. According to US consulting firm, Arthur Little, there are particular organizations that are more information dependent than others, such as banking, insurance, pharmaceuticals, utilities, computers and chemicals.

Amidon and Skyrme also write that, in 1997, chief knowledge officers were perceived to be more valuable in Europe than in the USA. The percentage of people who valued the function was 33% in Europe and 21% in the USA. The survey also noted that the chief knowledge officer's function was often executed by line managers, typically the research and development manager.

Amidon and Skyrme (1997 p. 59) note that the 'perceived value of a Chief Knowledge Officer' varies in North America and Europe by the percentages shown in Table 5.1.

Skyrme (1997) notes that '87% of the senior executives polled considered that their business was knowledge intensive'. According to Skyrme (1997 p. 5):

Managing a company's knowledge more effectively and exploiting it in the marketplace is therefore the latest pursuit of those seeking competitive advantage.

What is knowledge management?

Amidon and Skyrme (1997, p. 31) note two definitions:

Knowledge Management is something of a movement and theme, rather than something very definite. (Taylor, R., Unisys)

It's lots of concepts and framework, but I need help with practical knowledge problems, (Braddock, J., BNFL)

Amidon and Skyrme's findings (1997, p. 31) also note that the subject of knowledge management is:

typical of a subject in its infancy, where the definitions are not widely agreed, and there is not an established set of practices.

They did find that a 'growing number of companies were wrestling with the problems of knowledge' and that good knowledge management practice was critical to their success.

Amidon and Skyrme (1997, pp. 31–2) also note two other definitions:

Knowledge management is a natural evolution of our work in process management and total quality. It provides a vital focus on an important organisational asset. However, we try to avoid using the term knowledge management, because there has been a lot of hot air about it to date and is just as easily seen as another buzzword. As yet, there are not enough practical tools, methods and techniques. (Kilpi, E., Sedecon)

The central premise behind Knowledge Management is that all the factors that lead to superior performance – organisational creativity, operational effectiveness, and quality of products and services – are improved when better knowledge is made available and used competently. (Wiig, K., Knowledge Research Institute)

The philosophy underpinning intellectual capital

Skyrme (1997, p. 5) writes that knowledge and intellectual capital are the 'hidden' assets in a company and this mirrors the writing of Stewart (1997) who believes that firms create a 'competitive advantage' by managing their intellectual assets.

According to Roos et al. (1997, p. 15), intellectual capital is the latest in a line of thinking that has tried to tackle the problem of the management of knowledge. There are two streams of thought that have led to the development of intellectual capital as a concept, and these are strategy and measurement. Figure 5.1 illustrates this and shows how the strategy stream

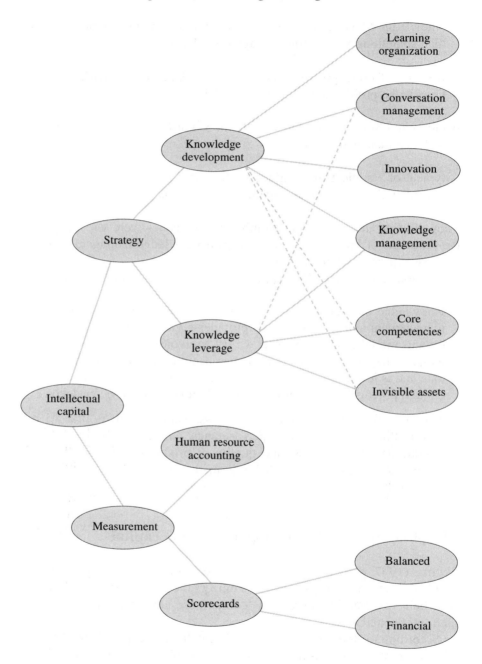

Figure 5.1 Conceptual roots of intellectual capital

Source: Roos et al. (1997) *Intellectual Capital – Navigating the New Business Landscape*,
Macmillan, Basingstoke – now Palgrave, p. 15

develops from knowledge development and the learning organization, plus the 'relationship between knowledge and success or value creation' (Roos et al., 1997, p. 15).

The lower stream depicted in Figure 5.1 tracks the measurement stream back to human resource management-led processes coupled with financial measurement techniques. The balanced scorecard developed by Kaplan and Norton (Roos et al., 1997, p. 21) attempts to assess financial and customer, internal and external growth measures. The perspectives are internal, external, present and future.

The upper stream follows a different pathway and uses the following concepts as stepping stones to intellectual capital. These stepping stones are:

1. Learning organization
2. Conversation management
3. Innovation
4. Knowledge management
5. Core competencies
6. Invisible assets.

Some of these areas link more directly into knowledge development and others into knowledge leverage. Invisible assets and core competencies tend to have a more direct link into knowledge leverage and less into knowledge development according to Roos et al.'s model. The learning organization, conversation management and innovation link more directly to knowledge development. The model suggests that knowledge management is equally linked both to knowledge leverage and to knowledge development.

Some of these conceptual areas have been examined and written about more extensively than others in human resource management literature, especially the learning organization and core competencies. Innovation is an area that traditionally sits in the marketing management arena and invisible assets in the sphere of accountancy. Moving down the list to the area of scorecards, financial scorecards were also developed for accountancy purposes and the balanced scorecard is more oriented towards human resource management.

There has been a debate emanating from HRM circles that knowledge management has taken over the baton from the learning organization (Scarbrough and Swan, 1999). This is possibly one of the most important areas to evaluate as it gives context and meaning to both concepts.

The learning organization achieved much popularity during the 1980s and 90s. According to Kelleher (1995, p. 192):

There appear to be difficulties in defining the concept of a learning organisation and Ceri Roderick (1993) argues that perhaps it might be more useful to understand that a precise definition may not be appropriate and that learning organisations display certain characteristics that distinguish them from more traditional organisations.

Belet (1995, p. 139) describes the learning organization as a new managerial concept and believes it 'conveys a new underlying managerial paradigm'. Belet also quotes leading academics on this subject.

A learning organisation is an organisation which facilitates the learning of all its members and continuously transforms itself. (Pedler et al., 1988)

The learning organisation can mean two things, it can mean an organisation which learns and/or an organisation which encourages learning in its people. It should mean both. (Handy, 1989)

An LO is an organisation skilled at creating, acquiring and transferring knowledge and at modifying its behaviour to reflect new knowledge and insights. (Garvin, 1993)

Scarbrough et al. (1999, p. 2) also give clear definitions of both knowledge management and the learning organization.

KM – any process or practice of creating, acquiring, capturing, sharing and using knowledge, wherever it resides, to enhance learning and performance in organizations;

LO – an organization that is able to discover what is effective by reframing its own experiences and learning from that process; by developing the skills of its people it continuously transforms itself (Pedler et al., 1991)

Scarbrough et al. (1999, p. 2) note that both knowledge management and the learning organization are labels and are not 'independent realities'. Therefore they treat them as 'language constructions used to articulate a view or a vision of the world'. They believe that the learning organization is more broadly based and is:

primarily concerned with the ways in which organisations design themselves to value, manage and enhance the skills and career development of
their people in order to ensure continuous organisational transformation.

They believe that knowledge management is different because it:

is more narrowly focused on the ways in which firms facing highly
turbulent environments can mobilise their knowledge base (or knowledge assets) in order to ensure continuous innovation in projects.

The above analysis suggests that knowledge management is most useful
during times of change where the business environment is experiencing
instability. This implies that knowledge management could be of real use
during particular phases of an organization's lifecycle; in particular during
mergers and acquisitions and periods of market consolidation.

Belet also writes that the concept of the learning organization has been
criticized for its ambiguity and its youth as a concept. All the writings
reviewed by Belet seem to position the learning organization into the
framework of organizational change and he associates it with a 'new
managerial philosophy' (1995, p. 141). What Belet fails to acknowledge
are the complexities of the learning process and how this relates to the
learning organization. Marsick and Watkins (1997) highlight the importance of 'informal and incidental learning' and provide a summary of
'reflective and transformative learning theories'. They note that, 'A sense
of inner discomfort requires a trigger' (Boyd and Fales, 1983) and that an
'openness to new information' (1997, p. 302) is useful. They also note that
'unfreezing' and 'refreezing' is part of transformation learning, according
to Argyris (1970).

Marsick and Watkins also note that 'individuals must learn continuously
in order to be competitive' (1997, p. 304). They note, along with many
other writers on the subject of management learning, that there has been a
general movement towards self-directed learning, increasingly promoting
the philosophy of self-reliance and self-development (p. 304; Tough, 1979,
1982; Pedler et al., 1994).

Conversation management, mentioned by Roos et al. (1997), alludes to
the work of Nonaka and Takeuchi (1995), whose research highlights one
of the fundamental differences between Western and Eastern (especially
Japanese) management thinking. They suggest that in Japan knowledge
expressed in words and numbers represents the 'tip of the iceberg' only.
They view knowledge as primarily 'tacit', something not easily visible or
expressible and highly personal. In Japan, according to Nonaka and

Takeuchi (1995), knowledge management is chiefly about converting tacit knowledge into explicit knowledge, so that it can be shared with others. This will be examined in Chapter 6, however, the underlying principle is that by sharing information and knowledge through conversation much may be gained by both the participants and the organization.

Innovation tends to be associated with new product development and thinking that is at the leading edge within a given industry. It is precisely due to technological innovations that knowledge management and intellectual capital have arrived. According to Seely Brown (Botkin, 1999, p. 221):

> Innovation is everywhere; the problem is learning from it. Where employees confront problems, deal with unforeseen contingencies, or work their way around breakdowns in normal procedures. The problem is, few companies know how to learn from this local innovation and how to use it to improve their local effectiveness.

SUMMARY

- Knowledge management has become more popular as a subject and concept in business and management circles

- Intellectual capital is intellectual material that can be put to use to create wealth

- There has been a belief that some economies are moving (or are about to move) into the information age

- Intellectual capital and knowledge management tend to be strategic organizational issues

- The aims and objectives of these concepts are to bring a competitive advantage to the organization

- The conceptual roots of intellectual capital derive from two streams: strategy and measurement

- The concept of the learning organization seems to have been the precursor to knowledge management in the UK

- Individual learning of employees in the 1980s and 90s became much more person centred, in terms of being self-directed, with a greater emphasis on self-development and self-management.

Department of Trade and Industry

PAT LANGFORD

Q: Is there anything unique about what you do in terms of knowledge management at the DTI?

A: In terms of a government department, we are unique in that there are nine people looking at issues which include knowledge management as part of our overall modernization programme. The project that I am dealing with at the moment (May 2000) from a change management point of view is the 'briefing@dti' system. This will give people in the department desktop access to current policy statements on the hot topics facing us at any one time. It's a completely new approach to how we handle our topical briefs and to get it accepted in the department will require a significant effort in terms of communication, education and training, which is what I view as change management. At the moment, this is a full-time commitment for me but other people in the unit are looking at other knowledge management projects.

To create briefing@dti we have more or less copied the Department of Health system that they have had for three years, however, it's been adapted significantly to fit into our own IT environment. This still has teething problems but, hopefully, when these are ironed out, we will be ahead of most government departments. There's quite a lot of pressure on other departments now to develop their own systems, as there is going to be something called the 'Knowledge Network', which is going to be a pan-Whitehall initiative. It will take all the individual departmental briefing systems and link them up, so that you can actually see everything that is going on in policy terms with each department.

Q: Do people have resistance to this?

A: Possibly. We launched the system on 3 May but we are doing the change management on a fairly softly, softly basis. We are training people how to put information onto briefing@dti. Not a lot of information has gone there yet because we need to answer people's 'what's in it for me?' questions.

Q: *So actually getting information from people is proving to be quite an interesting exercise itself?*

A: Yes. We need to get people to accept that in fact this is not going to create more work for them and it's really going to make less work. briefing@dti enables them to write a brief, put it on the system, and then they will not be asked to write a core brief on that subject again, providing they keep it up to date, whereas, at the moment, they may be asked to brief on the same issue over and over again. A very small number of people will see that brief. The author will see it, the people with whom they clear it will see it and the minister or senior civil servant for whom it has been written will see it. What we want to do is to make sure that the information is available right across the department, so everyone can see what's going on with Rover, BMW, Nuclear Power, and so on. briefing@dti is breaking down those communication and information barriers.

Q: *What have you done to promote and assist this cultural change?*

A: Various things. I have designed a workshop on 14 July which will bring together representatives from those who provide briefing and those from the Private Office who commission it. This meeting will be structured in such a way that we ensure that we provide answers to the questions we know people will ask. We shall put them up on posters and say 'Here's the question, there's the answer and you can add any other thoughts you have'. If we had done it in the traditional way, that is, we call the meeting and say 'Who wants to comment?', up go the hands and people have to sit back and listen to a stream of questions and complaints from others. This is because it's new, it's different, and they don't understand necessarily that it's going to cause them less work. It will eventually free them up to do more enjoyable things.

We have persuaded one of our ministers to do a short interview and photo shoot with me in which she will say 'As far as I'm concerned, this is the bees knees, this is what I expect people to be using from now on. It's a key component of e-government.'

briefing@dti is in its very early stages and it will be interesting to see how this develops. I am currently developing FAQs (frequently asked questions) and putting them onto the system to reassure people that we are aware of their concerns and to provide them with answers to the questions they ask.

Department of Trade and Industry

PATRICIA HEWITT *Minister for
E-commerce and Small Business*

*Q: Where do you think the UK is today in terms of international
competitiveness in terms of e-commerce?*

A: In terms of e-commerce, we have a clear idea of the UK's standing
compared to the other major economies, as for the past four years the DTI
has been producing an annual report, which benchmarks progress in use of
e-commerce by businesses in the UK and other G7 countries (and in
Sweden in this year's report).

From this benchmarking we know that the majority of businesses in the
UK are online and have access to the relevant online technologies. For
example, nine out of ten people work in businesses which have Internet
access. This is on a par with the USA. The proportion of businesses actually trading online in the UK is the highest in all the countries studied.
Overall it is fair to say that the UK is in a group of leading countries with
respect to online business.

*Q: Where do you think the UK will be in 20 years time in relation to other
economies?*

A: Since one of the greatest challenges of the knowledge economy is its
unpredictability, it is impossible to predict with any sort of accuracy how
the economy, markets and society will develop over the next 20 years.
What we can do is ensure that everyone in the UK is aware of the challenges and opportunities offered by the new technologies. To do this we
have launched the UK online programme which has a target of giving
everyone in the UK access to the Internet by 2005. Our 'UK online for
business' programme is also aimed at small businesses, to make them
aware of the benefits that online technologies can bring.

We also recognize that government itself will have to learn and adapt and
that is why we have undertaken a massive programme to get all government services online by 2005. We are also investing in the science base,
which is where all the new technologies and businesses will come.

Q: *What are the hurdles and barriers to overcome in order for the UK to achieve the government's vision?*

A: Internet access is growing fast, with over one-third of homes connected already. Digital television is also spreading quickly – about one in five homes today and one in two of families with children. The UK online programme is designed to get people, business and government itself online.

Many people are still worried about using a computer or trying the Internet. Our new UK online centres – 600 already, rising to 6000 by 2002 – are already encouraging people to have a go. There is also a very high take-up rate for basic IT courses, which are free to people out of work and very cheap (an 80% discount) to people in work.

One of the barriers to the growth of online business is the fear of giving credit card or other personal details online. We're publicising consumer tips for safe e-shopping. And we have encouraged industry to develop a 'Trust UK' scheme – hallmarking good Codes of Practice, which protect online shoppers, for instance by guaranteeing confidentiality and offering online dispute resolution if anything goes wrong.

Q: *The skills shortage appears to be demand led from industry. How can we reverse the situation to where UK citizens can be skilled enough to anticipate future demand?*

A: This government is determined to close the digital divide. We have a role to play in ensuring that businesses and individuals can make full use of e-commerce. There should not be a society of information have and have-nots.

That is why we are making sure people have the IT skills and access they need to be full citizens of the modern world. We are doing this by first ensuring that every community has access to new technologies. We are creating a new technology of online centres, where you will be able to surf the Net, and get advice if you need it. We are aiming to open over 2000 centres around England by the end of 2002. (The devolved administrations have their own policy initiatives in this area.) And we are encouraging the recycling of computers to those who cannot afford new ones. Second, providing IT training. This autumn, the learndirect services will open for business, delivering its courses online. By 2002, learndirect aims to provide one million courses a year. Finally, raising standards in schools – over 98% of secondary schools and 86% of primary schools are now connected.

6 Knowledge Creation and Sharing

For the Japanese, knowledge means wisdom that is aquired from the 'perspective of the entire personality' (Nonaka and Takeuchi, 1995, p. 29).

Japanese companies have steadily increased their world market share in consumer goods and this is not due to extraordinary entrepreneurial powers, or because of an efficient liberated economy, according to Nonaka and Takeuchi (1995). They explain that it is due to the skills and expertise of 'organizational knowledge creation'. The authors recognise that manufacturing prowess and access to cheap capital has played its part in Japan's growth, however, they also see the importance of close and cooperative relationships with customers, suppliers and government agencies. Nonaka and Takeuchi also mention the importance of lifetime employment, the seniority system and other human resource practices, however, they still put forward the view that Japanese companies are especially good at 'bringing about innovation continuously, incrementally and spirally'.

For Nonaka and Takeuchi, knowledge is the basic unit of analysis for explaining organizational behaviour. They argue for a fundamental shift in thinking about what an organization does with knowledge. More specifically, they start with the belief that the business organization not merely 'processes' knowledge but also 'creates' it. The two professors claim that management research and studies have neglected the subject of knowledge creation by the business organization and years of research into Japanese firms have convinced them that knowledge creation has been the most important source of Japanese international competitiveness.

Nonaka and Takeuchi also make clear the differences between *tacit* and *explicit knowledge* that many other writers have also explored. Explicit knowledge can be articulated into formal language including grammatical statements, mathematical expressions, specifications and manuals. This form of knowledge has been the dominant mode in Western philosophical tradition, according to the authors, and may be transmitted across individuals formally and easily. Tacit knowledge is arguably more important, hard to articulate with formal language and is personal. Its roots lie within an individual's value, belief and perspective system. It involves the intan-

85

gible factors and Nonaka and Takeuchi believe that 'tacit knowledge has been overlooked as a critical component of collective human behaviour'. They argue that tacit knowledge is an important source of Japanese competitiveness and this is why Western people view Japanese management as an enigma.

The goal of their study was to formulate a generic model of organizational knowledge creation (Figure 6.1). They believe that in Western philosophy the individual is the principle agent who possesses and processes knowledge and in Japanese organizations knowledge creation takes place at three levels: individual, group and organizational. From this they deduce that there are two major components of knowledge creation – one is the *form* and the other is the *level*. There are then two forms of interactions, *tacit* and *explicit*, which interact between the individual and the organization to bring together the four major processes which constitute knowledge creation:

1. Tacit to explicit
2. Explicit to explicit
3. Explicit to tacit
4. Tacit to tacit

1. Socialization: Tacit to tacit
2. Externalization: Tacit to explicit
3. Combination: Explicit to explicit
4. Internalization: Explicit to tacit

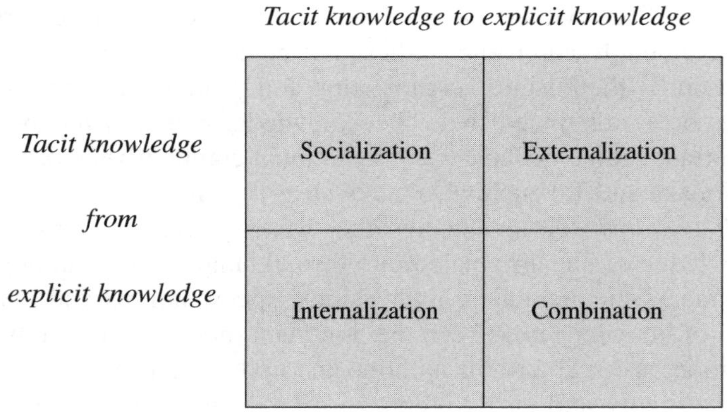

Tacit knowledge to explicit knowledge

Tacit knowledge	Socialization	Externalization
from		
explicit knowledge	Internalization	Combination

Figure 6.1 Four modes of knowledge conversion

Source: Nonaka, I. and Takeuchi, H. (1995) *The Knowledge-Creating Company*, p. 62

These four modes need further explanation.

From tacit to tacit: 'Socialization is a process of sharing experiences and thereby creating tacit knowledge such as shared mental models and technical skills' (Nonaka and Takeuchi, 1995, p. 62). One individual may acquire tacit knowledge from another without using language. Through observation, imitation and practice, the key to acquiring tacit knowledge is experience, according to this model. However, there are practitioners who refute this idea, suggesting that tacit knowledge is very personal and cannot be transferred. Nonaka and Takeuchi (1995, p. 63) point out that if there is no shared learning process, 'it is extremely difficult for one person to project her- or himself into another individual's thinking process. The mere transfer of information will often make little sense, if it is abstracted from emotions and specific contexts in which shared experiences are embedded'. Examples of socialization within a learning context are brain-storming exercises, and a classic example is the informal meetings set up at Honda to solve complex development projects. These were known as *tama dashi kai* (brainstorming camps).

From tacit to explicit: 'Externalization is a process of articulating tacit knowledge into explicit concepts. It is a quintessential knowledge-creation process in that tacit knowledge becomes explicit, taking the shapes of metaphors, analogies, concepts, hypotheses or models' (Nonaka and Takeuchi, p. 64). According to Nonaka and Takeuchi, after we have conceptualized an image, we generally tend to express it in language. The process of converting tacit knowledge into articulate knowledge is facilitated through writing. When there are gaps in our understanding of these concepts as we communicate them to each other, this promotes discussion and dialogue which leads to reflection and differing styles of interaction.

When the externalization mode is operational, it typically demonstrates itself in the form of concept creation and seems to be triggered by dialogue or a collective reflection. One frequently used method for concept creation is to use *deduction* and *induction*. Concepts may be deduced from information already known, for example when Mazda created the RX-7 concept, its corporate slogan was 'create new values and present joyful driving pleasures'. The RX-7 was conceptualized by deduction from its corporate slogan. At the same time, team members in the USA were attending concept clinics. These clinics were aimed at gathering information from experts and customers and helped to *induce* the concept of the RX-7.

Other means by which the process of externalization may be facilitated is by the use of analogy or metaphor. A good example used by Nonaka and Takeuchi describes how Canon were developing a disposable cartridge for a mini-copier designed for home use, which would eliminate the need for maintenance. The cost of an engineer to be available for troubleshooting across the country would be too costly and therefore Canon decided to eliminate the part that caused the most maintenance problems.

The taskforce responsible for solving this problem met on numerous occasions and after many 'heated discussions', the team leader, Hiroshi Tanaka, sent out for some cans of beer. After the team had enjoyed the contents, Tanaka asked, 'How much does it cost to manufacture this can?' The team then explored the possibility of applying the process of manufacturing the beer can to manufacturing the drum cylinder, using the same material. By clarifying similarities and differences, they discovered a process technology to manufacture the aluminium drum at a low cost, thus giving rise to the disposable drum (Nonaka and Takeuchi, 1995, p. 66).

Nonaka and Takeuchi describe these examples and explain the 'use of metaphor and analogy in creating and elaborating a concept'. In their opinion 'externalisation holds the key to knowledge creation, because it creates new, explicit concepts from tacit knowledge' (1995, p. 66). There is a 'sequential use of metaphor, analogy, and model ... Metaphor is a way of perceiving or intuitively understanding one thing by imagining another thing symbolically' (p. 66). Nonaka and Takeuchi quote Bateson (1979) 'it is often used in abductive reasoning or non-analytical methods for creating radical concepts'. Nonaka and Takeuchi further explore the notion of metaphor and describe how it should not be confused with analysis and they quote Donnellon et al. (1986) who argue that 'metaphors create novel interpretation of experience by asking the listener to see one thing in terms of something else' (p. 67). They also suggest that metaphors 'create new ways of experiencing reality'. Therefore, metaphors are 'one communication mechanism that can function to reconcile discrepancies in meaning'.

From explicit to explicit: 'Combination is a process of systemizing concepts into a *knowledge system*' (p. 67). The explanation given is that when individuals communicate through the various methods available such as, 'documents, meetings, telephone conversations, or computerized communication networks' (p. 67) they are able to exchange and combine knowledge. Usually this involves sorting, adding, combining and categorizing the explicit knowledge and Nonaka and Takeuchi note how formal education and training at schools leads to knowledge creation. They write that the MBA (Master of Business Administration) is a good example of combination processing.

From explicit to tacit: 'Internalization is the process of embodying explicit knowledge into tacit knowledge. It is closely related to "learning by doing". When experiences through socialization, externalization and combination are internalized into individuals' tacit knowledge bases in the form of shared mental models or technical know-how, they become valuable assets. For organizational knowledge creation to take place, however, the tacit knowledge accumulated at the individual level needs to be socialized with other organizational members, thereby starting a new spiral of knowledge creation' (p. 69).

Nonaka and Takeuchi then explain that explicit knowledge is usually converted into tacit knowledge by way of oral communication, written communication or illustrations and diagrams. Documentation assists individuals to internalize what they have experienced and also assists others to 're-experience' their events. Examples of this are when customer complaints are recorded and then read by other team members. Nonaka and Takeuchi describe how General Electric developed an answer centre in Louisville, Kentucky and documented all calls made in order to help the new product development team to re-experience what the product development team had experienced. Over 200 operators would respond to telephone calls which could be as many as 14,000 per day, which then resulted in General Electric programming a computerized database system. This system was programmed to solve around 1.5 million 'potential problems and their solutions' (p. 69). This computer system was then equipped 'with an on-line diagnosis function utilizing the latest artificial intelligence technology from quick answers to inquiries; any problem–solution response can be retrieved by the operator in less than two seconds' (p. 69).

This example from *The Knowledge-Creating Company* demonstrates how, through the use of technology, organizations may be more responsive to customer needs. Nonaka and Takeuchi put forward a compelling argument that competitive advantage is created when the 'four modes of knowledge creation' are acknowledged, recognized and developed within organizations.

SUMMARY

- Japanese companies have steadily increased their world market share in consumer goods

- One explanation is due to organizational knowledge creation

- A business organization may process and create knowledge

- There are two major components of knowledge creation, form and level

- There are two forms of interaction, tacit and explicit

- They combine and create four modes: socialization, externalization, internalization and combination

This Japanese view has been accepted by American and European academics and businesses and, if coupled with technology, may produce time, cost and profit improvements.

Case Study

Chartered Institute of Personnel Development

ROY HARRISON

Q: What can a chief knowledge officer and knowledge management add to a company?

A: Without knowledge management, knowledge is measured independently of people and so psychological issues are underplayed, it brings complexity of a relevant level to debates about knowledge and its uses and adds the people aspect to new IT resources.

Q: What are the differences between information and knowledge, for example on a company intranet of case studies? If one consultant looks up a case study previously undertaken and uses that as a model for a similar problem, is he using knowledge or just information?

A: I think that is an example of sharing knowledge because it is information that has been worked on, actioned and then reflected upon and so there is knowledge there. There is a definite aid to knowledge sharing through IT, but that is not the whole answer, people need to be involved in the process as well. For example, knowledge is great but you need people to learn it! Also these people must then be motivated to create and acquire knowledge which is of use to an organization. The problem is that not all people want to learn and in some companies the attitudes are very different. In a competitive organization, for example one where salesmen are rewarded on contracts and volume sold and so on, then I would not be willing to share my hard-earned knowledge with anyone else! It would be commercial suicide to share information within this industry.

Q: So any industry that operates like that has a natural aversion to knowledge sharing?

A: Exactly.

Q: *If a knowledge sharing system were introduced, would the company/ industry/personnel adapt to it, change their behaviour and make more money as a result?*

A: There are options, for example using a sales team that is rewarded on a team basis. What I'm saying is that the way in which organizations operate across the economy are many and varied, much of the assumptions currently underpinning knowledge management take only one model and somehow suggest it is generally applicable, this is not the case. In organizations without a trust culture, there is no easy way you can promote knowledge sharing, my point is that much of the people aspect of knowledge management is underexplored.

Q: *And where does knowledge management fit into the new economy?*

A: Knowledge management can build knowledge into a system that will be available to all workers within a company, although there maybe an emerging new economy of high-skilled jobs, knowledge management can be the foundation for these jobs. The two schools of thought, one being we are all knowledge workers now and the other being that there is a knowledge elite being supplied by everyone else, are still to be addressed. Will the gap between the rich and poor come together or widen? People management and development of all workers is now critical, how do you motivate a non-knowledge worker? Our research is not complete but the future is in the balance.

Q: *And your research is?*

A: Our studies currently are into intellectual capital, how learning takes place in knowledge-based organizations and the issue of knowledge management in the context of organizations living in uncertainty. We are also looking at linking knowledge management and how it affects business performance as well as working with financial institutions on human capital issues.

Q: *Do you think knowledge management is here to stay now?*

A: I think it's a fundamental issue and will stay, however I think the title will change because knowledge management is a top-down concept, putting emphasis on the management and control of systems, much of what we've discussed is more complex. We want to ensure that people's personal knowledge adds value to organizations and therefore to society.

Q: *So you have a fundamental belief that there is a connection between business and society?*

A: Yes, very much so. I believe that in the end business, economy, society, politics are just different ways of looking at the same thing.

Q: *Do you see knowledge management as a learning tool or more of an IT-based initiative?*

A: We're still at a stage thinking about the advanced principals and methodology of knowledge management, what's happening in BT, Casio and the Post Office and so on are a mixture but the really valuable ideas are bringing both together.

Q: *Is knowledge management something much deeper than just 'selling training' for the Chartered Institute of Personnel and Development?*

A: Yes, it's part of the underlying corporate identity of an organization. What is that organization? What's it for? What are its objectives? What is its core knowledge and values and how does the knowledge within that organization deliver? But it's only one part of a wider corporate management issue.

Q: *So does this mean that there's a gap in the knowledge of senior management about knowledge management and that there is a lot of education necessary for these people who run our corporations?*

A: If the corporate board doesn't understand about knowledge management they will miss the trick. This is the importance of having the chief knowledge officer at the board table so that, as issues are debated and decisions are made, knowledge dimensions are part of the input and part of the output.

Q: *Is the chief knowledge officer just going to be a human resource manager in disguise or will he/she have a very different role to an orthodox human resource or personnel director?*

A: It is very different; although the chief knowledge officer will have a big impact on human resources, he or she will also have an impact into the financial and IT area and will have to be part of the production processes of an organization. It is an independent role and if an organization sees that its competitive edge is represented by its core of knowledge, it will be dealt with in its own right.

Q: *Is someone who had a personnel role and moved into business information systems a good example of a chief knowledge officer but without the label?*

A: Yes I think you're right, I could name several people who are really chief knowledge officers but without the title!

Wolff-Olins

SLAWA SHUMOWSKI
Futurologist

Q: *Is the whole notion of knowledge management itself just a consulting fad that has been with us for a while and will just fade away?*

A: That's a difficult question, at the moment I don't think it will disappear but only if people continue to treat knowledge as a major commodity.

Q: *Is it possible that in developing markets, such as the East European markets, new economy companies will be welcome?*

A: Yes definitely, just look at India, which is now a major software power.

Q: *Do you think that the traditional oil companies are planning for the day when oil is no longer a major commodity?*

A: I guess, these companies do not just deal in oil, of course they must be looking at different industries.

Q: *As a futurologist, do you have the next 15 years of your career planned out for yourself?*

A: In human resources there is a famous saying, 'You always have to know what is the step up to the next step'. If you know what you want then you should know what to do, a very philosophical question!

Q: *Do you think that certain companies' and industries' style of business will become more influential over the next decade as a result of being knowledge intensive? Can you think of any examples?*

A: There will be a change, with new winners, as long as the story behind the products can be maintained, knowledge intensive dot.coms must be able to supply their products.

7 Knowledge Management and Measurement

How to measure and manage both

There is increasing pressure for companies to measure intellectual assets and recent statements by leading financial business leaders describe why this is the case.

> We're very much moving into a knowledge-based economy, and the proper measuring and accounting of assets that create wealth in a knowledge-based economy is critical. It is the whole underlying foundation of our economy going forward. [Steven Wallman, former Commissioner, Securities and Exchange Commission] (Skyrme, 1998, p. 13)

The recent interest in dot.com companies has been an interesting learning process in knowledge management. Some of the Internet start-ups are now folding and the reason, according to some, is due to their lack of general management. Islam and Farrelly (2000) write:

> Boo.com sale hopes suffer early blow ... Deutsche Post and UPS are among creditors owed a total of $25 million for their services. Boo has no assets other than its tarnished brand, intellectual property and the website, which has been kept running as a showpiece for potential buyers.

According to Skyrme (1998, p. 14), there are three main motivations for managers to measure their intangible and knowledge assets:

- It provides a basis for company valuation (asset focus)

- It stimulates management focus on what is important (action focus)

- It may be used as a baseline for justifying investment in knowledge management activities (benefit focus).

Nicholas Bahra is grateful to Karin Breu, David Grimshaw and Andrew Myers for assistance and for permission to quote extensively from *Releasing the Value of Knowledge: A Survey of UK Industry* (2000). Much of the material in this chapter is adapted from that paper.

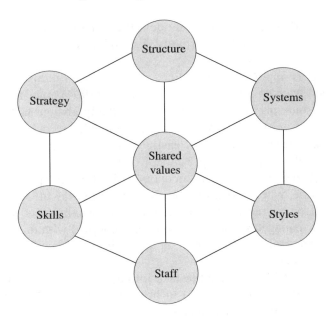

Figure 7.1 McKinsey's 7-S framework

Source: Peters, T.J. and Waterman, R.H. (1995) *In Search of Excellence: Lessons from America's Best Run Companies*

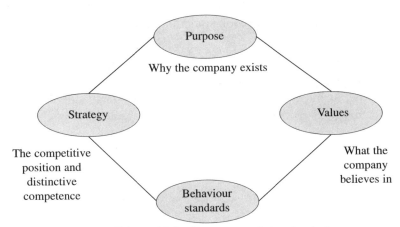

Figure 7.2 The Ashridge mission model

Source: Campbell, A. (1996) *Mission and Management Commitment*, Ashridge Strategic Management Centre

There are numerous theoretical models that have been created to help managers to manage more effectively. Two of these models are depicted here (Figures 7.1 and 7.2).

Both models apply to organizations working in an industrial economy and are good ways to assess strategic fit. Kotler (1994) notes that the environment surrounding organizations will inevitably change faster than the 7-Ss. Similarly with the Ashridge mission model, the behavioural standards that are necessary may not easily translate across various cultures. One idea would be to develop a model that can be used across cultures and, in particular, in developing economies in, for example, Central and Eastern Europe, where the issues are complex in terms of developing the economies from agrarian to information. It is usually how intercultural sensitivity is managed in these environments coupled with the emotions of people that are trying to survive in an increasingly competitive world that determines success.

This new model would need to take into account the fact that an information infrastructure would need to be developed, which would need a specific focus for project management. Also, the feelings of people would need to be considered. Funding is the key to the success of such projects, as various stakeholders need to be involved at various levels. Finally, fellowship is necessary to ensure that real trust is created. This does not imply a male gender focus, but applies to both genders, as it is often the women in many communities who bring people together in a spirit of cooperation. The model could look something like Figure 7.3.

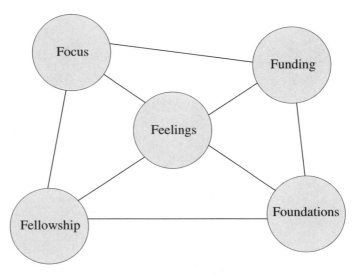

Figure 7.3 The five Fs model

What are knowledge-based business benefits?

According to Dr Karin Breu at Cranfield School of Management, respondents to their recent survey were asked to highlight from a list of business benefits those which their organizations had achieved to date, as well as to identify potential, future benefits. This list is represented in Table 7.1.

Table 7.1 Knowledge-based business benefits

■ New products/services	*Innovation and growth*
■ Research and development	
■ New business opportunities	
■ Developing new markets	
■ Innovative capability	
■ Reducing geographical barriers	*Organisational responsiveness*
■ Organisational integration	
■ Organisational flexibility	
■ Sharing ideas	
■ Organisational learning	
■ Speed of decision making	
■ Customer retention	*Customer focus*
■ Customer service	
■ Meeting customer needs	
■ Product/services quality	
■ Supply chain efficiency	*Supply network*
■ Integration of logistics	
■ Supplier relationships	
■ Sustaining existing markets	
■ Time-to-market	
■ Process innovation	*Internal quality*
■ Capability for change	
■ Operational efficiency	
■ Project management	
■ Product/services management	
■ Staff morale	
■ Quality of decision making	

Source: Breu, K. et al. (2000) *Releasing the Value of Knowledge: A Survey of UK Industry*, p. 9, Cranfield School of Management

Based on their analysis, certain themes emerged that factored the set of business benefits into five classes of higher level business benefits. These relate to the following areas:

- Innovation and growth
- Organizational responsiveness
- Customer focus
- Supply network
- Internal quality.

According to the study (Breu et al., 2000, p. 10):

> Innovation and growth describes the business benefits that emerge from a market-facing innovative impact that leads to new products and services, increased research and development output, new business opportunities, new markets, and innovative capability.

> Organisational responsiveness relates to the business benefits that result from reducing geographical barriers, achieving organisational integration and organizational flexibility, sharing ideas and organisational learning, and improving the speed of decision making.

> Customer focus summarises the business benefits that result in customer retention, good customer service, meeting customer needs, and product and services quality.

> Supply network describes the business benefits organisations can drive in their supply chain management in increasing supply chain efficiency, in integrating logistics, in tightening supplier relationships, in sustaining existing markets, and in reducing time-to-market.

> Internal quality encapsulates inward-facing business benefits that result from process innovation, developing and sustaining a capability for change, operational efficiency, better project management, effective product/services management, improved staff morale and quality of decision making.

Organizations then rated their performance in terms of achieved versus potential business benefits of knowledge exploitation and the following picture emerged (Figure 7.4).

The spidergram represents views of organizations in relation to the achieved (see grey line) versus the potential (see black line) higher level benefits of knowledge exploitation. The axes represent the percentage of

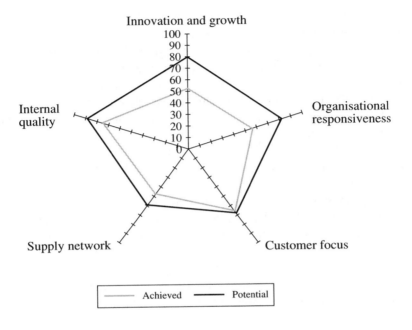

Figure 7.4 Business benefits of knowledge
exploitation: an overall business view
Source: Breu, K. et al. (2000) p. 10, Cranfield School of Management

organizations identifying the degree to which a higher level benefit has been achieved. For example, while approximately 80% of the surveyed organizations identified innovation and growth as a potential business benefit of knowledge exploitations, just over 50% of the surveyed organizations felt they actually had achieved that business benefit.

The 'spidergram' is an effective method of compiling a performance profile based on the empirical data. The shape of the grey line graphically represents organizational performance of knowledge exploitation to date. The shape of the black line, in contrast, is indicative of the potential performance of knowledge exploitation that organizations envisage as possible in future. For example, as the grey profile clearly shows, with the exception of customer focus, organizations currently are underperforming consistently, with innovation and growth and organizational responsiveness revealing the biggest performance gaps.

The identification of the performance gaps helps business decision makers in realizing the areas in the business where the potential for value creation is not being fully exploited and in directing future investments in knowledge exploitation. Moreover, the size of the performance gap as indicated by the difference between the black and the grey line expresses the degree of investment, resource allocation and senior management commitment required to seize the opportunity for knowledge exploitation. And, finally, peaks on the axes, whether potential or achieved, represent those areas in the business with the highest potential for value creation. For example, nearly 90% of organizations consider internal quality as the top business benefit of knowledge exploitation and, thus, as the peak area of value creation.

A more detailed view of achieved versus potential business benefits of knowledge exploitation at the overall level of the total sample is depicted in Table 7.2.

The primary performance gaps in knowledge exploitation relate to innovation and growth and organizational responsiveness. The secondary performance gaps are in internal quality and supply network. Notably, customer focus is the single business benefit where all the surveyed organizations almost achieved their perceived potential (p. 12).

The analysis of the business benefits of knowledge exploitation in the Cranfield survey are undertaken in the following way:

1. Presentation of the top three potential business benefits of knowledge exploitation as identified by the respondents and ranked in terms of their potential for value creation.

2. Presentation of the top three gaps in terms of the discrepancy between the business benefits that have been achieved to date and the potential business benefits that still can be achieved in future.

3. These gaps, while they may not be identical with the primary business benefits as identified in 1, constitute the most significant areas for future value creation through knowledge exploitation. Hence, for each of the

Table 7.2 Business benefits of knowledge exploitation: an overall business view

	Achieved %	Potential %	Gap %
Innovation and growth	53.2	80.7	27.4
Organizational responsiveness	57.3	83.4	26.1
Internal quality	75.2	89.0	13.8
Supply network	46.8	59.0	12.3
Customer focus	66.9	68.1	1.2

Source: Breu, K. et al. (2000), p. 11, Cranfield School of Management

top three gaps in benefits realization, specific areas will be identified to help organizations to focus their attention in order to drive the highest value of future investments in knowledge exploitation.

In the Cranfield survey, a more detailed picture of the organizations' performance on achieved versus potential business benefits of knowledge exploitation is formed from the analysis of the data at a functional level. The functional areas for which the data were analysed include:

- customer services
- operations
- finance/accounting
- product/services development/R&D
- general management/strategy/business development
- sales
- marketing
- human resources.

Another established method to measure whether your organization has a knowledge based culture is to use a well-designed questionnaire such as the one supplied by Amin Rajan at Create (see Appendix at the end of this chapter).

12 ways to measure intellectual capital

The Montague Institute has identified several approaches for measuring intellectual capital (Graef, 1997):

1. *Relative value.* Bob Buckman of Buckman Laboratories and Lief Edvinsson of Skandia Insurance are proponents of this approach, in which the ultimate goal is progress, not a quantitative target. For example, have 80 per cent of employees interacted with customers in a meaningful way?

2. *Balanced scorecard.* Supplements traditional financial measures with these additional perspectives: customers, internal business processes, and learning or growth. The term was coined by several Harvard Business School professors.

3. *Competency models.* By observing and classifying the behaviours of successful employees and calculating the market value of their

output, it   is possible to assign a dollar value to the intellectual capital they create   and use in their work.

4. *Subsystem performance*. It can be relatively easy to quantify success or progress in particular aspects of intellectual capital. For example, Dow Chemical was able to measure an increase in licensing revenues from better control of its patented assets.

5. *Benchmarking*. Involves identifying companies that are recognized leaders in leveraging their intellectual assets, determining how well they score on relevant criteria and comparing your own company's performance against their performance. Example of relevant criterion: leaders systematically identify knowledge gaps and use well-defined processes to close them.

6. *Business worth*. This approach centres on these questions: What would happen if the information we use now disappeared? What would happen if we doubled the amount of key information available? How does the value of that information change after a day, a week or a year? Evaluation is focused on the cost of missed or underutilized business opportunities.

7. *Business-process auditing*. Measures how information enhances the value of a business process, such as accounting, production, or marketing.

8. *Knowledge bank*. Treats capital spending as an expense instead of an asset and treats a portion of salaries (normally a 100 per cent expense) as an asset because it creates cash flow.

9. *Brand-equity evaluation*. Measures the economic impact of a brand (or other intangible asset) on such factors as pricing power, distribution reach and ability to launch new products as line extensions.

10. *Calculated intangible value*. Compares a company's return on assets (ROA) with published average ROA for the industry.

11. *Microlending*. A new type of lending that replaces tangible assets with such intangible collateral as peer-group support and training. Used primarily to spur economic development in poor areas.

12. *Colonized reporting*. Suggested by SEC (Securities and Exchange Commission) commissioner Steve Wallman, this approach supplements traditional financial statements (which give a black and white picture) with additional information that adds colour. Examples: brand values and customer satisfaction measures.

SUMMARY

- Many leading financial experts believe that we are moving into a knowledge-based economy

- There are three reasons for managers to measure their intangible assets: asset focus, action focus, and benefit focus

- Knowledge-based business benefits can be classed into five key areas: innovation and growth, organizational responsiveness, customer focus, supply network, internal quality

- By conducting professional surveys you can discover how knowledge management relates to various organizational achievements

Case Study

Intellectual Capital Services

DR STEVE PIKE

Intellectual Capital Services (ICS) has developed a methodology to measure intellectual capital. Dr Steve Pike of ICS notes the relative importance of resources in value creation for a financial services company (Table 7.3).

Table 7.3 Importance of resources in value creation

Type of resource	Percentage
Human	43
Monetary	19
Organizational	17
Relationship	15
Physical	6

Pike depicts how navigators can assist as a conceptual map of a company.

Q: What is a navigator?

A: A navigator is a conceptual map of the company (Figure 7.6). It is not used to show business processes as such, although at more detailed levels it can, but is a view of how the intellectual capital elements that are used in real processes are valued. The size of the 'bubble' in the diagram is a measure of how important the resource is for the value creation of the company, but more important, are the arrows that connect them. The thickness of the arrow represents the importance of the 'transformation' of one 'stock' of intellectual capital to another. For example, the transformation of human competence and intellectual agility to IP is a measure of the importance of this aspect of R&D.

Q: *How do you create a navigator?*

A: The navigator is drawn from numerical data (Figure 7.5). Several other pieces of information can be drawn from it, notably the figures for return on intangible resources (ROIR). As the navigator is a conceptual map depicting relative influence in value creation, the ROIR figures are a management guide to how a company treats its resources; does it invest in them or simply use them.

The final diagram (Figure 7.8) shows the ROIR (actually the negative of the logarithm of ROIR) on the y-axis and the importance of the stock on the x-axis. You can see that the ROIR for the most important stock – the clients – is close to 0, which means that the investment the company puts into its client relationships is in proportion to the benefit obtained from them.

Q: *Could you explain the significance of the competence score?*

A: Competence has a high score (Figure 7.8), which means that the company is not investing in training its staff; it probably just recruits in its talent. Cash on the other hand is at the bottom meaning that it is readily generated but its use is a problem. If management is happy to have unused cash and distribute it to shareholders then that's fine, otherwise it could be used to invest in other resources.

Q: *How would you describe knowledge management?*

A: Knowledge management is a 'meta-activity' of the company and can be analysed using more detailed navigators in the same way as my simple example. However, the 25% figure (Figure 7.5) means that that when considered at that level, the components of human capital are responsible for 25% of the value creation influence of the company. The ROIR figure is the ratio of the importances of the flows into and from human capital. The figure of 7.29 indicates that human capital is a source of value creating influence. Looked at another way, you could say that there is insufficient investment in human capital in the company.

Q: *Does the word relational refer to relational capital?*

A: Relational (Figure 7.5) means relational capital and is a coarse top-level category of intellectual capital (the other top-level categories being human, physical, monetary and organizational capital). Relational capital is a composite of the importance to the overall business of customers, agents, potential agents, competitors, the financial community and so on. Navigators and the next level down are far more revealing.

Q: *What do the figures inside the spheres represent?*

A: Figures inside spheres (Figure 7.5) represent the relative influence of that stock in creating value. Figures of influence are filtered to show only the most important flows – this keeps the diagram simple. Low figures are excluded and the remainder renormalized. The figure of 1.2% is the importance placed on the outflow of funds in value creation. The inflow will have gone in small elements to various parts of the navigator and were almost certainly filtered out.

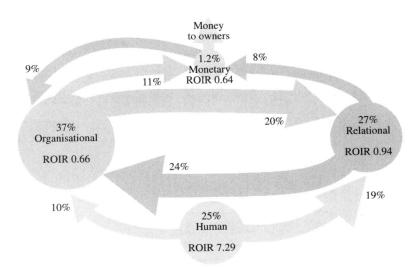

Figure 7.5 The navigator depicting the return on intangible resources

Source: Intellectual Capital Services Limited

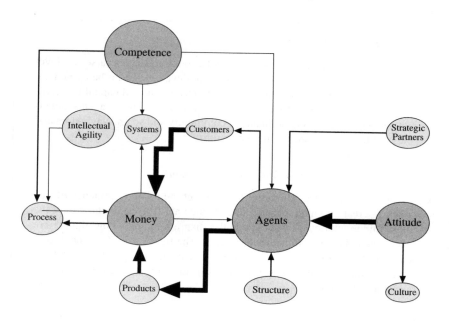

Figure 7.6 The navigator depicting relationships
between agents, attitudes, culture and finance
Source: Intellectual Capital Services Limited

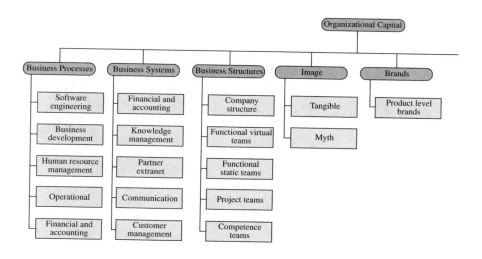

Figure 7.7 Where knowledge management is
within a financial services company
Source: Intellectual Capital Services Limited

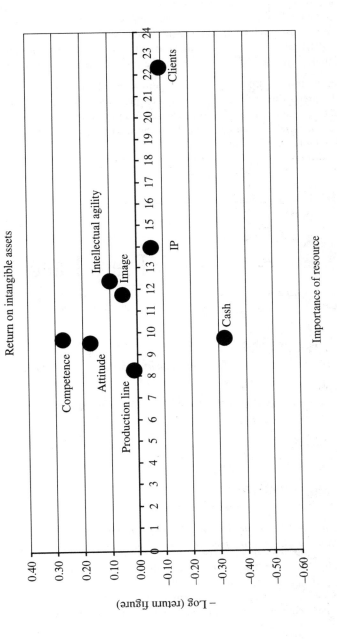

Figure 7.8 Some simple results from the navigator process

Source: © Copyright ICS Ltd, 2000

Q: If the ROIR figures are less than one, what does that mean?

A: Since the navigator is a conceptual map, individual flows do not represent real business processes or meta-processes such as knowledge management in themselves (although these things can be deduced from navigators with care). ROIR figures less than one mean that the item is a sink for value. That is, more is put into the resource that the resource affects elsewhere.

At the crude top level, knowledge management can be organizational-to-physical representing the use of process or explicit knowledge in a production process. It can be organizational-to-human in training and mentoring, and it can be human-to-human (visible at the next level down) in knowledge sharing between people.

Pearn Kandola

BINNA KANDOLA
Occupational Psychologist

Q: Can you explain how knowledge management relates to organizational psychology?

A: As occupational psychologists we have to keep up with business, in effect all we have is knowledge.

Q: Is your product the knowledge of the people in your firm? Is this what you sell?

A: Yes, that's our expertise, our product.

Q: So you're a classic example of a knowledge-intensive company. Do you transfer that knowledge effectively to your client?

A: Our working partnerships are one of our values, if the client requires that knowledge, then we supply it. Often they lack resources. That's why they look outside their organizations. Clients do not always want in-house psychologists. They use us as and when required, to not employ us all the time is really cost effective.

Q: Are there too many competitive threats to an individual to communicate and share their knowledge?

A: People like to protect their positions. Knowledge is power. The processes that organizations have to protect their knowledge actually stifle the creative use of that knowledge.

Q: Can knowledge management relieve these problems of stifling knowledge sharing?

A: It can help with knowledge sharing, but what you do with it is affected by other factors such as company attitude. To have more knowledge is one thing, putting that knowledge to some benefit is something else.

Q: What does knowledge management mean within Pearn Kandola that is different from other consultants?

A: We have our own knowledge, the knowledge of psychology. Other consultants don't have any knowledge to manage, they offer a process and that is their knowledge. Knowledge management is about networks and sharing of information.

Q: Is there is a genuine shift towards an increasingly knowledge-based economy, both in Britain and internationally?

A: I returned from America in April where I met a professor who said that the new dot.com type industries will soon face difficulties because they are unconventional and do not have the types of structure in place to enable them to survive. (N.B. This prediction was correct.) New economy companies will only succeed if they learn from old economy companies.

Q: So you don't really believe there is a shift in the old and new economies happening here?

A: Oh no, there is a shift but the shift is because of technology and not that big.

Q: As a psychologist, do you think that all this new technology and increasing office work has created a happier, healthier Britain or perhaps a harder working, more stressed out nation?

A: Well for me there is no difference, technology has helped, we can work from home and find information much more easily, we now can type our own letters and do our own filing.

> **Q:** *So your industry has become more knowledge intensive?*
>
> **A:** I suppose so, yes, although we've always been able to work from home, it's just easier now. Before, if working from home, we'd have to come in instead of just clicking a document to send it here.
>
> **Q:** *What types of firm do you work with?*
>
> **A:** Large multinationals.
>
> **Q:** *What sorts of assignment do they ask you to do for them?*
>
> **A:** Our three areas are assessment, development and diversity. Ensuring that people have the competencies, skills and abilities to meet their objectives is a key determinant of organizational effectiveness.

Appendix: Self-assessment toolkit

Guidance notes

This toolkit is designed to help you to audit your company's practices on maintaining and enhancing your company's corporate memory. It does this by focusing on two aspects of the elements identified under knowledge culture:

- Relevance: how relevant are the identified elements to the current circumstances of your organization?
- Implementation: to what extent are each of these elements currently being implemented in the organization?

In each case, your are invited to give a three-point score, as follows:

Relevance	Score	Implementation	Score
None	1	None	1
Some	2	Some	2
Large	3	Large	3

After scoring, please deduct the relevance score from the implementation score for each category to give you the difference. Areas where the net score is negative are the ones that need specific actions.

A Knowledge Culture: Systems

	(A) Relevance 1 or 2 or 3	(B) Implementation 1 or 2 or 3	(B – A) Difference (+) (–)
A *Competitor benchmarking:* Identifying and implementing best practices by competitors			
B *Groupware/intranet:* Using technologies across the organization to assist the knowledge sharing process			
C *Search engine:* Moving towards creating an internal market in knowledge			
D *Knowledge coordinators:* Giving individuals the responsibility for coordinating knowledge within a division or an organization			
E *Staff selection criteria:* Ensuring that new recruits are able to subscribe to the values conducive to knowledge sharing			
F *Competencies* Ensuring that knowledge sharing competencies are part of training and developmental initiatives			
G *Contractual obligations:* Getting senior management to actively endorse knowledge management			
H *Virtual teams:* Bring together employees from different divisions and/or locations via video conferencing to offer different approaches to thinking and working			
I *Communities of practices:* Promoting self-organized groups where employees exchange ideas and thoughts on common work practices and aims			
J *Team-based rewards:* Recognizing and rewarding teamwork			
K *Metrics:* Measuring the impact of knowledge sharing in different areas of the business			
L *Balanced scorecard:* Ensuring that the impact of knowledge management is assessed in financial and non-financial terms			

B Knowledge Culture: Values

	(A) Relevance 1 or 2 or 3	(B) Implementation 1 or 2 or 3	(B − A) Difference (+) (−)
A *Broad vision:* Aligning knowledge management to a 'guiding star'			
B *Business as community:* Making sure that employees see their company like any social entity in which they have rights and responsibilities			
C *Knowledge champions:* Securing support for knowledge sharing from senior staff			
D *Role models/gurus:* Singling out and praising people for their exemplary work in knowledge management			
E *Coaching and mentoring:* Encouraging personalized methods of training and development which unlock employees potential to maximize their own performance and that of their own organization			
F *Cross-functional teamworking:* Getting employees from various functional silos to work together to pool different ways of thinking and working.			
G *Encourage experimentation:* Providing the opportunity for employees to try out new ideas and working methods			
H *Learning by trying:* Enabling people to develop a can-do mentality			
I *Tolerate mistakes:* Supporting a no-blame culture which acknowledges that experimentation inevitably results in mistakes			
J *Recognize successes:* Ensuring that good knowledge management practices attract recognition			
K *Real-time feedback:* Providing employees with immediate feedback to help their own learning			
L *Honest feedback:* Giving constructive feedback on which people can act			

	(A) *Relevance* *1 or 2 or 3*	(B) *Implementation* *1 or 2 or 3*	(B – A) *Difference* *(+) (–)*
M *Retain 'reject' pool:* Providing the facility for people to retrieve and develop ideas in the future that may not be relevant today			
N *'Gut-feel' index:* Using surveys to ascertain whether employees feel that the above values are implemented in daily activities			

C Knowledge Culture: Behaviours

	(A) *Relevance* *1 or 2 or 3*	(B) *Implementation* *1 or 2 or 3*	(B – A) *Difference* *(+) (–)*
A *Action learning:* Arranging work in ways that encourage experiential learning by doing			
B *New language:* Moving away from highly specialized terminology towards universally recognized vocabulary			
C *No jargon:* Avoiding ambiguous, meaningless terms which cause confusion and irritation			
D *True stories:* Publicizing real life experiences which people can learn from rather than having to rely on textbooks and detailed reports			
E *Metaphors:* Using images of pictures to stimulate mental and emotional intelligence			
F *Identification:* Making people aware of how knowledge sharing will help them			
G *Values:* Showing how sharing has a worthwhile impact on the entire organization			
H *Beliefs:* Demonstrating the fact that knowledge sharing is a workable and practical activity throughout the organization			

	(A) Relevance 1 or 2 or 3	(B) Implementation 1 or 2 or 3	(B – A) Difference (+) (–)
I *Reciprocity:* Showing that it is only by giving that one receives			
J *Interdependency* Making sure that people are aware that knowledge is power only if it is shared			
K *Soft rewards:* Highlighting the fact that knowledge sharing means immediate gains such as less hassle or reduced working hours			
L *Personal legacy:* Encouraging employees to do worthwhile things that leave a lasting impact			

Source: Rajan, A. et al. (1999) *Good Practices in Knowledge Creation and Exchange*, Create, Tunbridge Wells

8 How to Recognize Success

This chapter draws extensively on original research undertaken by Cranfield School of Management. Copies of the full report may be obtained from Microsoft UK. A complete exposition of this research can be found in Karin Breu and Geoff Smith (forthcoming 2001) *Selling Knowledge: Making Knowledge Management Mainstream in Today's Connected Enterprise, Financial Times*/Cranfield Management Research in Practice Series.

My personal belief is that you will know success when it arrives, provided that you are in tune with yourself and your market. Perhaps that is a little bit like saying that 'gut feel' is the best way to make business decisions, when we know that gut feel is really not enough to satisfy all the various stakeholders in your business.

There are various methods to assess the psychological, emotional and organizational state of being of a corporation or firm at any one moment in time and these are some possibilities:

- An attitude survey
- Training audit
- Quality circles
- Internal communications audit
- Structured staff selection processes, including exit interviews
- Feedback processes
- 360 degree appraisal
- Intuition.

The chances are if you are working in a highly charged, profitable and dynamic environment and you have not implemented any of the above, then you may not see or feel the need to introduce them.

However, the mark of exemplary management is the use of any of the above initiatives in a failing company to turn it into a successful one.

One of the most important and useful theories which could contribute to this area is how 360 degree appraisals can help. Although I would not

Nicholas Bahra is grateful to Karin Breu and Geoff Smith for their assistance and for permission to quote extensively from their forthcoming book, *Selling Knowledge: Making Knowledge Management Mainstream in Today's Connected Enterprise.*

115

always advocate the use or implementation of such an appraisal, its theory is something to consider. According to Professor Warner Burke:

> It is an important assumption of many leadership and management training and development programmes that if a manager is to be maximally effective, he or she must be made aware of (a) his or her own actions and (b) the consequences of those actions on others through some form of individually directed feedback process. Such belief is also reflected in the ever increasing popularity of multi-rater or 360 degree feedback systems for managerial assessment and development purposes. (quoted in Bahra, 1997)

High performers in organizations tend to lead to high-performing organizations. In the Cranfield survey, Karin Breu noted the profile of high-performing organizations.

Benchmarking business performance in knowledge exploitation

Benchmarking is the process by which organizations can discover the specific practices that are responsible for high performance and adapt and apply them to their organization. The Cranfield survey reported on the findings of how organizations actually perform, in their view, on each of the practice items. In this way, current business performance in knowledge exploitation can be identified. Performance was then contrasted across functions and industries to uncover variations and to later elicit the characteristics of high-performing organizations.

Current business performance in knowledge exploitation

The analysis at the overall level elicited a contrast in what organizations consider best practice in knowledge exploitation (see dark grey bars in Figure 8.1) versus their actual performance on each of the practice items (see light grey bars). The mean scores for performance are plotted in rank order. Again, scores ranged from 1 = very poor performance to 7 = very good performance.

The analysis of the full sample produced a consistent message: the higher the importance of a particular practice was regarded, the lower the organizations' tended to rate their performance and vice versa. The crossover in the performance–importance pattern indicates where organizations

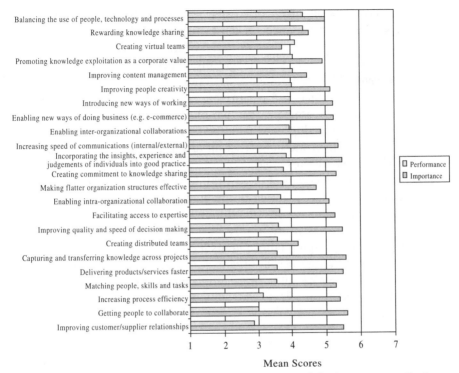

Figure 8.1 Business performance in knowledge exploitation: an overall view

Source: Breu and Smith (forthcoming 2001) Cranfield School of Management

need to focus their attention in order to improve current knowledge exploitation practice.

While this elicits the performance gaps on best practices at the overall level, there are more detailed differences in what constitutes best practices in functions and industries. Managers seeking to increase performance in value creation through knowledge can thus take one of two approaches: they can either direct their attention to the top practices in knowledge exploitation identified for their own function or the key practices in their industry sector.

Benchmarking best practice in knowledge exploitation

To help organizations to improve their performance in knowledge exploitation, a benchmarking tool was developed by Cranfield. This tool is designed to visualize an organization's performance and allow it to relate its performance against other organizations. The benchmarking process as extracted from this survey thus involves a two-step procedure. In step one, organizations assess their performance on the best practice indicators. Step two graphically represents the results in terms of the five best practice themes (knowledge-driven culture, knowledge infrastructure, distributed working, knowledge transfer, working practices). In order to achieve this, a score was calculated for importance and performance. The ensuing analysis plotted importance against performance in a two-dimensional matrix.

This analytical procedure was undertaken for the whole sample as well as each of the functions and industries surveyed. In the following, the most significant findings are presented.

The results of the analysis at the overall level are depicted in Figure 8.2.

Ratings in the top-left quadrant of the matrix indicate that, while importance of a practice item is considered high, the associated performance is low. Conversely, ratings in the top-right quadrant indicate that an organization is performing high on those items it considers important. Ratings in the bottom-right quadrant reveal organizations that perform high on items they actually consider of subordinate importance. And, finally, ratings in the bottom-left quadrant reflect organizations that perform low on items of low importance.

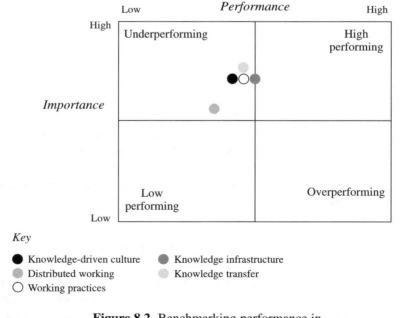

Figure 8.2 Benchmarking performance in
knowledge exploitation: an overall view
Source: Breu and Smith (forthcoming 2001), Cranfield School of Management

The analysis by Cranfield reveals that, at the overall level, the sample organizations are consistently underperforming. On four of the key practice themes, namely, knowledge-driven culture, knowledge transfer, working practices, and distributed working, organizations are not, overall, creating value through knowledge exploitation. Their performance in the practices underpinning knowledge infrastructure constitutes some exception as it is positioned on the boundary between the high-performing and underperforming quadrant. This result suggests that organizations, overall, still need to improve performance in knowledge exploitation.

At the cross-functional level, the analysis revealed no significant variations in their performance in knowledge exploitation. The pattern for each of the functions was very similar to the overall picture and hence they are not reported here. However, at the industry level, significant variations were discovered. For example, the financial services sector shows high performance, going against the norm, on knowledge infrastructure and working practices (Figure 8.3). By contrast, the public sector shows the lowest degree of performance in knowledge exploitation (Figure 8.4).

Distributed working represents a group of practice items that are rated fairly low in importance in the public sector relative to other sectors and

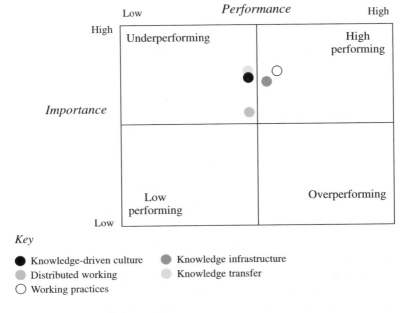

Figure 8.3 Benchmarking performance in knowledge exploitation: a financial services sector view

Source: Breu and Smith (forthcoming 2001), Cranfield School of Management

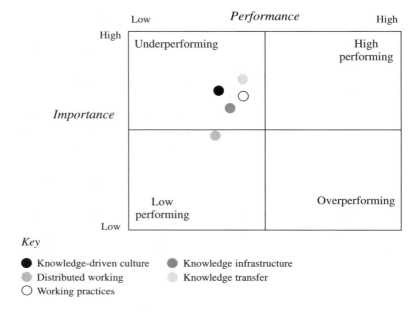

Figure 8.4 Benchmarking performance in knowledge
exploitation: a public sector view
Source: Breu and Smith (forthcoming 2001), Cranfield School of Management

functions. In sum, the public sector features lowest in realizing value from
knowledge exploitation.

The potential of technology in supporting
knowledge exploitation

The survey further addressed the question of the role and relevance of
technology in supporting value creation from knowledge. Respondents
were asked to rank in terms of effectiveness and ineffectiveness a set of
the most prevalent technologies applied in knowledge exploitation. The
analysis overall established that, in view of the capability of technology
applications for supporting the exploitation of knowledge, there is a clear
shift identifiable between what was considered effective in the past and
what will be effective in the future (Table 8.1).

While the overwhelming majority of respondents considered e-mail
(74%) as the leading technology for knowledge exploitation in the past,
only a minor proportion (31%) continues to view it as effective in the

Table 8.1 Views of effectiveness of technology applications
in knowledge exploitation: past versus future

Top ten effective applications overall	Past (%)	Future (%)	Top ten effective applications overall
E-mail	73.9	47.8	Internet
Management information systems (MIS)	36.4	35.3	Intranet
Shared databases	30.4	31.0	E-mail
Intranet	23.4	27.7	Shared databases
Audio conferencing	22.8	26.1	Customer relationship management (CRM) software
MS office environments or equivalent	20.7	23.9	Desktop video conferencing
Internet	18.5	17.9	Management information systems (MIS)
Document management	13.6	14.7	Extranet
Workflow management	10.9	13.6	Enterprise resource planning (ERP) systems
Enterprise resource planning (ERP) systems	10.3	10.9	Document management

Source: Breu and Smith (forthcoming 2001), Cranfield School of Management

future. While management information systems (MIS) and shared databases ranked among the top three technologies in the past, in future, the Internet is considered the foremost environment for effective knowledge exploitation, followed by intranet environments and e-mail. The shift from leaner to richer technology environments is indicative of the shift from data and information management in the past to knowledge exploitation today and in future. The complexity and ambiguity of knowledge requires rich technology applications that are capable of supporting the management and sharing of complex content as it is incorporated in people's experiences, expertise and understanding of the business context.

Similarly, regarding the overall view of ineffectiveness of technology applications for supporting knowledge exploitation, there is also an identifiable shift between what was considered ineffective in the past and what will be ineffective in the future (Table 8.2).

Comparing views of ineffectiveness of technologies in supporting knowledge exploitation in the past and in the future, it is notable that audio conferencing features as the most ineffective. Overall, desktop video

Table 8.2 Views of ineffectiveness of technology applications
in knowledge exploitation: past versus future

Top ten ineffective applications overall	Past (%)	Future (%)	Top ten ineffective applications overall
Audio conferencing	35.9	50.5	Audio conferencing
Desktop video conferencing	29.9	33.7	Interactive TV
Document management	26.6	27.2	Personal information management systems
Handheld devices	23.9	26.1	Document management
Shared databases	23.4	25.5	Desktop video conferencing
Customer relationship management (CRM) software	20.7	20.1	Groupware
Interactive TV	19.0	19.6	Handheld devices
Workflow management	17.4	18.5	Workflow management
Management information systems (MIS)	15.2	13.6	Enterprise resource planning (ERP) systems
Personal information management systems	15.2	12.5	Customer relationship management (CRM) software

Source: Breu and Smith (forthcoming 2001), Cranfield School of Management

conferencing, that commentators frequently promoted as a key knowledge management tool for its richness in combining text, visual and audio channels, has apparently not proven particularly effective in business practice to date.

Views of the role of technology in knowledge exploitation were also analysed with specific reference to the realization of business benefits (Table 8.3).

As can be seen, Internet, intranet, followed by e-mail environments were considered key technologies for supporting value creation in future. For the key areas for future value creation as identified in the previous analysis, namely innovation and growth and organizational responsiveness, a very similar representation of the top five technologies emerged. Customer relationship management (CRM) software and shared databases are seen to play a secondary role. A view across the five areas of future value creation, however, reveals that the Internet is consistently viewed as the top technology for supporting knowledge exploitation.

Table 8.3 The future role of technology in supporting value creation: an overall view

Innovation and growth	%	Organizational responsiveness	%	Customer focus	%	Supply network	%	Internal quality	%
Internet	46	Internet	45	Internet	43	Internet	47	Internet	46
E-mail	37	Intranet	36	E-mail	36	E-mail	34	E-mail	36
Intranet	35	E-mail	35	Intranet	35	Intranet	32	Intranet	35
CRM software	24	CRM software	25	CRM software	28	Shared databases	27	CRM software	26
Shared databases	24	Shared databases	24	Shared databases	23	CRM software	25	Shared databases	24

Source: Breu and Smith (forthcoming 2001), Cranfield School of Management

The Cranfield report presented the findings on the business benefits, key performance indicators, best practice, benchmarking and the role of technology in supporting value creation through knowledge at the overall, functional, and industry level. The final section presents the profile of the high-performing organization on all dimensions.

The profile of the high-performing organization

Organizations were defined as high performing that demonstrated a consistent performance on all five best practice themes in knowledge exploitation: namely, in creating a knowledge-driven culture, in designing a knowledge infrastructure, in enabling distributed working, in fostering knowledge transfer and in introducing new working practices (Figure 8.5). The profile of the high-performing organization in exploiting knowledge is reflected in the top-right quadrant. This represents a total of 35 organizations, constituting approximately the top 5% of the total survey

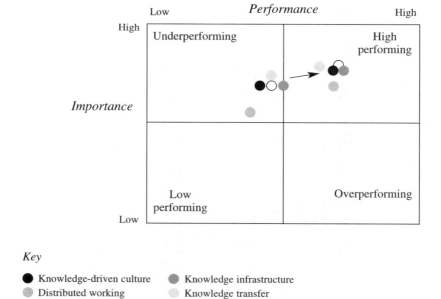

Key

● Knowledge-driven culture   ◍ Knowledge infrastructure
◍ Distributed working   ◌ Knowledge transfer
○ Working practices

Figure 8.5 Profile of high-performing
organizations in knowledge exploitation
Source: Breu and Smith (forthcoming 2001), Cranfield School of Management

sample. The top-left quadrant depicts the profile of the total sample. The arrow indicates the performance distance between average and high performance. Despite the relatively small subsample, a profile can still be elicited that may be indicative of the more general characteristics that high-performing organizations display. What makes the high-performing organization different from the average?

Best practice in high-performing organizations

First, a difference was identified in terms of best practice in high-performing and average-performing organizations. Table 8.4 shows, at a greater level of detail, the performance difference on the top ten best prac-

Table 8.4 Best practice items in knowledge exploitation: a comparative view of high-performing vs. average-performing organizations

Rank	Best practice items in knowledge exploitation	High performing mean	Average performing mean	Gap mean
1	Delivering products/ services faster	6.17	5.46	0.71
2	Capturing and transferring knowledge across projects	6.14	5.57	0.57
3	Matching people, skills and tasks	6.06	5.25	0.81
4	Getting people to collaborate	6.06	5.59	0.47
5	Increasing process efficiency	6.06	5.37	0.69
6	Improving quality and speed of decision making	6.03	5.45	0.58
7	Improving customer/ supplier relationships	5.94	5.46	0.48
8	Enabling new ways of doing business (for example, e-commerce)	5.91	5.19	0.72
9	Creating commitment to knowledge sharing	5.91	5.28	0.63
10	Incorporating the insights, experiences and judgements of individuals into good practice	5.89	5.46	0.43

Source: Breu and Smith (forthcoming 2001), Cranfield School of Management

tice items in knowledge exploitation between high-performing and average-performing organizations.

As can be seen, the mean best practice scores for high-performing organizations are significantly higher than those for the average-performing organization, especially for matching people, skills, and tasks, enabling new ways of doing business, delivering products/services faster, and increasing process efficiency.

Strategic importance of knowledge exploitation in high-performing organizations

The analysis of the data also revealed that high-performing organizations were more likely to recognize the strategic importance of knowledge exploitation, in contrast to average-performing organizations. High-performing organizations stated that:

■ Knowledge exploitation is on the board agenda

■ An organization-wide knowledge strategy is in place

■ A cost-benefit analysis is undertaken prior to investments in knowledge exploitation.

The difference in the strategic importance of knowledge exploitation in high-performing and average performing organizations is reflected in Figure 8.6. The differences between high-performing and average-performing organizations on these dimensions are striking in amounting to over 20%.

Business benefits in high-performing organizations

High-performing and average-performing organizations further revealed variations in the business benefits they had realized from knowledge exploitation to date. High-performing organizations outperform the average in creating value through customer focus, followed by innovation and growth and internal quality. Benefits realization is fairly similar in the areas of organizational responsiveness and the supply network.

Although there are currently quite pronounced performance differences between the high-performing and the average-performing organization, perceptions of the future potential of knowledge exploitations are strikingly similar as depicted in the dotted lines (Figure 8.7).

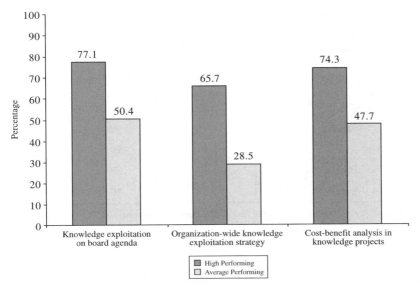

Figure 8.6 Strategic importance of knowledge exploitation: a comparative view of high-performing vs. average-performing organizations
Source: Breu and Smith (forthcoming 2001). Cranfield School of Management

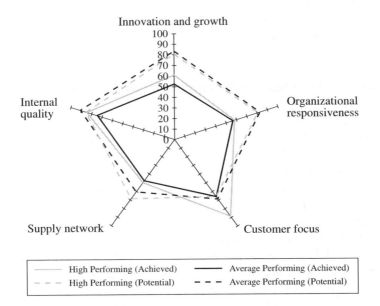

Figure 8.7 Business benefits of knowledge exploitation: a comparative view of high-performing vs. average-performing organizations
Source: Breu and Smith (forthcoming 2001), Cranfield School of Management

Table 8.5 Achievement of business benefits from knowledge exploitation: a comparative view of high-performing vs. average-performing organizations

Business benefits achieved: a comparative view	High performing %	Average performing %	Gap %
Customer retention	51	34	17
Meeting customer needs	51	39	13
Customer service	49	39	9
Competitive market awareness	40	38	2
Campaign effectiveness	37	20	17

Source: Breu and Smith (forthcoming 2001), Cranfield School of Management

More detailed analysis of the specific business benefits reveals that high-performing organizations display further performance differences to the average trend.

Table 8.5 reflects the top business benefits in rank order that high-performing organizations have achieved in comparison to average-performing organizations. As can be seen from the table, the contrast in performance is particularly striking on customer retention, campaign effectiveness and meeting customer needs.

Key performance indicators in high-performing organizations

Significant contrasts were further identified in view of the top key performance indicators for high-performing and average-performing organizations (Table 8.6).

Over 90% of high-performing organizations identified customer satisfaction as the top key performance indicator, compared with 77% of average-performing organizations. Contrasted with average-performing organizations, high-performing organizations further differ on customer value, project delivery and product/service quality.

Most notably, cost saving is significantly less relevant as a performance indicator in the high-performing organization. The concurrent pursuit of customer satisfaction and cost savings appears to represent conflicting goals. This is supported by the profile of average-performing organizations that were found to be far less focused on customer satisfaction and far more on cost savings. This suggests that organizations have to weigh

Table 8.6 Key performance indicators: a comparative view of high-performing vs. average-performing organizations

	High performing %	Average performing %	Gap %
Customer satisfaction	91	77	14
Customer value	66	43	23
Project delivery (time/cost/quality)	66	43	22
Product/service quality	63	47	16
Cost saving	57	68	−11

Source: Breu and Smith (forthcoming 2001), Cranfield School of Management

priorities in terms of deciding whether they are primarily driven by customer satisfaction or cost savings.

Future role of technology in high-performing organizations

Also, in view of the future role of technologies in supporting knowledge exploitation, significant differences emerge between high-performing and average-performing organizations. The role of technology was analysed with a view to its perceived capability for supporting the realization of business benefits from knowledge. The perceived effectiveness of technologies was reflected in rank order for each of the earlier identified higher-level benefits. As can be seen from Table 8.7, intranet, Internet, CRM software, desktop video conferencing and e-mail are the top five technologies for supporting knowledge exploitation in high-performing organizations.

The same analysis was undertaken for the sample of the average-performing organization. As can be seen in Table 8.8, the key technologies for supporting knowledge exploitation are Internet, e-mail, intranet, shared databases and CRM software.

A comparative analysis of the role of technology in knowledge exploitation in high-performing versus average-performing organizations reveals that CRM software and desktop video conferencing feature prominently in high-performing organizations, with e-mail assuming an strikingly inferior role. Average-performing organizations, in contrast, rely predominantly on Internet, e-mail and intranet environments.

Table 8.7 The future role of technology in supporting value creation in high-performing organizations

Innovation and growth	%	Organizational responsiveness	%	Customer focus	%	Supply network	%	Internal quality	%
Internet	50	Intranet	58	Intranet	60	Intranet	55	Intranet	64
CRM software	50	Internet	50	CRM software	40	Internet	45	Internet	45
Intranet	42	CRM software	42	Internet	40	CRM software	36	CRM software	36
Desktop video conferencing	25	Desktop video conferencing	33	Desktop video conferencing	30	Desktop video conferencing	36	Desktop video conferencing	36
E-mail	17	E-mail	17	E-mail	20	E-mail	18	E-mail	18

Source: Breu and Smith (forthcoming 2001), Cranfield School of Management

Table 8.8 The future role of technology in supporting value creation in average-performing organizations

Innovation and growth	%	Organizational responsiveness	%	Customer focus	%	Supply network	%	Internal quality	%
Internet	46	Internet	45	Internet	43	Internet	47	Internet	46
E-mail	38	E-mail	35	E-mail	37	E-mail	35	Internet	37
Intranet	34	Intranet	35	Intranet	34	Intranet	31	Intranet	34
Shared databases	25	Shared databases	25	CRM software	28	Shared databases	27	CRM software	25
CRM software	23	CRM software	25	Shared databases	23	CRM software	24	Shared databases	25

Source: Breu and Smith (forthcoming 2001), Cranfield School of Management

Business implications

The results of this survey confirmed theoretical propositions of the performance-critical role of knowledge in the business context and its impact on organizational competitiveness

New opportunities for value creation

One of the strongest messages from this Cranfield survey is that organizations are still striving to realize value from knowledge exploitation and that opportunities for value creation have shifted. The biggest new opportunities for value creation through knowledge were identified in *innovation and growth* and *organizational responsiveness*. While *customer focus* continues to be an area of significant value creation in future and organizations are currently performing well, organizations have discovered new areas of value creation that are driven by the exploitation of intangible assets such as people's expertise, experience and knowledge. The discovery of these new opportunities for value creation is driven by two important trends: first, business decision makers increasingly realize the value they can drive out of the exploitation of intangible assets, and second, economies of scope, typified by increasingly sophisticated and demanding customers, require organizations to shift from what has been referred to as the traditional 'make and sell' to the emerging 'sense and respond' paradigm.

Recognizing the strategic importance of knowledge exploitation

Organizations seeking to improve their performance on knowledge exploitation, it was found in this survey, need to recognize the strategic importance of knowledge exploitation. Knowledge exploitation needs to be a board-level concern in order to get senior management commitment. An organization-wide strategy for knowledge exploitation is absolutely essential to drive value creation in this new way. The evaluation of where best to invest in knowledge projects is clearly important in order to direct resources effectively. Ideally, priorities should be placed on those areas with the highest gaps in benefits realization as they offer the highest opportunities for value creation.

The model of the best-in-class in knowledge exploitation

High-performing organizations are best-in-class in knowledge exploitation. Their practices are instructive for managers who seek to improve the performance of their organization in knowledge-driven value creation. High-performing organizations value customers above all, use rich technology, such as CRM software and desktop video conferencing, to support the building of intimate customer knowledge and to use that knowledge to achieve maximum customer satisfaction. Indeed, customer satisfaction is the foremost key performance indicator with best-in-class organizations. Compared to average-performing organizations, they are far less concerned with cost saving.

Future technologies for knowledge exploitation

The survey established that e-mail, while considered the leading technology for knowledge exploitation in the past, is being outdated by the arrival of Internet and intranet environments. The technology profile of the best-in-class clearly suggests that rich technologies that merge multiple channels, in integrating text, audio and video, are most effective in supporting the capture and use of personalized, highly contextual knowledge, particular to an individual business context. The shift in the expectations of future technology environments clearly reflects a shift from a primary concern with data and information management (lean content) to a focus on knowledge management (rich content).

Benchmarking knowledge exploitation for improved performance

Organizations should use the benchmarking tool developed in this research to identify their current performance in knowledge exploitation and to assess themselves externally against the performance in business functions, industry sectors, businesses overall and best-in-class organizations. This will force organizations to examine their existing processes in knowledge exploitation in an external comparison, revealing areas for improving performance. As well as leading to creative thinking by drawing on practices developed in other businesses, organizations avoid reinventing the wheel and thus save time and cost in the development of best practice. As the benchmarking tool will be made available on the Internet, the existing database will grow and, thus, firm up its currency and relevance.

Overall the findings of this, to date, largest survey of knowledge exploitation in the business context confirms the continuing and increasing significance of intangible assets to organizational performance and competitiveness. While value creation in the traditional economy was primarily driven by the exploitation of *tangible* assets, as they are epitomized in the classic production factors of labour, capital and physical assets, value creation in the emerging knowledge economy will primarily be driven by *intangible* assets such as data, information and intellectual capital.

The striking underperformance in knowledge exploitation identified in this survey could be related, in our view, to the continuing application of management methods and tools that have been developed and were effective in the past. For organizations to develop a high-performance profile, they need to recognize the strategic importance of knowledge and assimilate new practices to continue to create value in the knowledge-driven economy.

SUMMARY

- There are various ways to assess the psychological, emotional and organizational state of being of a corporation
- You can benchmark business performance in relation to knowledge exploitation
- High and low performing firms can be identified through the use of structured research and analysis
- Best practice in high performing organizations can be identified and the contribution of this best practice can be assessed

McKinsey & Company

JONATHAN DAY *Principal*

Q: *What is the attitude towards knowledge management at McKinsey?*

A: I am speaking as an individual, not as McKinsey. What I can give you is my opinion.

Q: *Refreshing to hear, as some people will say that McKinsey is almost a cult. It's a privilege to have this door opened for me.*

A: All I can say on the cult issue is that our first priority is the protection of client interests. If you interview many people here you will get a range of views. I do not regard myself as an expert on knowledge management. I have some views on it and have done some writing on it but I know that there are people who have spent lots more time on this. We have a research project going with Ikujiro Nonaka, Professor of Knowledge Management at the Japan Institute of Science and Technology. We have a number of such projects going on around the world with academics. We do not have a resident expert on knowledge management here. It has never deemed to be necessary.

Q: *If you look at the work by Edvinsson at Skandia and Kenichi Ohmae, they seem to be suggesting that knowledge management in the past has been in the arena of information technology, but in future people in human resource management are taking 'ownership' of this as a business issue. Companies' knowledge-based systems are not really working quite as they thought they would. IT-led knowledge management is very systems orientated. HR-led knowledge management revolves around people, which has been described as human or intellectual capital. How does knowledge management affect McKinsey's clients? Have you been able to help them to manage their knowledge with or without the use of information technology?*

A: The quick answer is that we do relatively few projects with clients specifically on knowledge management. I can think of a handful around the design of joint ventures and organisational structures, and in new economy work. It may be that you have heard of the early work we did in managing our own knowledge.

Q: *Is this described in the work of Sumantra Ghoshal?*

A: Yes, it was third parties that tended to write about it, as in *Thriving on Chaos* by Tom Peters. It has a whole section on McKinsey's knowledge management system. *The Individualized Corporation* by Chris Bartlett and Sumantra Ghoshal has a chapter on McKinsey's internal knowledge management.

The old model for knowledge management in McKinsey was chaotic and not highly structured. So instead of a big, visible knowledge management department there was a department in the firm's office in New York that looked after these things behind the scenes. They developed a sort of internal *Yellow Pages*, called the *Knowledge Resource Directory*, which is now more and more common in other firms. You could call a central number, say I want a copy of document such-and-so, and within an hour it was on your desk.

Q: *It was an expedient solution, given the technology of the day.*

A: This was long before the days of e-mail and the Internet. Another thing they did was to create an enormous cross-reference database on a mainframe in the USA that could be accessed from around the world. You would feed in any key word or topic and it would produce a list of a dozen documents. Let's say you had an issue such as pricing strategy. You would feed in the subject and within an hour you would have a stack of data, drawing on work done around the world, sanitised for client confidentiality. You got a pile of paper but it was amazingly effective and simple. There was a scheme that encouraged people who had experienced a minor victory. If you worked with a client and they had some success with your recommendations, you were encouraged to write a Practice Bulletin. It arrived on every consultant's desk, printed on distinctive paper, and it said something like 'we worked in the steel industry in Asia, and this was what we learned'. You shared this information with other consultants and you gave them a contact for further information.

Q: *Consultants such as Arthur Andersen are also doing this. Is there a moral or ethical responsibility for consultancy firms today? When consultants sell knowledge, what impact does that have on their employees? What ethical responsibility do consulting firms have, given the power they have over companies?*

A: I suspect that you overstate the power that consulting firms have. It is less than you think. Knowledge creates value for people ultimately because of what they do with it. You said that McKinsey sells knowledge. Let's step back for a second. About four years ago I did some work on knowledge management that in a crude way tried to come up with a taxonomy of different kinds of knowledge: we called it K0, K1, K2, K3.

K0 was predominantly about knowledge that was only difficult to access because of the cost of gathering it. This was explicit knowledge. There is an enormous amount of data floating around; for example, the government has made a lot of public data available. You can observe the number of windows on house fronts; this is freely available information, but there is a high cost to collect it. You could call these public goods. K1 is explicit knowledge that you can copyright, for example, books. K2 is knowledge that is private because it can only be delivered through people. You have a particular expertise in a particular area. I can only access this expertise by hiring you. K3 is tacit knowledge embedded in an organisation rather than an individual. The individual needs the company to access the knowledge. One of the problems investment banks had was that there were K2 holders who could say 'I have in my brain a list of all the people who want to do this kind of deal and if I go to another bank, the knowledge goes with me'. With K3 the knowledge belongs to the firm, it's part of the culture or the social network. No one can take it away when they leave.

Q: *Does this touch on corporate memory?*

A: Corporate memory is part of it. The technical solutions I was describing, the *Knowledge Resource Directory*, for example, certainly enhance corporate memory. Because the more that I try to make the tacit knowledge explicit, the more I convince people that in fact it is the knowledge of the collective they are drawing on. Some companies have mechanical systems but they still cannot share knowledge. We try to ensure that McKinsey is above the individual consultant, and this makes the technical systems work effectively. For example, this morning the phone rang from Singapore and I helped the team that was calling, even though I had no reason to help them. I didn't know them, they got my name from one of our knowledge directories. I didn't even ask them for a charge number. That is just the culture of the company. It increases the tacit knowledge within the organisation.

Four years ago what I missed was this increasing phenomenon that this kind of knowledge is now spreading across corporate boundaries. I don't know if you have looked into the movement of information in the field of software. An interesting book on this subject is *The Cathedral and the Bazaar*, by Eric Raymond. It is basically about knowledge that wants to be free. When we first put the K0-K3 taxonomy together, we assumed that people always sought to privatise knowledge. That's one interpretation of Microsoft's strategy: you adopt a standard, then you modify it and appropriate it to yourself. Now we're seeing that it doesn't always work this way.

Q: *Can consultants solve every problem for their clients in this way?*

A: Absolutely not. We work with lots of outside firms. We've done quite a lot of work with communication and training firms, it's important because in order to implement strategies people need to learn new ways of working. For many years we've happily worked alongside the big five. My point is that there are skills that we do not have or never will, in-house.

We are probably at times more arrogant than we should be. I think the one thing I would ask is 'what are things that lead to client organisations being healthier and ultimately more productive with happier customers and employees?' When more value is added the bottom line tends to follow. You cannot get there simply by providing answers. We rarely get clients that come in and say 'we want to do x or y' and we then go in, stir the cauldron, crunch the numbers and say 'do x' and give them a bill.

It is important that organisations learn about themselves. It is now more of a mutual arrangement to explore the constraints, and the avenues for progress. I consider the most rewarding job is when the client says 'we feel this is the way to go'. After speaking with consultants they themselves have discovered that the way forward is this.

It is a process of joint learning rather than providing answers. You have not gone to the vending machine and sold them a slice of K1. The point I was trying to make about free knowledge is that providing a lot of free knowledge is not a substitute for creating a lot of value through tacit knowledge. You can download the whole of Linux free, from the Internet. But there are some very prosperous companies that have grown up around it providing services and systems. Oddly enough, the more free knowledge that's out there, the more it is valued. The Microsoft strategy of appropriating knowledge is not the only one out there. An example of a contrasting company would be Nokia. When standards come along they try to encourage people to follow them. They open themselves to standards.

Q: *What about K2? Are we developing knowledgeable managers? Is this getting better?*

A: A colleague and I did a seminar for Gordon Brown on managerial talent in the UK. My sense is that a lot has improved during the ten years I have been here in the UK. Ten years ago the UK was not a place where ideas could flow easily and quickly. It's different today. It's now much easier for entrepreneurs to get funding. It does not depend on who you are but the idea that you have, which is a big step forward. Not just through banks but venture capitalists as well. The tension between trades and professions is gone, but there is a long way to go. The vector is pointing the right way, the question is are we moving fast enough or are the Asian economies overtaking us?

Q: *What about the smaller firms who have to operate in this marketplace?*

A: A lot of economic and social value gets created when these smaller firms work well. There's an interesting piece of work that Sumantra Ghoshal gave me not long ago, a rigorous economic analysis showing that large firms and small firms are not substitutes but in fact complement one another to provide what an economy needs. Large firms are the places where resources can be gathered. Small firms drive the engine of innovation. Together, good things happen.

Q: *Is it important to provide skills training or organisational development to owners of small firms? For example, could there be a need for a specialist 'international management development centre' for small and medium enterprises?*

A: I think a lot of what you describe is happening. Before I came to McKinsey, I worked in a small consultancy in the USA. Our clients were much smaller; the largest had a turnover of $300,000,000. Many of our clients were hospitals, non-profits and things like that. Even back in the 1980s there was a huge community of what was called technical assistance providers; I don't know if you have any thing similar here. But in the USA we had SCORE, which was the Service Core of Retired Executives. If you were running a small business, you could call on them. We called on some of the SCORE people to help our clients because they had run businesses of various sizes and their skills were helpful to the non-profits.

Q: *I still believe there is a gap in this market sector for learning and training development in this country; do you agree?*

A: Not necessarily. I believe there is a lot of work going on in this area. I know people who are doing distance-learning courses, for example, an innovative legal training programme, an Internet-based continuing education service. Solicitors and barristers can go to the web and download courses, information on case law, and so on, and meet their requirements for continued training. In medicine this is very common and in business management it is increasingly common for basic functional disciplines in accountancy, HR and so on.

If there is a gap it comes from a different place. For learning to be effective there has to be what we describe as reflective episodes in one's life. I think you as an author take this for granted as you live a more reflective life than most of us. But if you think about most business people there is not much time for reflection or reading. Hanging over them is constantly the phone, the e-mail, the full diary; once in a while you can have people at the top of the giant companies taking sabbaticals. But that is rare. McKinsey is big enough to allow this, especially as it runs on K3 rather than K2, tacit rather than private knowledge. Some day I hope to step away for a few months to think and write. McKinsey's teamwork system and our K3 means that I can do this without my client work collapsing around me. But the gap is there for a small business. Once in a while I communicate with my former partner in the USA; in that smaller consulting firm, it's all go, go, go. The staff there have no time for those reflective episodes.

Q: *Do you think they need to make the time?*

A: Yes this is not a gap in provision, this is a gap in receptivity and I have seen business grow to the point where their managers will make the time. For example, Harvard has an 'Owner Manager Programme'. Owners or senior mangers can step away and reflect on what they are doing and then come back to a more active mode. Perhaps what they have to say is when you are running this small business that's an active period in your life. It's not a time for reading and reflection, it's a time for action and doing. If the business fails, you take a couple of months to consider what you are going to do, and then you go on to the next venture. The market creates the opportunity for reflection.

9 How to Avoid Failure

Jim Tucker is a Director at the Corporate Recovery Practice at KPMG, London. He was one of the team that dealt with the first dot.com disaster that happened on 18 May 2000. The company was Boo.com. According to Chris Ayres, writing in *The Times* (2000): 'There were tears, naturally; breakdowns, possibly. There was even a subdued round of applause, if one report is to be believed.' When Boo.com went out of business, 300 young people lost their jobs and during its 18-month life as a company Boo managed to eat up £85 million, around a £1 million a week. This is a company that generated lots of interest, but no profits. The company's founders, Kajsa Leander and Ernst Malmsten, saw their dream turn into the business nightmare that we all want to avoid.

By October 2000, the sun was setting on the dot.com darlings, according to Garth Alexander and Dominic Rushe, who reported in the *Sunday Times* (2000) that: 'In the last few months more than 60 dot.com companies have folded. A hundred more are on the critical list, laying off workers and desperately looking for new financing to keep their dreams alive.' According to Birinyi Associates, a Connecticut research firm, during the period 1999–2000, the 25 worst performing online stocks lost US $114 billion in value and their shares were down 95.7% on average from the year 2000's highs.

So, are these corporate failures any different from the failures of the old economy? Tucker at KMPG, says not. His job is to restructure companies that have encountered problems. By restructuring, Tucker means: 'Redesigning underperforming companies in order to reposition them to return to profit and generating cash.'

He believes in a simple four-point assessment of a company to keep it on track, comprising:

1. a viable business model
2. adequate funding
3. strong management
4. a contingency plan.

Nicholas Bahra is grateful to Professor Sue Birley from Imperial College, London for permission to quote from her paper, 'The failure of owner managed businesses: the diagnosis of accountants and bankers'.

Tucker believes that these are overriding themes that apply to both the new and old economy firms. Although all four factors are of great importance and are 'must do's', according to Tucker, the single most important factor for any new start-up is a viable 'plan b', and then a 'plan c', for when trading starts to head off-track – upwards or downwards.

The crisis management methods and processes that must be built into thinking at the most senior of levels, along with key personnel, are of great importance and although most firms spend time planning how to succeed, time needs to be devoted to the failure route, if only to know how to recognize the signs and then confront and deal with the issues and problems.

Investor relations, public relations, customer relationships and suppliers all need to be addressed. How and by whom? The answer is to constantly re-evaluate the business model, prepare robust forecasts for funding and sources and ensure that management have a range of experienced people available at the crucial times. Tucker adds: 'Normal business rules do apply in a new economy.'

Professor Sue Birley (1995) at Imperial College, London, conducted a study over an 18-month period into why some firms fail. She examined 486 independent owner-managed businesses that had failed, where failure was defined as businesses that had gone into formal insolvency proceedings.

The respondents were given a list of 87 possible reasons for the failure of their businesses and then asked to score the extent to which each reason contributed to their most recent client failure on a scale of (1) 'to no extent' to (5) 'to a very great extent'. The 87 individual reasons for failure were grouped into 24 common themes.

The top 10 failure themes, in order of importance as measured by their mean score, were:

1. Capital structure
2. Management team
3. The economy
4. Customer diversity
5. Financial management
6. Owner attitudes
7. Rising costs
8. Lack of planning
9. Pricing
10. Suppliers.

A key finding in the report was that two-thirds of respondents were of the opinion that the business failure could have been avoided if remedial action had been taken to address the following problems:

■ autocratic, inflexible owners making decisions based upon emotion, who either failed to seek outside help or who resisted that which was offered

■ a poor management team with insufficient experience

■ inappropriate mix of skills

■ failure to delegate managerial responsibility

■ poor operations management

■ lack of family succession

■ a weak business concept and lack of planning.

It is naturally easier to identify why a company has failed with hindsight, and although this study does not aim to merely criticise management, it does highlight that, on occasions, some of these businesses could still be trading if professional intervention had occurred at the right time. Other key findings were:

■ almost 80% of the identified failure themes related to managerial issues

■ poor management of debt and poor forecasting were internal managerial deficiencies contributing to failure in more than 70% of cases

■ 41% of owners were perceived to have relied too heavily on intuition and emotion in their decision making, to such an extent that their business failed

■ in 20% of cases, inflexibility of the owners was a serious problem

■ lack of planning was a significant contribution to failure in more than 60% of cases

■ 23% were felt to have paid themselves amounts greater than the business could afford

■ while the poor state of the national economy contributed to collapse in 41% of cases, it did not dominate and was nearly always combined with other internal factors which had already weakened the business

- one-third of the businesses had not asked for help prior to the failure, and those who did were more likely to have approached their banker than their accountant

- 62% of businesses who requested help were given that help

- banks and accountants represent two sectors of the economy often accused of being directly responsible for the success or failure of the small business sector – the banks for failing to invest and the accountants for failing to provide adequate and appropriate support. While this may be so in some cases, there is no evidence in the report to support this view.

In this report, Professor Birley found no case where a single factor caused the demise of the business but, rather, the cause was part of a complex pattern of interrelated factors. Analysis of these patterns identified seven clusters of businesses, which had suffered similar fates.

Key findings from these clusters were that two-thirds of the businesses failed primarily due to managerial deficiencies. Also there was no bias towards younger businesses, the research demonstrating that age was no defence against failure.

Commenting on the report's findings, Peter Hemington, partner at BDO Stoy Hayward, said:

The report provides independent confirmation that weak management is the primary cause of business failure. The reasons for business failure cited reflect the failings of management. As organizations grow and markets change, the organizations outgrow the capabilities of their management to control them. Managers in growing businesses, therefore, must be trained and prepared for the crises that accompany the various stages a business passes through in its development.

It is interesting to note that those managers who did ask for help were more likely to approach their banker than their accountant. This suggests that owner-managers believe additional funding will solve their problems whereas they should be looking at the more fundamental business issues highlighted by this report. There is no doubt that, of the two groups of advisers, the accountants are best placed to provide this type of advice and even to influence the dynamics of growth itself. As a profession, it is an important challenge for us to break down the barriers in the minds of today's entrepreneurs.

Professor Birley of the Management School added:

> Owner-managers are often single-minded and very independent. They have to be in order to survive the early ravages of the marketplace. However, as this research has shown, many do not have the management skills necessary to successfully grow the business, nor are they necessarily inclined to take remedial advice. Perhaps the most important finding from this study is that their clients had not consulted the bankers and accountants in one third of cases, and in a number of these the failure could have been avoided. It is clear that there is a need to build stronger bridges in the network, to develop greater trust on the part of owner-managers and more robust diagnostic and counselling skills on the part of the advisers.

From this report and numerous other studies, there is sufficient evidence to suggest that owner-managers and businesses generally have numerous hurdles to overcome if they are to stay in business. This means that if staying in business is difficult enough, then even greater challenges present themselves after the survivor stage. The game changes from staying alive to competing with the other survivors who have mastered the art of staying in business. These organizations now realize that to survive is not enough. They have to win market share through their competitive edge.

Dr Graham Wilson (2000, personal communication) has offered an interesting analysis of the psychology of dot.com failures. Wilson, Director at The Insight Partnership, notes that there are differences in the personality traits of dot.com entrepreneurs. He suggests that the reasons for the high number of dot.com failures are both simple and complex. The simple answers are:

- Overzealous lending
- Payback expected too early
- Inexperienced management
- Pressure to perform.

A more complex answer could be:

- Lenders assume these entrepreneurs behave/think like others
- Dot.com entrepreneurs are not the same as other entrepreneurs.

Wilson believes that traditional entrepreneurs are typically compulsive, which means they:

■ Never give up, despite many failures
■ Have expertise
■ Are limited by their practicality
■ Are not proven academically
■ Maintain strong control
■ Cannot relax.

He also believes they are dramatic, which means they:

■ Draw attention to themselves
■ Crave activity and excitement
■ Are excessive.

The dot.com entrepreneurs appear to be different, because while they are still compulsive, they are less dramatic and more schizoid. By 'schizoid', Wilson means, they are:

■ Detached; they expect bad relationships
■ Indifferent to feedback, positive or negative
■ Unconcerned for the future.

According to Dr Wilson, the solution is to balance these schizoid tendencies. They will need a mentor whom they can trust, but it will not be easy to build this relationship. They will need someone who will help them to 'get a life' without threatening them. Wilson believes that the dot.com entrepreneur will reject the dramatic marketing specialist unless this taps into a model of early relationships. The dot.com entrepreneur could be thinking, 'I became like this to defend myself against people like you'. Wilson also writes that they will also reject most impositions from lenders on their board.

■ 'Father doesn't understand how clever I am'
■ 'Mother won't leave me alone'
■ 'Older brother makes me feel inadequate'
■ But may respond to older sister.

This whole area of individual and organizational psychology deserves time and patience to understand its real contribution to people and businesses. Chartered psychologists study for around eight years and many of them have developed specialist skills and knowledge-based processes that can help individuals and organizations to succeed.

Business psychology and organizational learning

Personal experience teaches us that the school of hard knocks is one way to learn. For example, when we fall off a bicycle, we remount and persist in developing our powers of balance. If we can translate that learning process to the organization, the chances of running a successful organization are greater.

Chris Argyris is an influential writer and a proponent of the learning organization, whose essay, 'Teaching Smart People How to Learn' (1998) is thoroughly recommended as a guide to examining what makes a learning organization. Although there has been much debate as to the differences in meaning, philosophy and organizational model and behaviour of the learning organization and the knowledge-based organization, there are times when some of their respective conceptual principles are interchangeable, and for our present purpose, this is one of them.

According to Argyris (p. 81):

Before a company can become a learning organization, it must first resolve a learning dilemma: competitive success increasingly depends on learning, but most people don't know how to learn. What's more, those members of the organization whom many assume to be the best at learning – professionals who occupy key leadership positions – are, in fact, not very good at it.

Argyris argues: 'Effective learning is not a matter of the right attitudes or motivation. Rather, it is the product of the way people reason about their own behaviour' (p. 81). Argyris writes that people who are confronted about their own role and how it connects with an organization's problems will often deny that the fault is theirs. The likely response is to be defensive and this posture does not allow people the intellectual freedom to be critical enough about the very problems they are trying to solve. For Argyris, the solution is for companies:

to make the ways managers and employees reason about their behaviour a key focus of organizational learning and continuous improvement programmes. Teaching people how to reason about their behaviour in new and more effective ways breaks down the defences that block organizational learning. (p. 82)

Argyris makes a distinction between single loop and double loop learning and uses the analogy of a thermostat (p. 83). He writes of a thermostat that 'automatically turns on the heat whenever the temperature in a room drops below 68 degrees' as being a good example of single loop. The thermostat that poses the question, 'why am I set at 68 degrees?' and then attempts to find whether another temperature will or will not heat the room more economically, is his example of double loop learning.

However, there are several points to raise. First, the notion that *all* organizations *need* to be learning organizations has to be challenged. For example, in the new economy, it is perfectly acceptable for teams of professionals to align themselves for particular tasks or projects and work together for periods of time and then to close down those relationships. In the event of expediency, creativity, knowledge creation and innovation being the key drivers for this style of team, is it then important for this particular team to internalize the lessons learned from this project and then to share and communicate this learning with a view to building it into the psyche of the entire organization? This very much depends upon the team itself and the needs of their respective organizations, however, perhaps this process could take away some of the fun and the impulsiveness of this style of working for the people involved.

Another challenge to Argyris's thinking and that of John Burgoyne and Peter Senge is the idea that if the process of learning within an organizational context is too systemized or rationally driven, it might take away the very spontaneity that the creative personnel involved like to work in from an organizational cultural perspective. One can imagine an environment where people are given plenty of room to manoeuvre intellectually and the time and budget to develop creative and innovative solutions. These same people may perform brilliantly and yet if they were constrained in their working activities by being asked to follow a corporate 'learning model', this could inhibit their thinking and perhaps take away the vital sparks that make their intellects work.

John Verrill is a lawyer at the City firm, Lawrence Graham, a firm of solicitors with the benefit of over 130 years of corporate history and identity. According to Verrill (2000, personal communication), some new economy companies or dot.com firms have far too many problems in the way they are structured financially and managerially:

With many dot.coms, cash goes in to stimulate demand The entrepreneurs have a new idea and then find a way to match buyers with sellers. It can be a cost effective way to bring these two parties together. Often, new economy firms are exploiting 'multi layers of rights'. Protection of what they are doing in the new economy is essentially a paper trail. In the USA there has been a difference in emphasis on the way government has treated and encouraged the new economy. For example, development costs in the UK for taxation purposes have a 25% writing down allowance. In the US, 100% is allowable. This provides a great incentive, which results in creating 70 millionaires every week in Silicon Valley, many of them being under 40 years of age.

The Keynesian ripple effect is taking place in the UK. One new economy employer has recently acquired 600,000 sq feet of space near Reading, which is about 30 miles from London. They will employ over 150 personnel with a salary of at least £75,000 per annum. This new economy hot spot will naturally have an impact upon the local house prices. Verrill believes that as the trend moves towards people working from home, there will be an increased demand for new economy properties. According to Verrill, if you are working from home, you are more likely to be comfortable doing this with a property spacious enough that is fit for the purpose, rather than a tiny room in bedsit-land. 'Pension funds are big investors in commercial property and if the demand and value shifts from commercial to residential property how will this be addressed?' He also adds some thinking to the way investors are thinking about new economy firms:

Perhaps there have been some 'over-grandiose plans' and 'ludicrous ideas' presented to venture capitalists, however, what you are going to spend and where it is coming from is critical to the financial management of these firms. There is no substitute for bean counters. The more you ignore them, the more problems you are storing up.

Boo.com is the classic example and some have learned the lessons of the consequences of champagne, caviar and Concorde. The 'loss–reward' ratio is the pinhead of those who get rewarded as opposed to those who have funded the rewards and lost their investment.

Failure is important in the management mix or within the business's organizational processes. According to George Cox, the Director General of the Institute of Directors: 'Innovation is a never ending commitment' (this being the title of his essay in the IOD's *Director's Guide*). He writes:

The concept of innovation is often associated with the single big new idea: the dramatic one-off breakthrough. However, in today's world, innovation has to mean more than this. It has to become a continuous way of life. Only those companies that recognize this, and are equipped to deal with it, are going to succeed. (p. 5)

Cox writes of the 'entry ticket' into the game of business. If a company has one innovation that might make a financial killing, it could open the door to it being able to trade on the stock exchange, for example. However:

Long-term success requires a change to the fundamental nature of the business. After all, innovation is not only about creating new and better products and services. It also means identifying and forging links with other organizations, to secure funding or tap into special expertise or knowledge. Equally important is the safeguarding of intellectual capital and business profits through the proper use of IP [intellectual property] law. (p. 5)

Dr Geoff Nicholson is Staff Vice President of Corporate Technical Planning and International Technical Operations at 3M. For almost 100 years, innovation has been the reason that 3M has enjoyed success in the business areas of healthcare, telecommunications, industrial, electrical, transportation safety and many other markets. Nicholson, who was part of the team involved with the 'Post-it' notes, believes that innovation occurs when an organization creates the conditions necessary for it to happen.

'Scientists have a constructive disrespect for management', Nicholson says. He adds, 'At 3M, they can use 15% of their time every week and devote it to a personal project of their own choosing. The results of these projects are never measured, it's a message that it's their programme' (2000, personal communication).

According to Adam Brand (1998), Manager of Business Information Services at 3M, this 15% rule is flexible at 3M. 'Not everybody uses it – and some take far more than 15% of their time, especially when a promising idea takes form as a likely product'.

In order to innovate constantly, Nicholson believes it is important to 'change the basis of competition. Our scientists have both determination and passion for their jobs. I tell them, don't try to avoid failure, failure is an essential part of progress'.

According to William E Coyne, 3M's Senior Vice President for Research and Development:

Innovation has become part of our brand promise ... To sustain the flow of new products, we continue to invest about $1 billion a year in R&D, and as a manufacturer we are particularly proud of our patent portfolio growth. During 1998, we were awarded 611 US patents, placing us 10th among US companies. In 1999, 517 US patents were awarded to 3M. (IOD, 2000)

SUMMARY

- Normal business rules apply to both the new and the old economy

- One definition of restructuring is 'redesigning under-performing companies in order to reposition them to return to growth'

- Four points to consider are: a viable business model, adequate funding, strong management, contingency plan

- Weak management and poor capital structures have been discovered to be the cause of owner-manager business failures

Case Study

Arthur Andersen

LIZ MARTIN

Q: So what is Arthur Andersen's knowledge management initiative about and where are you in terms of developing and implementing it?

A: We are working on both the technological aspects of knowledge management, for example virtual learning networks, and the people and organizational development area, for example succession planning, retention of top talent and the learning environment in which people work.

Q: Like a holistic approach?

A: Exactly, to support people in moulding their jobs to suit themselves and the business rather than the traditional approach of narrowly defined roles and very specific job descriptions. People are being hired as much for their potential as past experience and need the support in their working environment to explore and position their role, skills and knowledge within a wider learning and knowledge framework.

Q: *So recruitment is not necessarily competency based?*

A: It needs to be, because if you hire someone for their potential, you need to focus much more on their competence as opposed to hiring someone to fill a specific job role, as the role may well change.

Q: *What does knowledge management in the new economy mean to you?*

A: I think the work of Tom Peters, and Peter Senge on branding yourself, your skills and knowledge and continuous learning is influential. Generation Y are regarded as more mobile, less loyal and expect to change jobs several times during their career, therefore they will be more inclined to do what best suits their own portfolio of skills and knowledge. In business this translates into providing an environment where employees can continue to develop skills and knowledge, but are required to learn and develop each other to the benefit of the business.

Q: *What key things do you want to see implemented to help knowledge management work for Arthur Andersen?*

A: Besides the use of navigation systems and learning networks we are focused on the individuals within the framework and helping them to understand 'how I can contribute to business objectives' and 'what it means to me to be part of the business'. It is about helping an individual to understand their strengths and weaknesses. Helping individuals and managers to understand how they can use their skills and knowledge within a role and in the business context will deliver maximum return to the business. In performance terms this is a shift to focus on what an employee does well and how they can do more of 'it'.

Q: *Do you use 360 degree appraisals here?*

A: We do internally and we develop 360 degree solutions for clients.

Q: *What other aspects of knowledge management are you exploring?*

A: Maximizing enabling tools such as intranet strategies, virtual learning networks and the principles of good employee communications.

10 How to Maintain Market Position

BP Amoco was the largest industrial merger in corporate history. The intent to merge was announced in August 1998, less than 60 days after being proposed by Sir John Browne. The deal was to merge British Petroleum with the North American oil giant, Amoco, and this extraordinary task was achieved within 100 days. Preserving the value of both of the former companies' key intellectual capital, while instituting new processes within the combined companies, was recognized early in the game as a key priority. Dave Barrow, one of the leaders in the company's knowledge management initiative, likened the intensity and importance of the effort to the success of the new company to that of the Marshall Plan in mapping the reconstruction of post-World War II Europe. The merger plan was fundamental to the success BP Amoco has achieved and maintained through to the time of this writing.

BP Amoco has developed a real knowledge sharing culture that has resulted in what shareholders and board members like to see. In an article by Margaret Coles (2000) in the *Sunday Times*, Chris Collison, the internal knowledge management consultant was quoted as saying:

> Sir John Browne, the group chief executive, initiated a knowledge management programme in 1996 and we have saved millions of dollars by sharing know-how. The organisation is very flat now. We have 150 business units in 150 countries, so there is tremendous potential for one isolated business unit to repeat things.

When mergers take place on this scale, the style and manner in which two or more organizations bring their people together will be the most important

Nicholas Bahra is grateful to Professor John Burgoyne for assistance and for permission to quote extensively from 'What are the implications of the virtualisation of organisations and the emergence of knowledge management for management development'. Much of the material in this chapter is adapted from that paper. Nicholas Bahra is also grateful to Karin Breu for assistance and for permission to quote extensively from 'Europe's Competitive Future in the Knowledge Economy: The Need for a European Contribution to the Emerging Knowledge-based Theory of the Firm'. The latter part of this chapter consists of material adapted from that paper.

151

factor as to whether the new organization succeeds or fails. The sensitivity relating to knowledge sharing and knowledge transfer is critically important and Dave Barrow describes some of the fundamental processes that he and his team facilitated during 1999 (2001, personal communication).

> It was important to respect the views of people in the organization related to common, high level issues and processes. Regarding knowledge transfer, the central message was that the process was fundamentally a human one that occurs most successfully via peer to peer relationships.

> We have targets for improving productivity and there are clear linkages to rigorous measures. During the next twenty four months in fact, the company expects to double staff productivity.

Dominic Rushe, reporting in the *Sunday Times* (2000), probes into which companies are actually delivering shareholder value. Rushe describes the measurements of EVA (economic value added), MVA (market value added) and FGV (future growth value). These measures, provided by Stern Stewart, a leading firm of management consultants, list the top 100 companies and their ranking in terms of these three measures, plus other traditional ratios, for example the return on capital employed and the cost of capital.

Calculating the EVA is quite straightforward. It is the difference between the profit a company makes and the cost of its capital. According to Stern Stewart (*Sunday Times*, 2000), the point of EVA is to 'align the interests of shareholders, management and workers'. Actual performance is measured using MVA, which attempts to measure whether or not a company is giving shareholders value for money. In 2000, Stern Stewart added a new measure (FGV), which tries to define what percentage of a company's value is the product of expectations that it will grow in the future.

At the top of the list is BP Amoco, followed by British Telecom and then Shell.

One of the most revered management specialists, Peter Drucker, wrote of the coming information-based organizations in the *Harvard Business Review on Knowledge Management* (1987). He wrote:

> an information-based business must be structured around goals that clearly state management's performance expectations for the enterprise and for each part and specialist and around organised feedback that compares results with these performance expectations so that every member can exercise self-control. (p.10)

In the same essay he also writes:

to remain competitive – maybe even to survive – they [businesses] will have to convert themselves into information-based organizations, and fairly quickly.

According to Professor John Burgoyne (2000, p. 2):

the growing concern with knowledge management and the rapid emergence of virtual organisations are two of the main signs of a revolution in the functioning of organisations, which has profound implications for management development.

As part of the organisational learning process organisations are becoming virtual – new e-commerce firms are created as virtual from scratch, surviving traditional firms are rapidly 'virtualising' themselves to survive and prosper. There are three main aspects of organisational virtuality:

- A high proportion of virtual workstyles and workplaces for employees of all kinds.

- A high level of access to all organisational knowledge and resources for all organisational members – a dramatic fall in internal transaction costs if the necessary collaborative culture is achieved.

- The location of the organisation in its virtual context is increasingly critical to e-markets (both purchasing and selling), location in virtually managed just in time supply chains and industrial networks, web branding and imaging.

Organisational knowledge is differentially located – in people, records, culture, archives, technology, patents, expert systems, competency frameworks, training programmes, resource centres. There are new challenges in integrating and harmonising these.

For managers and employees there are fundamental new issues:

- Self-management and development as a knowledge manager and producer

- Working in mixed generational teams with radically differing work lifestyle orientations – pre-generation X, generation X and post generation X

- Linking personal knowledge and learning to collective knowledge and learning

- Finding mutually beneficial understandings and practices over intellectual property ownership

- Seeking and taking reward as equity as well as remuneration

- Access to knowledge creating situations as a necessity for maintaining career viability. (p. 2)

Knowledge management, knowledge intensive firms, knowledge work, organisational learning and virtualisation of organisations may be:

1. the latest events in the continuously changing world of organisational life, or,

2. the early stages in a quantum transformational change in the nature of business, organisation and management – similar in scale to the industrial revolution of the nineteenth century. (p. 3)

The argument Professor Burgoyne puts forward is that those of us who are concerned with management development should take the second possibility seriously. If we are now seeing the initial symptoms of an emergent revolution then this has fundamental implications for management development.

The fast generation of new knowledge approach demands a clear understanding and fostering of the research and creativity abilities of the organisation. The exploiting underlying knowledge approach requires an organisation to learn about its own distinctive knowledge and how to apply it in new situations while retaining ownership of it. (p. 5)

Knowledge management

The practice of knowledge management has been largely developed by the IT/IS function, whereas HR has largely championed organisational learning. Because of this the two may not be optimally integrated.

Two things are problematic:

- The knowledge generation and use process

- The diverse form, location and ownership of knowledge. (Burgoyne, 2000, p. 3)

The knowledge generation and use process

There appears to be some agreement that the key steps in knowledge management and utilization are as in Figure 10.1.

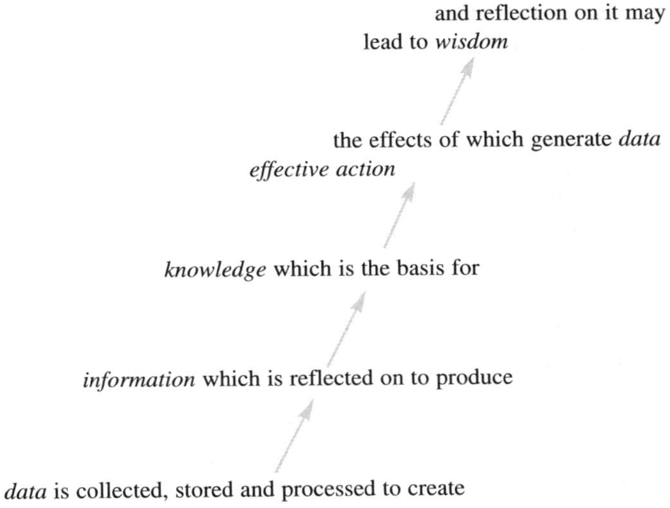

and reflection on it may
lead to *wisdom*

the effects of which generate *data*
effective action

knowledge which is the basis for

information which is reflected on to produce

data is collected, stored and processed to create

Figure 10.1 The knowledge generation and use process

Source: Burgoyne (2000) 'What are the implications of the virtualisation of organisations and the emergence of knowledge management for management development?' (p. 5), Lancaster University Management School

Data gathering and processing is now massively speeded up by IT/IS. Knowledge, application and wisdom are human learning processes – which are massively challenged by these new processes.

There is arguably a change of type that occurs between information and knowledge. This is the point at which human understanding, intuition, judgement and sense making comes into play.

Organisational knowledge is located in:

1. people's heads
2. technology and procedures
3. the tacit abilities of practitioners
4. archives, records, patents, reports
5. organisational culture.

For organisations to make use of its collective knowledge it has to relate, integrate and use these differently located and formed types of knowledge. These different kinds of knowledge vary in their accessibility to conscious use and their tendency to naturally belong to individuals or organisations. 1, 2 and 4 are relatively accessible to conscious analysis and control, 3 and 5 the reverse. 1 and 3 belong naturally with individual people, whereas 2, 4 and 5 are collectively located. (Burgoyne, 2000, p. 6)

Professor Burgoyne (2000, p. 6) believes that

The Internet is catching on three times faster than television did when it was new, and seven times faster than radio when it was new. E-firms are achieving leading positions at unprecedented speed – for example Amazon. Traditional firms are adopting e-practices equally fast. E-firm start up is a goldrush phenomenon; e-firms are valued on promise way beyond current revenues. E-workers are keen to work for maximum equity stake and survival salaries. This is the new phenomenon of equity culture, employees wanting material acknowledgement that they are or own the critical means of production – their own knowledge and brainpower.

There are three aspects of the virtual organisation:

1. Virtual work process and workplace for a high proportion of employees – workstations and remote working.

2. High levels of accessibility to all organisational information and resource by a high proportion of staff.

3. Firms dealing with customers, suppliers, labour market remotely, and significantly 'located' in virtual reality, for example on websites in virtually managed networks and supply chains'.

Burgoyne adds that:

the situation for corporate management development is changing rapidly from one in which managers have to be persuaded to learn in order that they can be useful in a different future, to one in which managerial employees are demanding, as a condition of employment, that they are involved in work that is developmental for themselves and their careers, and with reasonable access to qualification and non-qualification bearing formal learning opportunities. (p. 8)

Burgoyne also notes that:

the alternative to taking the knowledge from the people is keeping the people with the knowledge. Locking people with valuable knowledge into the organisation can be attempted through formal contractual arrangements; reward systems, which include deferred benefits, the fostering of strong culture of loyalty. In making these arrangements the incentive and material support of learning and development have to be maintained. (p. 8)

Dr Karin Breu at Cranfield School of Management writes of the ontological nature of knowledge in organizations. In her paper, 'Europe's Competitive Future in the Knowledge Economy: The Need for a European Contribution to the Emerging Knowledge-based Theory of the Firm' (2001), Breu explores some of the important issues facing European management research now and in the future.

Breu believes that:

The advancement of a knowledge-based theory of the firm, including models for knowledge management practice, is a compelling issue for European scholars if they seek to assist organisations to effectively participate in the new economy. The proposition draws on three core observations: First, the impact of knowledge in the new economy on organisational competitiveness. Second, the domination of the emerging knowledge-based view of the firm by a US American logic. Third, the ontology of knowledge as a socio-cultural phenomenon along with the impact of national cultures on business practice, which are leading to theory with limited transferability elsewhere. (p. 2)

Breu defines the concept of 'knowledge' in the business context as

broadly defined as synonymous with the concept of the organisation's intangible assets. These include intellectual capital, know-how, skills and expertise that are incorporated in individuals, groups, communities, processes, products, services, relationships with customers, suppliers and business partners, and the organisational history and identity. (p. 3)

It is of significance that Breu mentions both history and identity as this is the often the basis of the culture of the organization.

Breu builds on the assumption that a knowledge-based *theory* of the firm has not been articulated as yet and that, instead, we are currently observing the emergence of the knowledge-based *view* of the firm. The concept of 'knowledge management', according to Breu, is defined as a

practically vital aspect of the knowledge-based view of the firm to include the understanding of the purposeful acquisition, creation, dissemination and application of knowledge with the overall aim of improving organisational performance and competitive advantage. (p. 3)

Breu's argument draws on the following observations on the phenomenon of knowledge in a business context and the current state of theory development:

■ The increasing significance of intangible assets to organisations as the source of competitive advantage in the knowledge economy.

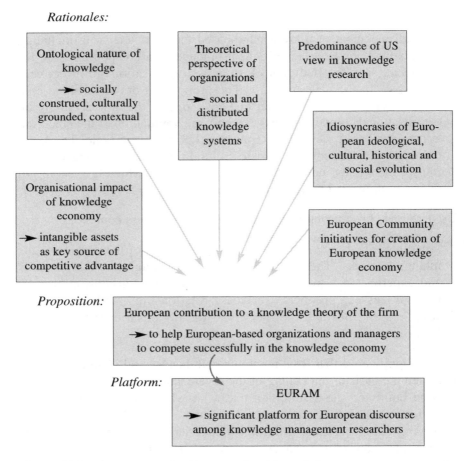

Figure 10.2 The argument for European-level knowledge management research

Source: Adapted from Breu, K. (2001, p. 4)'Europe's Competitive Future in the Knowledge Economy: The Need for a European Contribution to the Emerging Knowledge-Based Theory of the Firm', Cranfield School of Management

- The ontological nature of knowledge in organisations as not only scientific but also as socially construed, culturally grounded and contextual.

- The theoretical perspective of organisations as social and distributed knowledge systems to attend to the intrinsicality of knowledge in the business context.

- The idiosyncrasies of the European ideological, cultural, historical and social evolution with its implications for organisation design, culture and operations.

- The predominance of US knowledge theory and research with its limited transferability to the European business context.

- The European Community's initiatives for the creation of the European knowledge economy supported by the convergence of European resources in science, technology, and academia. (p. 4)

The above observations by Breu are also shown diagrammatically in Figure 10.2.

The ontological nature of knowledge in organizations

Ontology is the science of being or reality and Breu contributes to the understanding of knowledge management in her paper by exploring the ontological aspects of knowledge in organizations.

Breu associates organizational competitiveness with its 'knowledge of experience', and thus completes the connection with 'history, identity and embedded experience'.
Breu writes that (2001, pp. 5–6):

Knowledge in organisations is both scientific and social in nature. Although there is the strictly positivist view that scientific knowledge is objective and consequently context-free, it has been asserted that scientific knowledge is still an expression of culture, its values and beliefs, artefacts and symbols. Knowledge in organisations has been conceptualised, among many other approaches, along two dimensions. There is, on the one hand, the instance of 'knowledge of experience' where individuals acquire skills and knowledge through practical experience or learning. This type of knowledge is largely tacit. Its validity is context-dependent because it is developed according to the specifics of a particular context. Also referred to as 'knowledge-in-use', this type of knowledge is embedded in organisational routines and operating procedures, understood by members with shared experiences and values.

Much knowledge in organisations is of this tacit nature. In contrast, knowledge acquired through formal training, also referred to as 'knowledge of rationality' is more abstract and theoretical. It is rather standardised and tends to develop in line with the 'best practice' of the profession, rather than the specifics of a particular firm. Knowledge of rationality is far less specific to a particular context, is formulated in a logical way, and is generic and rationalised.

Although knowledge of rationality is an important element of the organisation's intangible resources, it is the contextual, embedded element, as incorporated in knowledge of experience, that protects it from expropriation and imitation and that generates those unique, imperfectly immitable resources that fuel organisational competitiveness.

SUMMARY

■ Knowledge sharing and knowledge transfer are of importance in order to achieve an organization's objective to maintain a high performing position

■ Respecting the views of senior personnel using a peer process assists with this endeavour

■ Shareholder value may be calculated using measures such as MVA, EVA and FGV

■ Trust is probably the key ingredient

Case Study

Cable & Wireless plc

KEITH MATTACKS *Knowledge Management Specialist*

Q: *Do you support the view that knowledge-intensive firms are more important than anybody ever realized?*

A: Absolutely, our business now is essentially moving away from plain old telephone services towards data and IP (Internet Protocol) and this makes knowledge and information at the centre of our customer's business and therefore by definition puts it at the centre of ours as well. We needed to take an analytical/strategic view of knowledge management.

Q: *Why? What is your vision and strategy?*

A: Our focus now is on business customers, future growth will come from IP and data services. We're operating globally and main markets for growth are America, Europe and Japan. Speed to market, customer service and continuous improvement are all vital and the sharing of knowledge is a key factor of production both for us and our customers. Explicit knowledge in our systems and processes can cause problems, the challenge is getting that to work.

Q: *Why is it a strategic issue?*

A: Cost benefits and other reasons such as share value, which can no longer be defined by earnings alone, intellectual capital, the talent of our people and our leadership are now prominent factors.

Q: *Do you feel knowledge management has been embraced as a concept right up at the top level of the organization?*

A: I think that's where we are at now. We are moving into an economy where the greatest value is in the recipes rather than in the cakes. The other thing that clinches it is that the effects of location and culture can impair knowledge sharing if we are not careful; we are moving from separate businesses where local knowledge was key to a single but dispersed and diverse operation. This makes knowledge creation and sharing more difficult. Cable & Wireless will continually transform itself in order to create value through a culture of innovation and learning, generating and freely exchanging knowledge.

Q: *Is knowledge management just another fad or will it be around for a while?*

A: Knowledge management is still relatively new and I think it's got a long future ahead of it. The business of organizations using what they know to continue to build and grow their business has always been around. Knowledge management doesn't ignore the complexity of reality like BPR (business process re-engineering) does.

Q: *Do you agree that knowledge management is organization development, management development, systems and processes and some other issues aligned together to form a holistic approach to managing people in an organization?*

A: Knowledge management includes strains of all those things, but I wouldn't say it encompasses them all. It includes threads of each of those things and weaves them together in a way which is different. I think we will start to see jobs in this area, chief knowledge officer and so on, but this is almost a project to create knowledge generation and sharing and make it part of our organization culture and not a long-term job. Technical support is important but, if we don't get this right, it's almost irrelevant. We've got a lot of work going on to change our culture, we need to invest in both organization and technology, the key word is both.

Case Study

BBC

EUAN SEMPLE
Knowledge Manager

Q: *Can you sum up in four or five key points how the BBC achieves on the hour deadlines every hour efficiently?*

A: Trust, sense of purpose, enthusiasm, socialization and different cultural backgrounds. All these things together create a workforce that can put aside self-interests and work as a team.

Q: *People are continually struggling to define knowledge management, do you think it is necessary to do that?*

A: Knowledge management is just a name for how many companies already work and what makes them tick. It is just a name, which is in fashion, for particular management skills. Knowledge management is about more than just information and data exchange. It is about creating a corporate culture where people relate to each other as parts of the whole. I think an analogy of knowledge management is music, where it's not the notes that make up the music, but the spaces in between the notes.

Q: *Do you think that industry is changing in terms of technology?*

A: Especially in terms of the Internet, yes. There are many changes occurring and we are constantly looking at new ways to tell a story.

Q: *Do you have any thoughts about the initiative started for 360 degree appraisals within the BBC?*

A: The process of self-reflection and self-awareness hasn't been high on the list of characteristics of senior managers and there is a need for it to become so.

Q: *Do you use any personality assessments and psychometric tests here?*

A: Yes, sometimes but not always. There are many new management techniques coming in. As an example, managers have asked me before how did I get so much work from my staff? And the answer was that we sat down and worked out how we as a group saw the world, saw the Beeb and how we saw ourselves adding value to that, then away we went!

Q: *So it's about the style as well as content of management skills?*

A: Probably considerable more about style than content in my case! But seriously, yes.

Q: *So do you see knowledge management as a beginning?*

A: Yes, we haven't achieved exactly what we want so far and I see knowledge management as a way of working that will be valid for several years.

11 What To Do If It All
Goes Wrong

It is all about confidence. If investors know that you are struggling, if the world tells your investors that you are struggling, if your customers and your suppliers know that you are struggling, then you are in trouble. Trouble cannot be ignored in business unless you plan to retire giving no thought and regard for any responsibility to the employees you leave behind.

> When the needs of one of the stakeholders are not being met and either consciously or unconsciously they pull the plug, is when an organization will fail. (Wilson, 2000, personal communication)

Crisis management is a style that can be learned through training and practice. MBA graduates at leading business schools are taught the art of how to deal with the media, investors, employees and customers. Traditionally, crisis management training has focused on human tragedies, for example rail disasters, food contamination problems and airline hijacks. During the past couple of decades, the media has expanded its coverage of business and local radio and television networks have grown in number. This means that if you are in business today, you cannot ignore the media and its impact on your business in terms of customer, investor, supplier and personnel relationships.

The dot.com experience demonstrated in the space of one year how a market could change from one of exponential growth to complete failure for many firms. In 1999, dot.com mania was spurred on by media interest in the Internet, venture capitalists and B2C (business-to-consumer) promises of success. Traditional companies did not fully understand the impact of how the Internet was going to affect their business and much of the year was spent trying to see the opportunity that this new technology was offering.

Nicholas Bahra is grateful to Jim Tucker, David Burlison, Mick McLoughlin and Phillip Davidson at KPMG for assistance and for permission to quote extensively from an article appearing in the November 2000 edition of *Recovery*, the quarterly journal of R3 (the Association of Business Recovery Professionals). Much of the material in this chapter is taken or adapted from that article.

Now the funding for B2C has dried up and investors have become more conservative about where to put their money. Many initial public offerings (IPOs) have been delayed or cancelled and traditional companies are starting to understand and use the Internet themselves.

David Burlison is the manager in charge of e-structuring at KPMG. According to Burlison, these established firms are 'therefore starting from a better position than dot.coms by having an existing customer base, a brand, and an internal source of capital to cross-subsidise the development of Internet capability'.

Although this book has examined the failure of dot.coms, the lessons learned will apply to entrepreneurs in the future. People will be setting up companies and organizations that are specifically in the government-to-business, business-to-business and business-to-consumer areas and many of these new economy firms will be collaborative projects bringing together disparate groups of people with a common interest. It is probable that these entrepreneurs will employ labour where the costs are low, for example in developing economies and if these entrepreneurs do not conduct their businesses responsibly and efficiently, the results could be devastating for the employees in their supply chain.

The message is quite simple. If you fail in the UK or the EU, there is some form of welfare system to help you and your family to survive. If you fail in other areas of the world, it could literally mean that you will be homeless. This means that the economic linkages between international entrepreneurs will need to develop some form of process or control mechanisms to ensure that unscrupulous operators do not act irresponsibly. This statement is contentious and international business does not need heavy policing to slow it down, however, as small and medium-sized businesses become more international, there will be a growing learning need to help these firms to succeed.

According to Tucker and Burlison at KPMG :

The options available for underperforming dot.coms are limited. The typical business model for dot.coms will often mean that insolvency options such as receivership can lead to a rapid dissipation in value for the company shareholders. Few physical assets are available to sell, there are not likely to be separable businesses which can be divested, there will probably be a higher than normal number of ransom creditors and there is unlikely to be a large debtor book to collect. Most importantly of all, the employees of these businesses are still highly marketable and are likely to be able to move on easily (or be purchased by headhunters as the television news showed during the boo.com liquidation).

Mick McLoughlin at KPMG was the liquidator for Boo.com. In relation to dot.coms, he believes that the options are limited in most cases to 'restructuring, administration or liquidation'. If your company is failing, perhaps the most important job of good responsible management is to be able to see the problems and address them before they become unmanageable, but the directors' responsibilities to creditors become paramount.

Tucker and Burlison write: 'As ever, restructuring relies on quality advice and decisive action being taken at a sufficiently early stage. This rule of thumb for traditional businesses becomes critical for dot.coms: few will die a slow death.' In understanding whether to pursue the restructuring route, three key questions should be addressed (Figure 11.1) The key question that is posed by the team at KPMG is whether the business model is still valid.

When a professional understanding of the validity of the business model has occurred, decisions can be made as to whether a restructuring exercise should be attempted. Due to the speed at which change occurs in the new economy, it is possible that the business model is no longer valid and therefore a restructuring is not recommended.

Tucker and Burlison also write of the importance of the customer life cycle. They recommend that:

One of the key analysis tools that should be used to assess the validity of the business model is to gain an understanding of how profitable the customer life cycle is. After the upfront technology investment the majority of funding provided to B2C dot.coms goes on the acquisition and retention of a customer base, if customers are lost to new competition before they even become profitable it is crystal clear the business model will never fly. Although customer acquisition strategies may require a

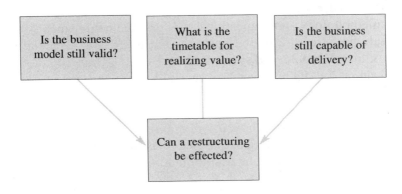

Figure 11.1 Customer life cycle
Source: Burlison, D., KPMG

large cash investment, strategies that offer a free entry into a prize draw if you sign up to a website, or offer a free CD with the first purchase rarely fail to attract a high level of customers. Where a number of dot.coms have failed is that once the customer has been 'acquired' they have not had 'retention' strategies in place to enable future profitable sales to that customer. Retention strategies aim to build up loyalty and ensure that customer is incentivised not to move on to the next dot.com that has £10m in the bank for customer acquisition.

Other important issues to be addressed are:

1. What is the timetable for realizing value?
2. Is the business still capable of delivery?

If the decision has been made that a restructuring appears capable of being effected, the second key question in assessing whether a restructuring should be attempted, according to KPMG, is to assess the likelihood of whether any further funding requirements will be made available. The sources of these funds for dot.coms are likely to be limited to venture capital and private equity and the key focus should be placed on understanding the options and timing surrounding an exit.

Tucker and Burlison also point out 'if a clear exit strategy is not worked out, then further funding required for a restructuring will not be made available'. Factors to be taken into account include 'market sentiment' at the time and if the plans of the company preclude an IPO (initial public offering), are there other options available such as a trade sale and how likely are these options to be successful?

In terms of delivery, this must also be examined for a successful restructuring to be undertaken. The analysis of this area uses traditional restructuring methodology, and questions the management capability, the organizational structure of the business and a key area especially for dot.coms, their technological systems.

The team at KPMG has identified several key themes, and these are as follows:

a *Weak and informal financial planning* – a common theme of dot.coms worked on to date has been the lack of financial planning specifically around cash. A combination of poor forecasting and irregular updates means that the actual cash position of many dot.coms is unknown, and therefore cash difficulties come as a surprise to both management and investors alike.

b *Company infrastructure unable to cope with rapid growth* – given the need to acquire customers, and therefore the emphasis on sales and marketing, there can be a lack of focus on the internal infrastructure and systems. This can be evidenced by the number of cases where dot.coms have attracted bad publicity due to systems failures leading to the inability to service customers. What value is a £5m marketing campaign to attract customers if the website can't be accessed or order fulfilment is unreliable?

c *Gaps in management strengths* – the assessment of the management team of dot.coms shows in many instances strengths around sales and marketing, but gaps in financial and operational skills. Counter-cultural it might be but most dot.coms would benefit from a wizened, grey-haired financial director.

The new economy, according to the team at KPMG, is having a very real impact on the world of business. Their view is that:

> this is a lasting phenomena and not a short-term 'blip' to normal business activity. Our experience at KPMG indicates that the approach to these [underperforming dot.com] cases is rather different from traditional cases with speed of assessment, planning and implementation needing to be significantly quicker. This is a great market opportunity for practitioners equipped with the right tools, methodologies and training'.

SUMMARY

- 'When the needs of one of the stake-holders are not being met and either consciously or unconsciously they pull the plug, is when an organization will fail'

- Crisis management is a style that can be learned through training and practice

- The dot.com experience demonstrated how a market could change from one of exponential growth to complete failure in the space of one year for many firms

- Restructuring relies on quality advice and decisive action being taken at a sufficiently early stage. The key question that may be posed is whether the business model is still valid

- Other important issues to be addressed are the timetable for realizing value and the question of whether the business is still capable of delivery

Ernst & Young

TIM CURRY *Partner*

Q: *Tell me about your approach to knowledge management at Ernst & Young.*

A: I think it is fair to say right up front that our approach here is pretty anti-academic, anti-intellectual and very pragmatic, so we don't have high theories or in-depth views on people you mentioned in your letter. This is very simple practical stuff, this is about making money. This is about driving professional productivity and the change that is happening in an organization such as ours is probably far less dramatic than it is in many other organizations.

Basically since we started we have been selling intellectual capital and therefore we have been spared the changes that have gone on in, say, the manufacturing sector, where, for example, these days 70% of the value of a motor car is not in its parts but in its intellectual capital.

Q: *Has this been recognized by your company for many years?*

A: No, I am not saying that but our core business has always been trading in intellectual capital.

Q: *So Taylorism is where you start your philosophy?*

A: Who was Taylor? What I am trying to say is that today all motor cars work. You take the quality for granted and the success of the motor car in the marketplace depends on a lot of very intangible things – it depends on some of the gismos, some of the packaging that goes with it, such as financial, it depends on the brand. Moving into a knowledge intellectual era has been quite traumatic for many manufacturers. We haven't had such change. We sell advice, insight, ideas and the intellectual skills of our people, that's what we were selling 150 years ago. I'm not saying there hasn't been change, but a change of emphasis rather than something more dramatic.

We are trying to drive professional productivity by recognizing, years after we should have done, that intellectual capital is an asset that we can store and take stock of and then push that stock around the organization so that everybody can have access to it. Then you can increase and enhance the quality and the quantity of the stock.

We are trying to do this here – to understand what we know as an organization and disseminate that – whether to a line person in the States or Hong Kong or Scunthorpe. We are trying to increase and enhance the value of our intellectual capital.

Q: *And that is a genuine shift in terms of openness, to allow the sprit of knowledge to be freely available to people at every level?*

A: You make it sound as if it is a major change – it isn't. In professional services, you have to be guided by your ability to work together, to exchange views and help one another. We are formalizing our procedures here, we know the position and importance of some of these behaviours. I would say it is evolutionary rather that revolutionary.

Q: *However, some are going to suggest that in a competitive organization people are going to be striving for success in a career structure. It is still not in their interests to necessarily expose the threat to their career to allow someone else to know what they know.*

A: Yes, this is so, if I tell you what I know, you are a smart guy and may see some of the flaws in it and it may not be quite as good as I think it is. I may have an insecurity problem and I may only share with you if I am pretty confident in my ability, that what I am telling you may not be perfect but it is pretty good.

Q: *That's a sign of a confident guy, someone who is willing to share?*

A: Yes it is, but when you put what you have got on display, you open up all sorts of vulnerabilities. I deliberately started with this issue as opposed to the knowledge is the power thing – if I tell you what I know, you will go and use it and I won't have it any more. That still exists, but is far less of an issue these days because the half-life of knowledge is so much shorter today than in the past.

Q: *Please explain this a bit more.*

A: Yes, people gain a piece of knowledge today but in a subsequent period it won't be worth anything – life will have moved on. For example – I have a guy who has a fabulous tax project – in five years time legislation will have changed and this won't be worth anything. Even in six months it won't be as useful as it was as others will have caught on. The pace of change is such that the half-life of knowledge has shrunk dramatically. In the past I might keep quiet about my product. These days I know in six months time it will be useless, so I may as well share with you so that you can enhance it. Admittedly you have got use of it, so I don't get all the brownie points any more but that's a risk worth taking.

Q: *This is straight out of* Smart Business, *a book by Dr Jim Botley in the States, where he talks about three reasons why people share – I think he says altruism can exist, as you say, by the sharing of knowledge. Second, people will become reputable if they become knowledgeable, and the third reason is the desire to communicate that knowledge.*

It is said that some markets such as the music industry are now old economy firms. This wasn't the case years ago, as it was said they had the leading edge, do you think is a rather ruthless comment about them?

A: I don't quite understand the distinction between old and new economy in knowledge management.

Q: *I agree – I am being constantly told that new knowledge management only applies to new economy companies*

A: No – I can't begin to understand that – knowledge management applies to all companies. Some of the leading exponents of knowledge management are oil companies and pharmaceutical companies. Are they new economy or old economy?

Q: *So does nobody know the difference between new economy and old economy?*

A: Not by my terms. New economy starts with dot.com, starts-ups and the Internet and presumably you've got to be making lots of losses. That is what the name implies as opposed to manufacturing, industrial-based companies.

Q: *Many are saying that new economy firms are different in many respects, but I fail to be convinced that there is a difference.*

A: Not a clue. Do you know much about BP?

Q: *Well they seem to be in the forefront of knowledge management.*

A: They seem to be in the forefront of being willing to change, to be flexible, and in this sense they would be right up among your new economy companies.

Q: *They introduced 360 degree appraisal before many other firms, the consultants were the Forum Corporation in the mid 1990s. I feel there is an issue here about how new economy companies are being described.*

People don't fully understand the term and if we can't explain the difference between new and old economy companies in such simple terms, then I think we do have a problem.

A: Well, I can't.

Q: *I need to clarify it.*

A: Is the distinction important?

Q: *Yes, it is if everybody is writing about it, because it is leading investors into all sorts of prejudices as regards to how organizations are going to be valued in the future, how shareholders and stakeholders have to make critical decisions, whether an organization had overvalued its intellectual capacity, or if there is an area in an organization which is no longer goodwill but intellectual capital.*

A: Let's come back to this organization. What is the market value of Ernst & Young? A huge sum. What is the number on our balance sheet? A very small sum. Virtually no physical capital at all. We have no stock and only a few fixed assets. Nor do we have much financial capital because as a partnership structure we distribute everything to our shareholders, so we don't retain it. So you could call the value of the firm intellectual capital or you could call it goodwill, assuming they are the same. But, of course, only a small amount of this intellectual capital is knowledge management.

Q: *So there is a massive difference in your opinion between knowledge management and intellectual capital?*

A: Under our definition of it, yes.

Q: *Can you offer me an indication if this will change in the future – most organizations seem to be bringing knowledge management into the arena of intellectual capital?*

A: It is a subset of it.

Q: *Have you identified this in a visual context? Do you have an organizational charge for this which shows where it sits?*

A: Well, we have an organizational structure which takes in some of the elements of intellectual capital as defined by Tom Stewart. For example, people manage our customer capital, the strength of our relationships with our customers and the strength of the brand. Structural capital and human capital would be closely aligned, but neither are part of my responsibilities.

Someone else has the responsibility to worry about our customers. The brand and image is someone else's. I wake up worrying about a subset of intellectual capital, the overall knowledge management infrastructure and the knowledge content that our guys need to help them to fulfil their tasks. Obviously, they themselves impact upon our customers, so everything is linked.

Q: *Do you see your role as a developmental role to assist your colleagues?*

A: Well, it's an enabling role, it's a second order role. My rationale is to help the guys out in the line do their core processes, which are, 'win work and do work'. So I am here to help them to win work and do work.

Q: *Now that's interesting. What if an employee of your firm comes back to you and says, 's/he could have done it better if this had been available to him or if she had approached it in another way'.*

A: We constantly ask our internal customers if what we do is working. Some of their answers will be subjective and many reasons will be given, but, on a good day, some of the knowledge content that they get from us will be recognized as a major assist. That is all we can ever be, because we are an enabling function. It is as difficult to measure the effect of knowledge management as any other enabling functions.

Q: *So the assessing of your knowledge management isn't as important as enabling people?*

A: I am not suggesting that at all.

Q: *Some people are saying that the only thing that is going to give their organization an advantage is their knowledge management. They are saying this is the key area to ensure their organization has a competitive advantage.*

A: This is what some writers say, but life isn't as simple as this – it can't be pigeonholed like this. They used to say that people were all that mattered, now it's knowledge but there is a huge overlap.

Q: *There does seem to be a huge emphasis on this – with a statement from the chairman's office to live and breathe these concepts.*

A: On an academic level – there are dedicated people who look after physical assets and others dedicated to the financial function – if you haven't got people dedicated to the intellectual capital, a large part of the answer is missing.

Q: *Do you have anything specific to Ernst & Young that is unique to your organization that your clients are happy to purchase from you?*

A: Yes, we have lots of things. That is the business we are in. In the knowledge management arena, I am not selling our solutions in the marketplace, I am doing this for Ernst & Young. Some think we have all the answers but it's not true. We have some, but not all.

Q: *So in its organizational structure, how can you be represented?*

A: Our corporate vision is summarized in a rocket emblem – our vision, competitive advantage, and a summary of the seven key building blocks which we have to get right. One of those is sharing knowledge. Everything is built round those building blocks. Visually it is the only thing that might help you. It has to be led from the top if change management is going to work, especially in relation to knowledge management.

In some ways we have a narrow view of knowledge management. We haven't defined it very carefully, we just need to get on and get things done, we don't mind that. Is it worth defining CV's – who cares – let's gets on and do it.

Q: *What would be your advice to people on how to avoid failure?*

A: To avoid failure, you need support from the top, investment and persistence. You won't get it right first time or the second time. And you need to get the right behaviours embedded into the reward systems and the culture of the organization.

12 Storytelling

This chapter looks at the concept of storytelling in business. At first, I wondered what relevance, if any, this had to knowledge management and business in the new economy. After reading documents supplied by David Snowden, Director at IBM's Knowledge Management Institute and also listening to a recording of his speech delivered to the MBA alumni at the University of Bath (Snowden, 2000), I realized how important this area is, especially to the people at IBM.

In 'The Cunning Plots of Leadership', an article by Thomas A. Stewart for *Fortune* magazine (1998), Stewart writes, 'Nothing serves a leader better than a knack for narrative. Stories anoint role models, impart values, and show how to execute indescribably complex tasks.'

Stewart writes of 'stories of identity', a term from Howard Gardner, professor of education at Harvard and co-author of *Leading Minds*, a study of the psychology of leadership. Stewart writes that 'Stories of identity convey values, build esprit de corps, create role models, and reveal how things work around here'. According to Gardner, stories are more important than memos, mission statements, newsletters, speeches, and policy manuals. They 'constitute the single most powerful weapon in the leader's literary arsenal'.

Stewart also writes of Charlotte Linde, a linguist at Stanford University and the Institute for Research on Learning in Menlo Park, California. Her research shows how 'stories of identity help organizations bring in new members, adapt to change, and, crucially, define who is 'us' (and who 'them') and why we're here'. Linde makes the connection between 'stories' and 'institutional memory'. For Linde 'they are the principal means by which groups remember' (quoted in Stewart, 1998).

Stewart then makes some direct points about how storytelling is about learning and can really make the difference to a company's performance and uses three examples.

Nicholas Bahra is grateful to David Snowden for assistance and for permission to quote extensively from ''Story telling: an old skill in a new context' (2000a) and 'The ASHEN model: an enabler of action' (2000b). Much of the material in this chapter is taken or adapted from those two articles. Nicholas Bahra is also grateful to Thomas A. Stewart for permission to quote from 'The Cunning Plots of Leadership' (1998).

The first is a South African electric company, Eskom, which was at the time, the world's fifth biggest electricity producer. Stewart notes that Eskom has put itself through 'remarkable transformations' through the use of training and development. In 1975 the business plan promised to double employment while increasing output at 5%. Instead, according to Stewart (1998):

> since 1988 it has cut employment and upped output by 30%, almost doubling labor productivity and nearing its goal of becoming the world's lowest-cost electricity producer. At the same time, the state-owned company has embraced the dramatically changed nature of the post-apartheid state. Eskom had suppressed non-white employees and neglected non-white customers. Now it is on track to having a management, professional, and supervisory group that is 50% black by the end of 2000 – while improving financial and technical measures of performance.

Credit for this success is certainly associated with the efforts of the head of learning at Eskom, Nomsa Mdakane. Apparently one-third of employees were illiterate and using Africa's tradition of verbal communication, the company managed to include personnel at all levels. Stewart quotes Mdakane: 'We do what you do in a village at a *mimbizo* – this is a Zulu word for "gathering".'

The story is developed to recount how clean mills contribute to making electricity more cheaply, which in turn benefits the community as a whole. According to Mdakane, the stories teach the lesson that 'we all need to be eating from one pot, which is the business, and stop protecting "what belongs to me"' (quoted in Stewart, 1998).

The second example provided by Stewart is of Xerox's technical representatives. These repairmen 'learn how to fix copiers not from manuals or classrooms but from swapping stories around the coffee pot, as a series of studies has shown'. These stories have been recorded in a database called Eureka, whose annual value to the company, according to chief scientist John Seely Brown, is over $100 million.

The third example from Stewart is of IBM. Stewart describes how selling global accounts at IBM may involve years of 'painstaking prospecting, courting and negotiating'. These are 'multiyear contracts across multiple lines of business' and Stewart notes that:

> Each deal is different, yet there are things to learn from past successes and failures, and the deals are so big that even a small improvement in the success rate or time involved could be worth millions of dollars. To

get at the knowledge, IBM has been reassembling the people who worked on a deal and asking them to relive the story-interrupting, correcting, supplementing, reminding each other of who did what when, and why – while video cameras record the event.

Storytelling: an old skill in a new context

Snowden (2000a, p. 2) notes two academic approaches to a definition of a story previously identified by Orton in 1995: the story feature definition that requires any story to communicate some form of causal resolution of a problem based on an explanation of the context that initiates the story, the emotions and actions of a protagonist and the actions – and their consequences – of the protagonist his/her reaction. This approach emphasizes the need to define the characteristics that determine story quality.

The structural-affect definition, which requires the addition of meaning and significance for the audiences, through empathy, suspense, curiosity, shock, all or any of which should create some form of learning or understanding. Here the issue is how a story is structured to affect an audience.

According to Snowden:

> these two definitions reflect one of the defining characteristics of Western academic thinking, namely the desire to create an explicit set of rules and associated process that enables something to be 'known' either through its proof, or the inability to disprove. This is both useful and dangerous at the same time. It is dangerous in that it attempts to create explicit rules for what is a tacit skill: we all know a good story when we hear it, without the need to deconstruct it. It is useful in that it can provide characteristics and contrasts which assist the process of deliberate story construction. (p. 2)

Some definitions of an anecdote are: 'a short story', 'a narrative of detached incident', 'unpublished details of history'. According to Snowden:

> Anecdotes provide a means by which an organisation or a leader creates a common identity by providing models and examples of good and bad behaviour. (p. 2)

Snowden also notes the difference between the 'good guys' and the 'bad guys': 'One of the ways of distinguishing the good guys from the bad guys is to look at the methods used for mapping or cataloguing knowledge. The bad guys will tend to use old methods, re-badged yet again with new language, but no real change of content. Unfortunately, new wine does not sit easily in old wine skins. Looking at different approaches to knowledge asset registers or knowledge mapping best evidences this.' Snowden writes:

1. There are two key lessons in respect of identifying what people know: if you ask people what they know, they will generally tell you what they think they ought to know, and it will generally be explicit knowledge – the knowledge that can be written down.

2. The more valuable tacit knowledge, and a substantial proportion of explicit knowledge is *only known when it is needed to be known.* It is triggered by a combination of events and circumstances that creates that 'I know what is going on' moment for the knowledge holder. (p. 4)

Snowden also writes of 'knowledge disclosure techniques', acknowledging their association with anthropological techniques and the 'direct observation of decision-making, the exercise of judgement and problem resolution over time'. He notes: 'By looking at decisions that were made, we can ask what explicit and tacit knowledge was used, in context.'

At IBM the approach is to select a sample of projects and then reassemble as many as possible of the original team for a one-day storytelling workshop. Storytellers are encouraged to reminisce, in the style of a reunion, creating a series of anecdotes, humorous incidents, lessons learnt, observations and plain narrative. It does not follow a linear sequence over time, but jumps around in time as the flow of the storytellers evolves and explores.

As the storytellers tell their story they are observed by trained observers who identify decisions, judgements, problems resolved or unresolved and chart these together with associated information flows. Once the story telling has come to a natural conclusion, the observers present their model for validation and then the group as a whole charts for each decision/judgement/problem resolution cluster what knowledge was used, and what was its nature: tacit in the form of skills possessed by individuals (experiences, intuition, relationships, understanding etc); explicit in the form of artefacts (pricing models, quality control procedures, rules, research etc).

The consolidation of the intellectual assets thus disclosed then enables a structured process to be followed. The artefacts that contain explicit knowledge can be optimized and distributed as appropriate. For tacit knowledge, the two big questions can be asked: Can we make this knowledge explicit? Should we make it explicit? The second is the most important, tacit knowledge is more powerful under conditions of uncertainty than explicit. Where we can and should make it explicit then we create or reuse artefacts to act as repositories. Where we can't or we shouldn't, then we urgently need to identify if the tacit knowledge concerned is the property of a limited number of individuals or of a community. In the former case – we are vulnerable to its loss and urgent action is required.

Experience leads to several interesting observations as to the manner in which the story telling takes place. In the above-mentioned case, the 'good' teams, those who had won good business, readily moved into story telling mode. They had enjoyed the experience and willingly reminisced, mining a rich vein of anecdotes, often humorous, self-deprecating and memorable. On the other hand, the 'bad' teams who had either lost business, or had won business that in retrospect their company would have been better without, found it more difficult. Stories were often told from very different perspectives, with little common understanding between players. Many stories carried themes of betrayal or well rehearsed excuse. However their stories were the most valuable for corporate learning. The best performing teams had often learnt the least and were in danger of propagating their lack of learning to new projects by telling stories of their success without recognising the elements of luck or unrecognized serendipity that were an essential component of that success. One 'anecdote about the anecdotes' was memorable from the project.

The best performing team, one who had won a major contract in the face of all expectations to the contrary, were telling their story. They had reached a key point, in which they had bucked the company's authorization process in order the close the business. History had proved them right and like all successful teams they felt that the whole world should be like them. They were painting a vision of anarchy that was intrinsically seductive. At the height of their enthusiasm, one of their number interrupted. 'We shouldn't be decrying the processes, they are there because in a company our size we can't always have brilliant and lucky teams. We should always remember that we can't presume that future teams will be as lucky'. The timing of this intervention in the story telling process was profound. It forced the circle to look at where they had been lucky to have the right knowledge in the right place at the right time. Where they had made good judgements on the basis of incomplete information, and how those judgements had been made. (Snowden, 2000a, p. 5)

Snowden then raises the question: 'Have we outgrown the 'tacit' and 'explicit' words?' He notes: 'In knowledge management the words *tacit* and *explicit* dominate most conversations. Although the use of tacit is normally attributed to Polanyi's 1962 Terry lectures at Yale University ... its de facto use is to a large extent determined by two authors: Nonaka globally and Probst in central Europe. The common reading of both these authors, whatever their intent, too easily leads to implicit assumptions about the way in which knowledge should be managed that are inappropriate and in some cases down right dangerous' (Snowden, 2000b, p. 1).

Snowden argues that the SECI model (Nonaka and Takeuchi, 1995) presents certain difficulties which are:

1. It is often used in complete isolation from its supporting material, including highly valuable but underused concepts such as Middle-Up-Down, to define the totality of knowledge actions in companies. While the model is useful, it is not universally applicable in Manufacturing let alone the service sector. (p. 1)

2. It has an implicit assumption that knowledge is some form of thing or entity that retains a coherent identity through the four transformations. Knowledge is seen as an asset that can be created and managed; replacing products and raw materials as the primary focus of strategic thinking. One of many problems with this is that the transformation of knowledge between the tacit and explicit states fundamentally changes its nature. (p. 2)

3. It leads to confusion between the *container* and the *thing contained*. Tacit knowledge exists in the heads of individuals or communities, explicit knowledge in documents and other artefacts. In practice most useful knowledge has both tacit and explicit aspects and needs to be managed holistically, the SECI model leads the average manager to manage the containers.

4. There is an implicit assumption that tacit knowledge can and should be made explicit. The two are separate questions ... the fact that we can does not mean that we should and more often we cannot without loosing something essential. Although many people use the Polanyi quote *'we can know more than we can tell'* ... few read on to understand that we can always know more than we can tell, and we can always tell more than we can write. They also fail to recognize that the initial emphasis on the word 'can'.

Snowden believes that 'Probst and his co-authors ... offer a seductive and simplistic, if not false, view of knowledge. Tacit knowledge gets little mention with the focus on a useful set of tools and techniques for managing knowledge, which can or should be codified. Knowledge is separated into two classes – that which can be codified and that which cannot which is held to be genius and beyond the bounds of structured management.'

Snowden also writes about 'knowledge disclosure points', and says 'These comprise decisions, judgments, problem resolution and learning. They are the points at which we use knowledge' (p. 3).

The ASHEN model

The ASHEN model was created as a means of providing a linguistic framework both to help organizations identify what they know and to move directly to action as a result of the meaning provided by the language. It is designed to prevent the need for argument about the management of its outcome. The mnemonic form facilitates consistent use in the field. The five ASHEN components are: Artefacts, Skills, Heuristics, Experience and Natural Talent, and these are now discussed in detail.

Artefacts

Definition – A product of human art and workmanship.

The term 'artefacts' encompasses all the existing explicit knowledge and/or codified information within an organization – the processes, documents, filing cabinets, databases and other constructed 'things' that encompass the codifiable to varying degrees of success. The management issue here is the removal of duplication and the general optimization and ready distribution of such artefacts to communities that need them. The artefacts will always need to be in the right place at the right time – even though most people may be unaware of their existence for most of the time – this is a non-trivial management challenge for which technology can only support, but not provide, answers. Many artefacts exist but are not known. They may be notebooks of exceptional past events in the drawer of a staff room of a supermarket, a diary in a café frequented on a regular basis by field engineers or a website using the free space in Hotmail used by individuals in competitive companies who shared a common interest. All three of these examples come from Snowden's own experience, and in each case were probably one of the most valuable assets identified in a knowledge disclosure exercise.

Their value is in their natural occurrence; they developed based on the real needs of individuals. According to Snowden, attempting to change their nature would be dangerous. To take the example of the field engineers; the book in question was used daily to communicate valuable information about health and safety procedures, work arounds on technical parts, gossip about managers, information about customers. The mechanism of its maintenance was that each engineer would casually read it over a cup of tea and then write their own observations before leaving. One of the solutions proposed when it was discovered was to enhance existing hand-held computers to capture the same information in the field. This missed the point, the artefact was a part of a social setting and involved social obligations. The solution was to endorse the use of the café in return for managers being allowed to photocopy the book on a weekly basis; and to sell the idea to the engineers by telling them to keep *two* books.

The key is to respect naturally occurring artefacts and separate the creation and capture of knowledge from its analysis and distribution. It may not be neat and tidy to do so and appear to be anti-rational and sub-optimal; but Snowden writes that it works.

Skills

Definition – Practical ability, expertness, practised ability, facility in doing something, dexterity.

In this context skills are those things for which we can identify tangible measures of their successful acquisition. Snowden draws upon the example of employing a plasterer where he can measure the deviation from a vertical plane of his work and the time taken to complete. Snowden writes that 'Customer relationship is a more different thing to measure and although it has aspects of "skill", the term is not enough in its own right. The time element is an important aspect of the skill measurement' (2000b, p. 4). Snowden writes that he is a 'reasonably accomplished carpenter, but a skilled chippie can accomplish in one hour a task that is a weekend's work for the amateur'. For Snowden:

Skills are something that organisations know how to manage. They are the most readily codifiable of the knowledge assets of an organisation. Training needs and skills analysis are well known techniques. Training courses, moderated work experience – the gambit of techniques available is wide and well proven. However there is always the danger of the codification heresy: the belief that once something is written down, then it is shared. Most of the published 'success' stories of Intellectual Capital Management often suffer from this heresy. To illustrate it let us return to the plasterer. Any one who has tried to plaster a wall based on the codified knowledge of a book, say, *The Ten Easy Steps to Perfect Plastering*, will know the issue. Following the instructions does not mean that the plaster will stay on the wall, or that you will not have to burn out several sanding machines to achieve any smoothness. Too many organisations in building their Intellectual Capital Management Systems are actually creating legions of amateur plasters. While skills can be codified, time has to be take to internalise them. The management task is to catalogue the skills, understand the time horizon and resource requirements for their acquisition and plan accordingly. (p. 4)

Heuristics

Definition – Serving to find out or to stimulate investigation, serving to discover. ~method, system of education under which a pupil is trained to find out things for himself.

Heuristics or rules of thumb are one of the most valuable of assets and may be articulated without the need to render them fully explicit. They are the effective way by which we make decisions when the full facts are not known – or knowable in the time available. A good example is the CEO looking at a range of investment proposals without sufficient time – or the inclination – to go through the detailed case. The decision criteria often take the form of a simple rule set: Has someone I trust checked this out? Will it impact on my targets for this year? Will it distract key staff from other more important targets? These may or may not be articulated, but they are often known to the CEO's inner circle. They are also the means by which experts and/or professionals make decisions in conditions of uncertainty. An example would be 'If the gauge goes above that level, in these circumstances then I'll look at the problem again'. The essence of heuristics is that they have fuzzy edges and therein lies their power. They allow greater consistency in conditions of uncertainty but follow the Pareto principle that 80% is good enough. Over time they may become fully explicit and become artefacts, or they may remain tacit – only available to an expert community. Recent work with a group of engineers revealed some interested heuristics, some of which could be codified and distributed – but the general comments about their use were summed up by one engineer who said 'Its a good rule and I use it all the time – but I wouldn't let anyone with less than ten years experience anywhere near it. Until then they can do it by the book!'

For management, identifying and codifying heuristics is a fast track and generally cheap way to spread valuable knowledge quickly. The act of making the heuristics explicit can also clear away false assumptions and out of date working practices, where the context in which the original and mostly unstated heuristics were developed no longer appertains.

Experience

Definition – Actual observation of or practical acquaintance with facts or events; knowledge resulting from this.

Experience, according to Snowden, is the most valuable and most difficult of the tacit assets of an organization. Snowden believes it is difficult for two reasons: (i) the experience may be collective rather than individual, and (ii) replication of the experience may not be practical or sensible.

Snowden uses this case to illustrate this:

A major UK company knew one of their key assets was the ability to manage cash but they didn't know why. Using the ASHEN model artefacts were readily identified in the form of management reports and the like. Skills were also evident, they were all Management Accountants. The Heuristics were clinically paranoid in their attention to detail, but made sense when the experience was identified: the common experience of three members of the finance team of living through a bankruptcy in a previous employment. That collective experience had given them an ability to spot trends, and take common sense actions faster and with more effect than others, no matter how intelligent or how well trained. The issue was two fold: (i) the experience was collective – they were a team and, (ii) although it could be repeated it does not make sense to plunge a company into bankruptcy every two years as a training exercise for the finance department! Over time story telling, war gaming and techniques derived from journalism can mitigate this problem, but organizations should be under no illusion – mitigation is possible, but there is no full substitute for the experience itself. Key then is to understand the dependence – and the consequent vulnerability in the event of change – to key experiences whether individual or collective. (2000b, p. 5)

Natural talent

Definition – (Natural) Based on the innate moral sense, instinctive. Inborn. (Talent) Special aptitude, faculty, gift, high mental ability.

Natural talent, the final component of our model according to Snowden, is unmanageable. 'We can improve our ability to spot it, we can foster its development and attempt to prevent corporate politics from stifling its realization. But we cannot manufacture or transfer it. We can build the skills necessary to spot it, and foster the experience that will allow us to use it. Like non-repeatable experience we need to understand our key dependencies and measure the risk and vulnerability to loss – and take appropriate action. The formal definitions quoted above speak for themselves' (2000b, p. 7).

A wider perspective

The ASHEN model is powerful in that it uses commonplace, or slightly unusual, words (artifacts and heuristics) and invests them with common-ense meaning. According to Snowden:

> It provides a different perspective, or creates an awareness of a required change in attitude. By asking the ASHEN question in the context of a KDP [knowledge disclosure point] we can achieve a meaningful answer which itself leads to action. When you made that decision, what *artifacts* did you use, or would you like to have? What *skills* did you have or need and how are they acquired? What *heuristics* do you use to make such decisions quickly, what is the range of their applicability? What *experience* do you have and what experience do the people you respect in this field have? What *natural talent* is necessary? How exclusive is it? Who else has it? Such questions allow the questioned to produce meaning full answers with minimal interference from the questioner.

> Most importantly ASHEN helps create a key shift in organizational thinking from key-person dependency to knowledge dependency. This essential step of depersonalization is critical to effective knowledge practice. It is the shift from *Only Linda can do X,* to *X requires this combination of artifacts, skills, heuristics, experience and natural talent and at the moment, only Linda has them.* The former statement has only crude solutions, the later permits greater sophistication and the potential for long lasting solutions and sustainable management action. It achieves this by using language that describes the situation at the right level of granularity to permit action without excessive analysis. (2000b, p. 6)

SUMMARY

- Stories of identity convey values, build esprit de corps, create role models, and reveal how things work

- Stories are more important than memos, mission statements, newsletters, speeches, and policy manuals. They 'constitute the single most powerful weapon in the leader's literary arsenal'

- If you ask people what they know, they will generally tell you what they think they ought to know, and it will generally be explicit knowledge – the knowledge that can be written down

- The more valuable tacit knowledge, and a substantial proportion of explicit knowledge, is only known when it is needed to be known

- Heuristics or rules of thumb are one of the most valuable of assets and may be articulated without the need to render them fully explicit

---

Burson-Marsteller

PER H. HEGGENES *Chief Knowledge and Insights Officer Worldwide*

Q: *Is training costly/expensive for firms such as Burson-Marsteller?*

A: Training represents a large expense in a professional services firm because turnover tends to be rather high. There is a vast investment in training people who then soon move on to their next job. Management consulting firms such as McKinsey hire graduates and most of them will only be there for three years because they won't make it to the next level. Well-defined methodologies and working procedures make it possible to leverage smart graduates effectively in this type of business. If you look at Burson-Marsteller it is somewhat different. There's less structure, it is not a science in the same way, it is more about counselling clients how to use communications more effectively and more strategically to achieve business results. That requires experience and a different set of skills.

Q: *How many people are we talking about at Burson-Marsteller?*

A: There are 2200 people worldwide. In the UK about 200. We have a total of 60–70 offices around the world.

Q: *Is it the accelerated learning processes that are going to be most helpful to an organization of this type where knowledge management may come into its own where experience is critical. Everybody wants to put a wise head on young shoulders. Does knowledge management sit in this area?*

A: It is partly to make young people learn fast, but it is just as much among equals, where we can all benefit and develop new tools. For example, we are developing a new concept called speed branding. This is for companies operating in the new economy. They are either Internet start-ups or old economy companies venturing additional business opportunities in the new economy. A key success criteria is to build the brand quickly in order to become the preferred partner/supplier. You must develop a stronger brand faster than any other competitor and that also means building it quickly so that all the seed funding isn't gone before the revenue stream is there. New economy companies need to build their brand quickly, they don't have five years, like Coca-Cola; they are living off borrowed money with a lot of competitors trying to do the same thing and the arena is the Internet and everyone owns the Internet, so differentiation is harder.

Building a quality brand that's differentiated requires you to understand how to build brands, a process of developing something that is clearly differentiated and relevant in the marketplace.

We use knowledge management tools extensively on a global basis, such as intranets and extranets with document tracking, chat rooms, bulletin boards and so on, to share knowledge more effectively and operate more seamlessly through time zones. We are under permanent scrutiny and need to focus on making sure we constantly look for ways to operate more efficiently in order to provide the best possible value for our clients and ourselves – that we are a differentiated as a company, that we bring insights that other companies don't bring.

Q: *You are now owned by WPP. Are you thinking of focusing more on Internet PR?*

A: Yes, definitely. We work for different clients – we are the number one in the world, have been for a long time and work for large international clients. Our new economy clients make up a significant part of our client base. We haven't positioned Burson-Marsteller as a new economy company. The Internet represents a new channel for communication with the marketplace and key constituencies – but that's all it is. It opens up some new opportunities for dialogue and increases the speed and outreach. We can campaign faster and more efficiently. By the way, this is the area where the young people teach the old people and not the other way round! We help clients to understand how to use the new media to get their message across, and how the Internet can change the way they are operating.

Q: *And the Internet is only one medium in the new economy?*

A: Sure. Digital TV is another and there will be new areas and opportunities that didn't exist a year ago.

Q: *Can we quantify the percentage of new media business that you do? More to give the reader a feel for what is really happening. And also to give the reader a feel of what you have said, to get traditional companies to learn the methodology associated with the new economy.*

A: It has happened very fast. We have built this from the inside, using our perception management platform. The new media is important, but the Internet is just another communication channel. There are advantages and dangers to Internet – for example it is much harder to control. Things can be posted on our websites that we know nothing about. We try to help companies to prepare themselves. We are trying to share with our global clients what we do and the experience we gather on the way. This requires effective knowledge sharing inside our own company first. We conduct the majority of the sharing around real client projects in addition to formal training workshops. Everything has to relate with real projects and real clients. We aim to develop better processes to facilitate this. Our intranet platforms are under constant redevelopment in order to better facilitate this learning process.

Q: *It is knowledge-intensive firms that are going to have the competitive advantage. How would Burson-Marsteller place themselves over other organizations to show how they are able to lead the field?*

A: We have spent a significant amount of resources developing knowledge sharing and knowledge management solutions. But rewarding positive behaviour is just as important. As long as I am the expert, my position is secure, but once I share, I make myself vulnerable. If I am good in a specific expertise area, then I am looked up to and I don't want to lose this position.

Q: *Therefore a whole set of behaviours need to be adopted by people in order for them to understand knowledge sharing and best practice in this area. By sharing it will make the organization stronger.*

A: Yes, people are different and their behaviour and that of the organization has to change. Rewarding knowledge sharing is the key to unleashing the untapped potential, which means that sometimes the way people are compensated must change. The more information you give away, the more powerful you should become.

13 The Future of Knowledge Management in the New Economy and its Relationship with Competitor Intelligence

In March 2001, Dr Marcus Speh Birkenkrähe, knowledge manager at Shell International, delivered a speech at the Hilton International, London. There are not many people who can talk about knowledge management in its most sophisticated form and link its theory to organizations. This man is one of the few.

For Speh:

> Knowledge management as a discipline is coming of age... The economy is at a true turning point, as 'old economy' meets 'new economy'. A number of challenges result from this fact – some of them known, many of them unknown and new. In order to meet these challenges, knowledge management, as a maturing discipline, must realize that it is at a turning point, too. Knowledge management professionals need to react to this situation by changing their whole attitude and approach to the theory and practice of knowledge management.

> Many of the challenges are inherently complex. This fact suggests that, in order to make knowledge management work, a holistic, or complex systems approach, needs to be taken. If knowledge management professionals take this new approach on board, then the discipline of knowledge management will be a powerful enabler of success in the future economy.

Nicholas Bahra is grateful to Dr Marcus Speh Birkenkrähe for permission to quote exclusively from his speech 'Turtles all the way down and all the way up'. Much of the material in this chapter is also adapted from this speech.

There have been a number of successes in the area of knowledge management over the past half decade, according to Speh, and he notes the high awareness of the concept of knowledge management and the fact that many more organizations are about to invest in this area. Speh mentioned the spectacular forecasts on the growth of the knowledge management sector, and the successes of knowledge-based businesses, for example the management consulting firms. Speh acknowledges the 'tremendous uptake in only a short amount of time'.

Knowledge and information are now totally synonymous with business. Dr Speh acknowledges that the connection between knowledge and competitive advantage had been made prior to the new economy and 'there are no doubts anymore that managing knowledge and knowledge creation are conditional to achieve innovation, or the introduction of anything new to an organization'.

Speh then describes why he believes we are at a turning point in the development of knowledge management and puts the successes into a new context. He chooses Kevin Kelly's description of the new economy.

This new economy has three distinguishing characteristics: it is global. It favours intangible things – ideas, information, and relationships. And it is intensely interlinked. These three attributes produce a new type of marketplace and society, one that is rooted in ubiquitous electronic networks. (Kelly, 1998)

Speh makes a number of key points including:

■ Globality is poorly understood. Everybody is aware of the struggle between local and global aspects – of culture, of the environment, and of organizations. Multinationals literally oscillate between decentralization and centralization. Communication technology is said to benefit the local agents – because it gives them access to the centre and other local agents, *and* it is also used as an excuse to eliminate local agents, because holding data and information centrally is so much more cost-effective. Likewise, everybody agrees that there are virtually no truly *global* organizations, only organizations with global presence. The rise of a new type of retailer like Amazon.com has complicated the issue even further. The point is, that knowledge management has not even begun to seriously address the issue of globality, which is central to knowledge management implementations – in both multinationals and locally operating firms.

■ Knowledge and information are firmly on the mental map of most organizations and we have an understanding that knowledge is context-dependent – hence we learnt to distinguish between tacit and explicit knowledge. Some even equate knowledge management with the theory and practice of conversion between tacit and explicit knowledge.

A lot of the terminology used is not clear. The current real economic world is used to thinking of itself as based on hard, tangible assets, not on intangible assets. Although companies are starting to accept that continuous innovation and managing knowledge are very important indeed – at the end of the day they still consider knowledge management a luxury, not something that keeps executives up at night. Speh noted:

> It is for a reason that we associate a higher potential for change with a discipline that refers to 'knowledge', to one of the highest achievements of individual and societal activity. To begin with, total quality management and business process re-engineering are non-integrative, they are management techniques that live off selection and restriction, not integration. Competitive intelligence, on the other hand, is an off-shoot of business intelligence, which is a civil version of military intelligence – not without merits, but very limited in scope, and exclusive by its very nature.

> So the first thing we must do is assume a different heritage. I will later get into more detail, but for now let me remind you that there are three very distinguished candidates among the sciences – physics, biology, and psychology. The sciences associated with the world of matter, of life, and of mind are all going through a similar process: they are trying to overcome the splits between each other and within themselves, to become more integrative, more holistic. To name only two examples of integration within: the integration of physics between Newtonian mechanics and quantum mechanics, spanning a period of over 200 years of intense research; and the integration of Freudian psychoanalytic theory with ancient Eastern theories of consciousness.

> One way in which Knowledge Management needs to change here and now is by accepting that the complexity of these questions requires that we focus more on integration of issues, and on transcending polarities, instead of thinking that there always needs to be one and only one answer. Which is how most of us have been brought up in business. Which is why we are often unwilling to deal with uncertainty by leaving decisions open, and by designing more flexible environments around great challenges.

The holistic, complex systems approach to knowledge management

Here, Speh explores what 'holistic' really means. This requires the introduction of a few theoretical concepts and a few of the implications of holistic or integrative knowledge management.

In many ways, I think knowledge management has suffered the fate of other so-called management sciences: it is developed too close to its own practice and therefore has a hard time getting away from itself. This doesn't sound like a bad thing, to be too close to practice – all business people are wary of theories that have no contact with reality at all. The trick, however, as so often, lies in the right balance between theory and practice.

Keeping this in mind, let's take a long step back from practice for a moment. We need to do that if we want to give proper meaning to the term 'holistic'. This word is in danger to become overused whenever a field of knowledge experiences the pressures I have described so far: it has matured enough to have gained some respectability, and enough to understand the size of the problems it is facing, but not quite enough to integrate these problems and address them with one language.

It is a situation that, I mentioned it earlier, other, larger sciences have encountered, and are encountering right now: the problem of integration is the same for physics, biology, or psychology, or the sciences devoted to matter, life, and the mind. So we're in good company here.

There is no time in this talk to go into the true origin of this problem, although it is a fascinating one, and I have to restrict myself to only a sketch of what a solution may look like. Many of the following ideas are originating from the work of a modern American philosopher, Ken Wilber.[1] His work comes closest to describing the integrative approach which I hope knowledge management will adopt from here on out.

For a long time, we thought that the problem with integration at the level at which we are talking here, came down to the famous mind–body split. It turns out, upon inspection, that this can be resolved by resolving the matter–body split, or the split between the laws that govern the physiosphere (the sphere of matter), and the laws that govern the biosphere (the sphere of life). The problem arises because systems in the physiosphere, matter systems, seem to only wind down over time in terms of order, which is captured in the laws of thermodynamics, while in the biosphere, living systems seem to wind up over time – for example in biological evolution, where amoebas evolve into apes, but never the other way around.

The solution to bridge the gap between these two contradictory observations marks the emergence of a whole set of sciences at the end of the 20th century – new sciences dealing with processes that bridge the gap between the two observations, systems that wind themselves up, or self-organising systems. These sciences are collectively known as the sciences of complexity – including general systems theory, cybernetics, non-equilibrium thermodynamics, cellular automata theory, catastrophe theory, autopoietic system theory, dynamic systems theory, and chaos theories.

To understand the complex system approach, we need to introduce a new notion which, interestingly, transcends one of today's problems in knowledge management – the issue between hierarchies and networks. Which is where holistic comes in.

As used in modern psychology, evolutionary theory and systems theory, a hierarchy is simply a ranking of orders of events according to their holistic capacity. In any developmental sequence, what is whole at one stage becomes a part of a larger whole at the next stage. A letter is part of a whole word, which is part of a whole sentence, which is part of a whole paragraph, and so on. Or in biology, any change in an organism will affect all the parts, no aspect of a structure can be altered without affecting the entire structure, each whole contains parts and is itself part of a larger whole.

The social philosopher Arthur Koestler coined the term 'holon' to refer to that which, being a whole in one context, is simultaneously a part in another. With reference to the phrase 'the bark of a dog' for example, the word bark is a whole with reference to its individual letters, but a part with reference to the phrase itself. And the whole (or the context) can determine the meaning and function of a part – for example in different meaning of bark in 'the bark of a dog' and 'the bark of a tree'. The whole, in other words, is more than the sum of its parts, and that whole can influence and determine, in many cases, the function of its parts.

Normal hierarchy is simply an order of increasing holons, representing an increase in wholeness and integrative capacity – atoms to molecules to cells for example. Or, to bring it back to knowledge management – individuals to groups to organisations. Hierarchy is central to systems theory, which is the theory of holism: to be a part of a larger whole means that the whole supplies a principle (or some sort of glue) not found in the isolated parts alone, and this principle allows the parts to join, to link together, to have something in common, to be connected in ways that they could not be on their own. In this sense, hierarchy is the fundamental structural principle, which is why they are sometimes drawn as series of concentric circles or spheres, or nests within nests.

How do networks come in? Well, within a given level of any hierarchical pattern, the elements of that level operate by heterarchy. That is, no one element seems to be especially more important or more dominant, and each contributes more or less equally to the health of the whole level.

But a higher-order whole, of which this lower-order whole is a part, can exert an overriding influence on each of its components. For example – when you decide to move your arm, your mind, which is a high-order holistic organisation, exerts influence over all the cells in your arm, which are lower-order wholes, but not vice versa: a cell in your arm cannot decide to move the whole arm – the tail does not wag the dog.

So in this language, networks operate along both dimensions – within each level of an organisation as heterarchies, and between levels of an organisation as hierarchies. Koestler in fact pointed out, after noting that all such hierarchies are composed of holons, or increasing orders of wholeness, that the correct word for 'hierarchy' is actually 'holarchy', or the 'governance structure of holons'.

And Knowledge Management itself becomes a holistic science if it uses an integrative vision and vocabulary like this to freshly describe its issues, questions and answers. The framework is suitable as it is. Let me demonstrate only two fundamental applications of this theory to knowledge management.

(1) Look at the most fundamental holarchy with which I began this whole argument: reality itself, which is made up of three smaller holarchies – the physiosphere, which is the holarchy of matter, the biosphere, which is the holarchy of living matter, and the noosphere, which is the holarchy of thinking matter, of mind and spirit. In this picture, reality itself is not composed of things, or processes, but of holons – composed, that is, of wholes that are simultaneously parts of other wholes, with no upward or downward limit.

The different spheres or holarchies, however, do correspond to the basic constituents that we have identified as core to our understanding of knowledge management as well: the physiosphere contains our *tangible*, or *hard assets*; the biosphere contains *people*; and the noosphere contains *intangible assets*, ideas, information, relationships. So this is rather neat.

(2) Now let us look at what Wilber calls 'pathological' hierarchies and heterarchies. You can already see how holarchies can go pathological. If the higher levels can exert influence over the lower levels, they can also overdominate or even repress and alienate the lower levels. Which leads to a host of pathological difficulties in both the individual and the society at large.

This simple thought gives rise to an intervention strategy: to root out any holons that have abused their position in the overall system, the arrogant holons, but not getting rid of holarchy per se. This is exactly the cure we see at work in psychoanalysis – neurotic holons refuse integration in the whole of the psyche – and in social theory – ideological holons that distort open communication – and in democratic revolutions – monarchical or fascist holons that oppress the political body – and in medical science interventions – cancerous holons invade a benign system. And also in knowledge management: arrogant holons correspond, for example, to individuals who abuse their position of knowledge by refusing to share with the rest of the organisation.

Networks, or heterarchies, as I called them earlier, can also become pathological. Heterarchy is holism within any level – it goes pathological when there is a blurring or fusion of that level with its environment: a particular holon doesn't stand out too much, it blends in too much; it loses itself in others – and all distinctions, of value or identity, are lost. In knowledge management, that's a familiar problem. Namely, what's the strategy to motivate people to share what they know, if they define their identity and value largely through the knowledge that they alone hold?

In other words, in a pathological hierarchy, one holon assumes dominance to the detriment of all – it assumes the role of the whole. On the other hand, in pathological heterarchy, individual holons lose their distinctive value and identity in a communal fusion and meltdown – it assumes it's only a part.

We have really only dipped into the theory of holons, which is a framework for any truly holistic theory. Two other interesting directions for investigation include the four fundamental capacities of holons: self-preservation, self-adaptation, self-transcendence and self-dissolution.

For the purpose of knowledge management, this opens a path to describe the building up, adapting, transcending and dissolving of knowledge in its agents – remember that organisations, teams, individuals can all be described as holons.

This theory is very much motivated by finding a consistent developmental perspective. Therefore, another interesting application is to look at the stages of knowledge management development. Any cogent or agreed model for these stages in the literature so far is notoriously missing. Complex systems theory offers a solution that distinguishes between different types of holons – individual or communal – and that represents what they look like from the outside versus what they look like from the inside. This simple structure allows one to fold in a wide spectrum of approaches to development and learning, ranging from Piaget's theory of the development of the child, over Argyris' left- and right-hand column description of the organisational learning process, to Habermas' critical social theory.

This scheme, which Wilber calls 'the four quadrants', can also be used though to trace the development of a thought from its origin in the individual to its communication and use. All the hierarchies of holons, or hierarchies, sit on the four diagonals of the graph. So there is a correspondence, for example, between the interior experience of sensations, and simple neuronal organisms, and likewise around the whole graph. This scheme is suitable for example to describe the management lifecycle of knowledge. It turns out, most of the stuff that's really interesting to KM is in the interior half of the chart, which is 'dialogical', 'right brain', as opposed to 'monological', 'left brain' and so on. In fact, the system is reported to have been used to describe potential future of NASA's space research, among other applications in organisational management.

This may look to you like a recasting of a process that we think we know very well already. But as I said earlier, we hardly understand what is really going on when people create and share or use knowledge. Putting it into the proper context, as a complex system, helps because it allows us to draw on a myriad of examples from other fields, not to mention the possibilities of modelling that come with the whole raft of complex system sciences; and there are other interesting new tools arising from such a perspective, including the so-called organisational constellations (for example – http://bertchile.iwarp.com/ InterviewChileOrg.htm).

Knowledge management as a powerful enabler for success in the new economy

Perhaps it is time here to stop and draw a fresh breath. As I said earlier, I have not been able to do more today than paint a very sketchy picture of the possibilities for a more integrative, or holistic knowledge management.

I have got two last thoughts and a joke that I would like to leave you with.

First of all, I hope you begin to appreciate the enormous advantage which an integrative and holistic approach like this offers. The particular framework, whose foundations I have outlined to you, has the benefit that it is itself built on the notion of wholeness. In the form in which I presented it today, this thinking makes a whole lot of approaches, that look very different, look not so different and, most importantly, usable for knowledge management theory and practice. But undoubtedly, there are other integrative theories out there. My point is that we must stretch ourselves to find a viewpoint from which we can integrate various approaches, or else we will fall short of the potential that knowledge management really holds – to get there will take focus, investigation and the will to change.

In fact, this is another nice demonstration of the meaning of holons: applying a sense of integration to knowledge management offers the field of knowledge management as a whole the opportunity to learn. That is, understand itself as part of a larger whole and understand its parts.

Next, I'd like to speculate that at the heart of the challenges that I listed earlier on, there is not just a problem with terminology, or methodology, or integrative capability of knowledge management, but a real split in our world that goes through our organisations. This also brings us back to where we began today – the role of KM for the new economy. The split that goes through organisations is very obvious where the so-called old meets the so-called new economy. By now it is becoming clear that we are not in an old versus new situation – the old economy won't just go away and make space for the new economy. In fact, they're not as different as they pretend to be – the clue here is, once again, integration across boundaries.

And the split, which goes across industrial, people and geographical boundaries, is perhaps more a fracturedness, a hierarchy of splits, than one split. If that's so, then I would like to see knowledge management act as one of the forces that help organisations heal their split.

Leo Burke, head of training at Motorola, is quoted in a book by Wilber with the following words that I think are relevant to this thought. He writes: 'At a meeting at the Santa Fe Institute I posed the questions, "What role do institutions of commerce, especially multinational corporations, play in the evolution of our species? And what potential, if any, does business have to support a vision of humanity that integrates spirit, mind and body on individual, organisational, and societal levels?"' There were no answers forthcoming, but asking the questions in a business context is a small step forward. Yet any exercise of considering such questions is quite limp without the questioners having a fundamental commitment to their own transformation. Ultimately, of course, this is a commitment not to incremental self-improvement, but to genuine self-transcendence.

There is an old joke about a King who goes to a wise person and asks how it is that the earth doesn't fall down? The wise person replies, 'The earth is resting on a lion.' The king asks: 'On what then, is the lion resting?' 'The lion is resting on an elephant', replies the wise person. 'On what is the elephant resting?' the King asks again . 'The elephant is resting on a turtle', says the wise person. And before the King can ask again, he says, 'You can stop right there, your majesty. It's turtles all the way down.' – It's holons all the way up, and all the way down.

Competitor intelligence vs. competitive intelligence

Letitia Andrewartha is Knowledge Management Director at Pricewater-houseCoopers and differentiates between competitor intelligence and competitive intelligence. According to Andrewartha (1999):

> Competitor intelligence is an important sub-set but nevertheless a sub-set of competitive intelligence. In essence it's all about focusing on products and services, how best to stay one – or preferably two – jumps ahead of the competition and ensuring that your strategy and tactics will enable you to defeat, deflect or devalue any challenge posed by your competitors in your chosen marketplace. Good competitor intelligence means you will be aware of, and prepared for, actions that your competitors may be planning and it will allow you to react quickly and effectively in response to the oppositions' moves.

Andrewartha goes on to explain:

Competitive intelligence requires a broader canvass as it embraces 'whole market' information and enables the analysis of data from many diverse sources to be employed in the design, development and implementation of your organisation's strategy. Although it should be client focused, the field of view should be as wide as possible. Trends which may, at first sight, be on the periphery of your business environment can be evaluated and incorporated into the planning processes that drives your R&D operations and provides R&D development experts with the information tools required to develop new products and services.

This whole area of competitive intelligence is set to become increasingly important and influential in terms of which companies survive in the new economy.

Shell Services International originated a content-based knowledge management framework. The framework divides the total knowledge space into three very different spaces. The density of information *increases* from collaboration to best practices, while the immediacy of the information *decreases* (Figure 13.1).

A few years ago a very different model was the basis of a knowledge management framework for the Shell Group (Figure 13.2). This model describes a four-step process, which every organization which wants to manage its knowledge better has to go through. The four process steps are related to both culture and technology and are aligned with knowledge management activities. They are:

- Capturing
- Sharing
- Using
- Learning.

According to Speh, the first step must be a realization of what the organization considers it's 'core knowledge' to be. Only if this can be identified, is there anything worth capturing. Second, the organization must then help to assemble 'knowledge communities'. Speh notes that the word community is 'meaningful'. 'Communities can and should cut across hierarchies, geographical and other barriers that stop the flow of knowledge. Once this has begun, a 'network-effect' sets in'.

Finally the last stage is more innovation, creativity and learning. The process works, according to Speh, 'at the level of the individual, the team, the department, and at the enterprise level'.

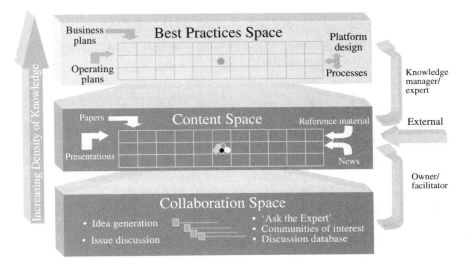

Figure 13.1 Content-based knowledge management framework
Source: Shell Services International, KMsolutions™ Content Architecture

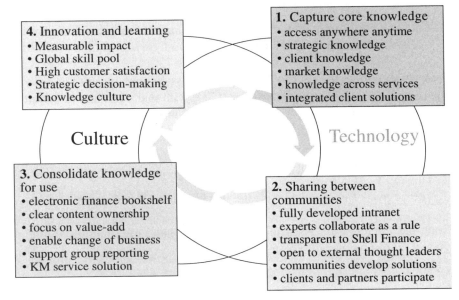

Figure 13.2 Process-based knowledge management framework
Source: Shell KM Framework

The differences between knowledge management and competitive intelligence are interesting. Knowledge management 'facilitates in the here and now', notes Speh, 'focusing on capturing and sharing, and emphasising the role of people, culture and process'.

> Competitive intelligence, and its twin business intelligence, are more focused on the future, on possibilities, helping to shape decision making, and emphasising trends, patterns, and what is currently uncertain, or unknown. Where knowledge management hopes to improve job effectiveness, there Competitive Intelligence hopes to lead to faster and better action. The Shell example, clearly lives in the bottom half of this pyramid. Shell's widely known scenario planning capability, for example, lives in the upper half. The activities of Shell's network of Competitor Intelligence Professionals represent a successful fusion of activities covering the whole pyramid (see Figure 13.3).

Similarities between knowledge management and competitive intelligence are:

- Both focus on intangible values
- Both require dedication and professionalism
- Both rely on larger communities and on sponsorship from the top to really make an impact on business.

A study conducted by the London Business School in 1999 compared the role of a chief information officer (CIO) with that of a chief knowledge officer (CKO). This comparison was made along four axes:

1. The need to be entrepreneurial
2. The understanding of technology
3. The ability to consult
4. The degree of interaction with the world outside the company.

Speh has depicted his assessment of where a 'head of competitive intelligence' would be placed (see Figure 13.4).

Speh also notes that:

> Competitive Intelligence has been recognized as a most important issue for Shell, and this insight has manifested itself in a powerful marriage of Knowledge Management and Competitor Intelligence. At the global

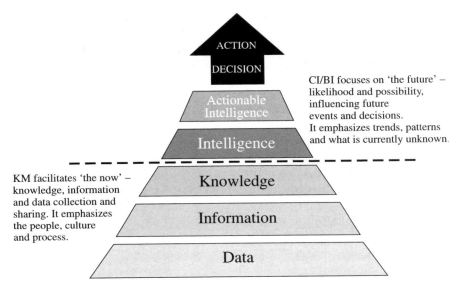

Figure 13.3 The intelligence pyramid
Source: Fuld; Rodenburg, Tillman & Associates 1999; Shell

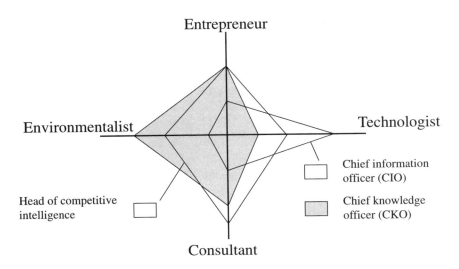

Figure 13.4 Roles of a chief knowledge officer, chief information officer and a leading head of competitive intelligence
Source: CKO research, London Business School, 1999 (modified)

level, there is a maze of smaller networks in each of the sectors, or businesses of Shell. The largest of the sector networks, is supported by the Exploration and Production, the EP sector. The Global Competitor Intelligence network brings all these networks together. (Figure 13.5).

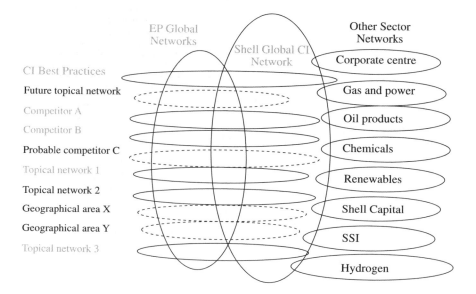

Figure 13.5 How Shell competitor intelligence (CI) is using knowledge management principles

SUMMARY

- For knowledge management to work, a holistic, or complex systems approach, needs to be taken

- Knowledge management will be a powerful enabler of success

- There is a high awareness of "Knowledge Management" and many more organizations are about to invest in this area

- Knowledge and information are now totally synonymous with business

- There are four process steps related to both culture and technology: Capturing, Sharing, Using, Learning

- There is a powerful marriage between Knowledge Management and Competitor Intelligence

Case Study

Shell International Limited

DR. MARCUS SPEH BIRKENKRÄHE *Knowledge Manager*

Q: *Is there such a thing as the old economy?*

A: I think there really is only one economy, but two quite different approaches to conducting business. Today, it is almost impossible to cleanly separate old and new economy – this is not made easier by the fact that the market itself seems confused after the recent Internet 'gold rush' that now seems to have come to an end. I suppose the easiest common denominator for all so-called old economy situations and companies is a very strong focus on the hard assets and tangible values. Kevin Kelly says that the three factors that distinguish the new economy are that it is global, it favours intangible things such as ideas, information, and relationships, and it is intensely interlinked.

By comparison, the old economy is not global. It has a number of large companies that have a global presence but it is not characterized by companies which run global processes. New economy companies are better positioned to be global. Many new economy companies are instantly global. The fact that they are instantly global doesn't mean that they are instantly successful as companies. So a company like Amazon has a global customer value proposition, but obviously goes through a process of conquering countries and regions just as any other company.

Connectivity is another important issue. I am not talking about connectivity in terms of technical connectivity, although that's part of it, but things can be run by self-organizing networks rather than hierarchies.

Q: *What about information flow in multinational companies in the past?*

A: That was purely through people. When I arrived at Shell there was one predominant knowledge management system and that was the expatriate system. The most effective way of pushing knowledge around the company was to relocate people. Information flow was through people (2–4000 people) who moved around and this was linked to the individual's potential value. As long as the company had complete control over that pool, everything was fine. The biggest hole came in 1996 when we were losing people.

Shell is a good example of the connectivity issue because it is very well networked. It runs on internal networks. The only problem with these 'natural networks' is that the networks are not normally self-aware: they are not aware of their potential. If the company as a whole does not realize that the networks are more important than the hierarchies, I would not call it self-aware. You need to foster those networks directly, rather than allow them to grow by themselves. You need to inject energy into them to help them survive and then switch them off when they have come to a close.

Everybody moans about how few new ideas there are, but the fact is that the system actually discourages people from having original ideas. In the new economy the processes by which companies come into existence and get revenue flowing are directly related to the speed and ease with which ideas are coming up from the ground and getting through to production and to the customer. They are directly related to transparency in a knowledge sense and in a decision-making sense of the company. In Shell, we have designed a process called 'gamechanger' which helps us submit ideas from everybody in the organization for rapid evaluation, decision and implementation.

Many new economy companies seem to be aware that they need to do things simply and quickly – for example a practical way of implementing knowledge management in these companies is to use Marshall McLuhan's proposition to make it easy for 'information to brush against information' – such as shoulder rubbing. The evolution cycles of new economy companies are also much shorter – there is less time to formalize them before another new economy company comes along and gobbles them up.

People management and human relationships have always been key to company performance. I am encouraged by the acknowledgement of emotional intelligence and the importance of having a 'soul' in your business. This makes talking about and implementing knowledge management so much easier, because people are already primed to revisit their old value systems.

What many people don't understand about the new economy is that it will lead to a massive freeing up of people's time. The customer gets a lot of power and the back office operations, which are where the people are employed in most of the countries, are in many cases just going to fold up, particularly white collar workers, not so much blue collar workers.

Q: *How should a 23-year-old graduate from university prepare for work in the new economy? What advice would you give?*

A: My recommendations to 23-year-olds would be (1) focus on what you know – the coming changes in the global labour markets will favour those who are aware of their capabilities and knowledge; (2) don't stop learning – and as a corollary, evaluate the quality of your environment and your own performance by the rate at which you are learning; (3) relax and keep a sense of humour – life is much too short otherwise. And while IT is not a panacea, it is true that technology is going to pull down many thresholds. Things are happening fast in this area and you've got the future on your side!

Q: *What do you think about measuring knowledge management?*

A: I think that measuring is highly overrated. In knowledge management I don't think that measuring can replace trust. When people say 'measuring' they want to replace trust. They are not brave enough to say there is a trust issue so they try to replace it with an automatic method.

Having said that, one cannot deny the need of business to place knowledge management in the present context of performance measurement. I think in effect I spend most of my time in knowledge management implementation assessing whether its promised benefits have actually been realized or not. This is appropriate, as long as business people also understand that measurement in the world of intangibles is quite a different beast from measurement in the physical world.

Q: *So, what about your background?*

A: The World Wide Web was developed by a small team of computer scientists at CERN, led by Tim Berners-Lee. I was a physicist at DESY, a sister lab of CERN, and I worked with those guys a lot around the time the World Wide Web was created. So I think I actually created the first 'virtual library' on the Web and was instrumental in pushing the Web out to large professional services firms and industry after I moved on from science. I was present at an historic moment – that's a nice feeling.

Notes

1. See for example Ken Wilber, *Sex, Ecology, Spirituality* (SES) (Shambala, Boston and London, 2000).

14 Knowledge Management and the Significance of Human Resource Management

Reasons for knowledge management failure

Personnel management, training and development or human resource management is the area of knowledge management that is new and relatively unchartered. Traditionally, people have associated knowledge management with information technology and latterly with brand management, intellectual property, patents and research and development. As organizational trends are pointing towards the knowledge-based view of the firm, as suggested by Breu and Kosonen, then it is logical to suggest that the importance of personnel and training within these organizations will increase over time.

Therefore, the importance of specialist recruiting firms, management development experts, organizational psychologists and academics cannot be underestimated. There are numerous reasons why knowledge management may fail within organizations, and most are linked to the importance of professional human resource management.

Professor Prabhu Guptara is Director of Organizational and Executive Development for the Union Bank of Switzerland. In the area of investment banking, Guptara has a unique perspective on the subject of knowledge management:

> The first point to note is that we are living, for the first time in human history, in a time when, in principle, we have the possibility of over-

Nicholas Bahra is grateful to Professor Prabhu Guptara for assistance and permission to quote from his conference paper, 'Relationship Marketing', first presented at the Annual Conference of the Chartered Institute of Bankers, Cambridge, UK, 14–15 September 1998, and subsequently published on the website of the Wolfsberg Executive Development Centre, Switzerland (www.wolfsberg.com). Also to Hannah Brown, Managing Director at Kendall Tarrant Worldwide and Karen Hand (Independent Consultant) for permission to quote from their paper, 'Staying Power'. Also to Korn Ferry International for permission to quote from their document, 'Strategies for the Knowledge Economy: from Rhetoric to Reality' – Davos 2000.

supply of all goods and services. Economics, business, society, pay and legal systems, politics and government are based on a rather different and outdated assumption of what kind of world we live in; their assumption is that we live in a world of scarcity. The business of living on outdated assumptions is true, especially of the world of banking. Management arrived rather late in the world of banking, and of course Knowledge Management has not yet arrived. The reason is that our attitudes and structures are still mired in the past world of scarcity of opportunity for customers to put their money into a safe haven.

Guptara adds that, 'in today's world of oversupply, relationships are up for grabs'. He also writes that knowledge management will 'never make up for poor products, poor strategy or poor systems'. In Guptara's experience, here are the most common reasons why knowledge management does not work.

Time. Most organizations, according to Guptara, cannot make knowledge management work because they are far too busy. Corporate anorexia has been good for the bottom line in the short run, but does not establish a sound foundation for sustainable success as individuals get burnt out and their knowledge dies with them.

Power. Probably the single greatest obstacle to establishing knowledge management in a company is the way in which power is accumulated and exercised in most organizations. For Guptara, career success is

not a matter only of ability and application: it is partly a matter of luck and, in most organisations, it is a matter of the quality of relationships with previous power-holders, of managing impressions, of politics, of starting high profile initiatives and jumping away from them before it becomes evident that there is more froth than substance. This is symptomatic of organisations which are not transparent, which do not face and address and solve real issues. Thankfully the number of such organisations is beginning to decrease, or at least more and more organisations are trying to implant honesty, transparency and a welcome for bad news.

The key point about the accumulation and use of power is that, in most companies, power is used to *lord* it over others. Knowledge management, however, requires power to be used to *serve* others: knowledge management requires an institutionalization of a fundamental unselfishness, a fundamental attitude of wishing to serve customers, not only outside the company, but, crucially, within the company.

Structures. The formal or organizational structures of most companies prevent knowledge management from operating. Most companies are organized along lines of function, region, division, or business unit, each complete with its own recruitment, induction and reward systems, based on their own bottom line. Of course this is not so for all companies, according to Guptara, however, he adds that the internal relationships across hierarchies must work.

Measurement systems. According to Guptara, 'Measurement systems too militate against knowledge management because they measure the wrong things. Usually, they measure bottom-line results though, in some enlightened companies, they have introduced a "balanced scorecard" and started measuring "key performance indicators".' Guptara also notes the significance of 360 degree appraisals and that 'contribution to and utilisation of company knowledge in pursuit of profitability versus that of competitiors' is an area worthy of exploration.

Organizational culture. Organizational culture, according to Guptara, 'vitiates the possibility of success with knowledge management in contemporary organisations ... These are the many things which create an organisation's "unspoken rules and ways of doing things".' Guptara assesses a number of areas of culture within organizations including recognition, reward and training.

Mohrman and Finegold (2000) report that:

> For an increasing number of companies, however, it is unquestionably true that human capital, rather than physical or financial capital, is the key to competitive success. This is particularly true for new high-tech and knowledge service enterprises that have been the key drivers of the new economy.

Mohrman and Finegold's report lists some of the key aspects of knowledge management as:

- Generating and applying knowledge
- Leveraging knowledge
- Connecting knowledge workers
- Importing knowledge
- Motivating knowledge contribution.

They also note from a leadership perspective that:

> To manage knowledge, leaders need to intentionally design the organisation and its processes to foster accessing, creating, growing, applying, leveraging and protecting knowledge for competitive advantage. Organisational knowledge is the essence of a company, and its purposeful management is a key executive responsibility.

Greg Smith, former head of information technology at Chartwell Land, notes the importance of both recognition and reward. Smith also notes how people and their knowledge are of critical importance in the property business. For Smith:

> Property is very much a people driven business and we set ourselves a challenge which was how we manage the contacts. If you look at what really drives a property company, there are the physical assets which are the properties. These physical assets generates an income stream through the occupation of those properties. What we are really interested in is the out-performance compared to the rest of the sector. Once you are start talking about the out-performance of a property you are into a different level of derivation.
>
> This means that you are into qualitative judgements about the future of the property which means you are into a knowledge based business rather than a physical asset based business. (2000, personal communication)

In terms of corporate memory, the implications are important if a company similar to Chartwell Land loses a key member of staff. An individual may have built up relationships with numerous people in the property business over a period of ten years or more. To capture these contacts is more about the quality of these business contacts rather than the quantity.

Another area that Smith mentions at Chartwell Land is the recognition of ideas. He notes that what has happened in academia for the last 200 years has yet to occur in business:

> If you use someone's idea, you say where it comes from. I think you have got to create value at the point of contribution, to the knowledge base. I don't believe that necessarily is financial. I know companies have developed systems to reward contributions to the corporate memory and some have moved on to rewards based on the utilisation of the knowledge. (2000, personal communication)

According to Hannah Brown and Karen Hand (2001) of Kendall Tarrant Worldwide, a leading headhunting firm specializing in the advertising industry:

> these should be good times for companies that deal in 'creativity'. The 1998 Institute of Management and Manpower study of UK Corporate Employment Strategies and Trends found that top British business leaders felt that creativity and innovation were the business skills in highest demand today.

Brown and Hand question whether communications companies are reaping the benefits of this surge in demand. They write: 'Specialists have undercut them. Management consultants have undermined them. Profit margins and industry self-esteem are eroding. Bad news for an industry whose stock in trade is "selling confidence".'

Brown and Hand ask: 'Is it now time that communications companies start to invest in people as the key to building stronger client relationships? It was this hypothesis that inspired Kendall Tarrant to investigate the case for people management within the communications industry. A questionnaire was sent out to 100 companies, 20 senior directors interviewed and comprehensive research undertaken to understand "best practice".'

It pays to look after your employees

There have been a number of studies (at M&S, BA and Birse Engineering) which have established that the best way to improve customer care and therefore satisfaction is by improving employee care. In the 1990s, Rank Xerox found that greater staff loyalty led to greater customer loyalty and that return on assets rose from 6% to 19% over the five-year period. When Frederick Reichfeld tried to calculate the 'loyalty effect' on company performance, he estimated that 'disloyalty' from stakeholders – employers, shareholders, staff and customers – can cut performance and productivity by 50% (Brown and Hand, 2001).

Employees' choices are increasing

There are many more choices available for existing employees and prospective employees/graduates within the communications industry. On one side, there are completely new industries like IT, where people can use

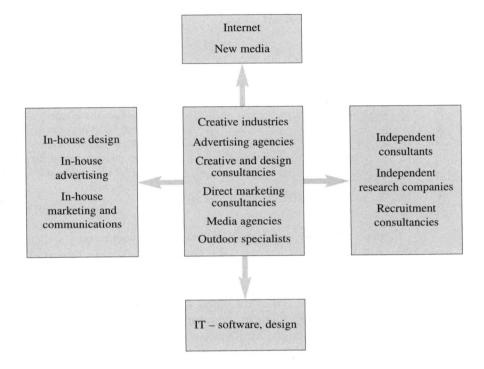

Figure 14.1 Employment opportunities in the communications industry
Source: Kendall Tarrant Worldwide

some of the skills that were traditionally used for communications. On the other, client companies and consultancies have set up in-house functions, which are frequently staffed with people that would have worked in the communications industry (Figure 14.1).

And competition for the best talent is going to get tougher

Brown and Hand (2001) report that the Kendall Tarrant Human Resource Survey supported IPA statistics in showing that 57% of employees were from the 25–34-year-old cohort. According to Mintel, by 2006 there will be a 17% drop in 25–34-year-olds in the workforce (from 7.5 million in 1995 to 6.2 million in 2006). If nothing else changes, this trend alone will put the communications industry under additional pressure to fight harder to retain a quality workforce.

Clarity of personal values

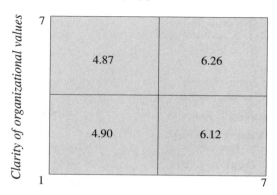

The cells represent the degree of clarity about personal and organizational values.

The numbers in the cells represent the extent of individuals' commitment to their organization on a scale of 1 to 7, with 1 being low and 7 being high.

Figure 14.2 Values congruence and individual commitment

Source: Posner, B. Z. and Schmidt, W. H. (1993) 'Values Congruence and Difference Between the Interplay of Personal and Organisational Value System', *Journal of Business Ethics*, **12**: 174

All these factors raise the stakes for hiring and keeping the best people, particularly for an industry such as communications, which relies on people for its ideas. Interestingly, McKinsey make the connection between business success and people management overtly in their stated mission: 'To help our clients make distinctive, lasting and substantial improvements in their performance, and to build a great firm that is able to attract, develop, excite and retain exceptional people.'

Organizational studies have shown that people have far higher levels of commitment to an organization if they feel the company is acknowledging their personal values (Figure 14.2). As Paul Donkersly says in his fore-word to Britain's Top Employers:

Enlightened employers know that the rules are changing ... and ... they are now grasping the nettle. Not out of some charitable gesture but out of simple business sense. Happy employees are productive ones and why in any case restrict your access to the 'best' people that every company says that it sets out to recruit purely by not being flexible.

People management is ultimately a set of principles rather than a specific set of policies. The application of these principles will vary according to specific cultures – from Abbott Mead Vicars to St Luke's, from Wolff-Olins to Tomato. The important thing is that people management becomes entrenched in the company culture so that it moves from being a 'nice to have' to being a 'must have'.

People management needs to become a key criterion for judging and evaluating the business

As Roisin Robothan Jones, strategic consultant observes: 'It's interesting that a CEO can be fired for mismanaging the financial assets but nobody seems to think of firing him for mismanaging his human assets.' It is important that the employee satisfaction is monitored and seen as a legitimate business goal rather than 'a luxury' when times are good. As one senior director in an advertising firm told us: 'The industry is ignoring these issues for as long as they possibly can. There is no appreciation of the fact that managing resources means people, not just desks. No one is really taught to do this.'

People management needs to be applied to every level of the company

A recent McKinsey report on people management has found that if you want to keep top calibre people you have to give them the bosses they deserve. This was supported by one of the agency managing directors, when he said: 'We never fully realized the true costs of having that mediocre person in that position – not only were the clients in jeopardy but we ended up losing three or four excellent people who had worked for him.'

SUMMARY

- We have the possibility of over-supply of all goods and services for the first time in history

- Economics, business, society, pay and legal systems, politics and government have, in the past, been based on the assumption of scarcity

- Some organizations are too busy to use Knowledge Management effectively

- Corporate anorexia is useful for short-term profits but not for sustainable success

- The single greatest obstacle to establishing Knowledge Management in a company is the way in which power is accumulated and exercised

- People have far higher levels of commitment to an organization if they feel their personal values are acknowledged

- People management will become a key criterion for evaluating a business

Centrefile Limited

BRUCE THEW, *Managing Director*

Bruce Thew is the Managing Director of Centrefile. The company first identified the value of knowledge management in the achievement of business success in 1997. A process of knowledge management (POKM) was gradually introduced over two years, and it continues to be an important part of the organizational culture today.

In 1999, Centrefile Limited won the *Human Resources Magazine* HR Excellence Award for 'the most effective knowledge management strategy in which HR is a key partner'.

Name of organization	Centrefile Limited
Address	Exchange Tower 2 Harbour Exchange Square London E14 9GE
Part of group	Ceridian Corporation of Minneapolis, USA
Number of employees	453 in 1999, 720 in 2001

A need for knowledge management

In 1997, we at Centrefile recognized that we had a number of significant issues which needed to be addressed. Our employee turnover was high and employee morale was low. In our 1997 employee survey, only 54% of staff agreed that they were satisfied with their jobs and worryingly, 24% were thinking of leaving the company within the next two years. To add to our concerns, the level of customer contract terminations was increasing.

We knew that we needed to take action and decided to go back to basics, redefining our vision and values. In order to achieve our corporate aim 'to be recognized as *the* payroll and human resources company' we needed to review the principles underpinning our operations. To help achieve this, the business identified a set of values designed to guide every person in the business in their daily decision-making processes. These values, agreed in 1997, have remained with us and are now regularly reviewed:

1. To sustain profitable growth

2. To delight the customer for prompt payment and profit

3. To develop and attract enthusiastic achievers

4. To act with honesty and integrity.

We recognized that developing and attracting enthusiastic achievers was a pre-requisite to achieving the other three values and that a successful process of knowledge management was a key factor.

To achieve this, we recognized that we needed to invest in training, development and recruitment processes and then work to retain our skilled and knowledge-able staff.

We knew that there were significant improvements which could be made by having a more structured approach, right across the business. For example, improving the process of knowledge management among help-desk staff would improve their service, both in quality and response time. Among managers it would help them to make their departments more effective and efficient. Improved knowledge management among the product development teams would make projects more likely to come in within budget and timescale. All these improvements would help in achieving the other values.

The board therefore created a new position of Training and Organizational Development Manager, reporting to the Finance and HR Director, to take responsibility for implementing a POKM in support of the values.

Training and development initiatives

Centrefile University

One of the first initiatives was the establishment of a Centrefile University. This provides information and financial support to staff to allow them to self-manage their own continuous professional learning and development, with an emphasis on externally recognized qualifications. Although a 'virtual' organ-ization, Centrefile University is structured along traditional university lines, with heads of faculties (relevant board members) taking an active role in iden-tifying suitable learning programmes, and in assessing and advising employees on their applications for training support through the university.

Linking performance and reward

A new personal development programme was devised and rolled out to all staff, branded 'MOTIVATE': Measurable Objectives for Teams and Individ-uals for Vision and values Achievement through Training and Education. This radically overhauled and brought together the three previously separate staff development processes (performance appraisal scheme, personal development plan and incentive scheme) to achieve the following:

■ link individual objectives to business plans and objectives

- provide a framework for effective performance management

- link recognition and reward to actual job performance

- identify specific individual training and development requirements

- link individual competence to effective job performance

Mentoring

A mentoring scheme has been introduced, whereby staff at different levels from different sectors of the business are linked together in pairs. This covers directors with senior managers, and middle managers with other employees who demonstrate significant development potential. The objective is to provide an experienced source of information and coaching for the less experienced, outside their normal line of management.

Induction

A new Induction programme has been implemented for new joiners. This is designed to ensure a sharing of knowledge from a wide cross-section of job-holders relevant to that position, leading the new joiner rapidly to understand the business and their role within it. It also includes a schedule of meetings with all the directors, one of the main objectives being to communicate the company's values.

Graduate scheme

A graduate entry scheme was created, which has proved extremely successful. The graduates are assigned to different departments for their first nine months, but encouraged to mix with each other to share their newly gained knowledge and experiences. They then move on to two more assignments of six months. By this time both they and the company have a good idea of the best initial permanent position for them, and also we have implanted a wide base of knowledge and contacts in our potential future management.

POKM within day-to-day processes

The strategic management of the business is broken down into five separate business boards, each responsible for one market sector of Centrefile's business. These boards are each headed by a Centrefile director, but the rest of the board comprises five to six middle and senior managers representing different functional roles across the company. This structure facilitates the sharing of experience and knowledge from a wide range of backgrounds, while focusing on one business/market sector. At the same time it provides a channel of communication about knowledge management directly through the business board's director to the Centrefile main board.

Within departments with specific skill areas, for example help-desks, they have developed their own training sessions to pass the expertise of the more experienced on to the more junior.

To assist staff who are studying for the professional payroll qualifications of the IPPM (Institute of Payroll and Pensions Management), clinics are run by staff who are qualified as IPPM tutors.

People Networks are an initiative whereby representatives from different locations but in the same type of function get together to hold discussions with their internal suppliers and customers. In this way any issues between departments can be understood and solutions agreed; also the representatives from different locations can learn from their counterparts' experiences, and take ideas back to their own colleagues.

Evidence of business improvement

Reduced staff turnover

- In 2001, employee turnover stands at 10% – almost 50% down on the rate in 1997.

Improved employee morale

- In 1997, only 54% of staff were satisfied with their jobs overall. By 2000, this figure had risen to 89%, with 92% of employees agreeing that they were proud to work for Centrefile.

Competitive advantage

- In the outsourced payroll business, the knowledge of our staff is the key differentiator which inspires customers to trust us with managing their payrolls. We have more qualified staff than any of our competitors, with over 100 holding a payroll professional qualification, including 7 MSc's in Payroll Management of which none of our competitors has more than one.

- Our business in this market has grown by 100% in each of the last three years, which we believe largely reflects the value of this investment in knowledge.

Improved service levels

- The increased expertise and professionalism of our employees is also helping us to improve the level of service on the help-desks. Through a call centre management system we are able to measure various statistics of help-desk performance, such as the average time taken to resolve a caller's query, and the number of calls which can be dealt with immediately without referral to someone else. These measures have shown consistent improvement and are resulting in improved customer satisfaction, assessed by responses to the quarterly customer survey and by Centrefile winning the *Daily Telegraph*/Energis Award for Customer Service.

New recruits

- The culture of learning and knowledge sharing is having a positive effect in attracting higher calibre applicants to our recruitment campaigns. Our first graduates, recruited in 1997, provided their views on what they liked about working for Centrefile for inclusion in new recruitment packs. They included reference to the continuous development programme, the mentoring scheme, and the opportunity to work on projects with people at the most senior level in Centrefile. These knowledge management-related benefits are now often cited by candidates applying for positions, and contribute to the consistently high number of applicants. This is helping us to achieve our third business value: to develop and attract enthusiastic achievers.

In conclusion

This structured approach to knowledge management has enabled us to develop a culture of open communication, where people work together to overcome problems with constructive, innovative solutions.

Centrefile now has a culture where people are valued as individuals, with a strong focus on reward and recognition for achievement and success. For us this has resulted in a strengthening of our knowledge base and has led to improved customer satisfaction.

But there is no place for complacency. This is a process which we need to work at constantly and we have lots of plans for the future including:

- developing our skills matrix

- refining the measurement of knowledge sharing and gathering

- introduction of computer-based training

- setting up a learning centre through the company intranet

- assessing the opportunities for sharing knowledge with our customers via the Internet.

15 Conclusion and the Future

There is so much more information, data and knowledge that I would like to include in this book. After many interviews with leading professionals on the telephone, the net and in person, it has been concluded that knowledge management and intellectual capital are here to stay as management subjects. Knowledge management may change its guise during the next decade or so, but it will reappear in various ways. The following pages contain snippets of some of these conversations.

I think it is important to mention one of the most significant reasons for this development in management thinking, which will prove to be the management theme of this decade. Seven years ago, an article appeared in *The Atlantic Monthly* (1994). 'The Age of Social Transformation', written by Peter Drucker, was an insightful essay exploring the geopolitical changes that were affecting business. Drucker writes:

> To be sure, this century of ours may well have been the cruelest and most violent in history, with its world and civil wars, its mass tortures, ethnic cleansings, genocides, and holocausts. But all these killings, all these horrors inflicted on the human race by this century's murderous 'charismatics', hindsight clearly shows, were just that: senseless killings, senseless horrors, 'sound and fury', signifying nothing. Hitler, Stalin and Mao, the three evil geniuses of this century, destroyed. They created nothing.

He then writes

> Indeed, if this century proves one thing, it is the futility of politics. Even the most dogmatic believer in historical determinism would have a hard time explaining the social transformations of this century as caused by the headline-making political events, or the headline-making political events as caused by the social transformations. But it is the

Nicholas Bahra is grateful to Seija Kulkki and Mikko Kosonen for assistance and for permission to quote extensively from 'How Tacit Knowledge Explains Organizational Renewal and Growth: The Case of Nokia' (forthcoming 2001), and also to the Indian Society for Training and Development (ISTD) 'Human Resource Development – Global Strategies in 2000 AD' copyright 1994.

social transformations, like ocean currents deep below the hurricane-tormented surface of the sea, that have had the lasting, indeed the permanent, effect. They, rather than all the violence of the political surface, have transformed not only the society but also the economy, the community, and the polity we live in. The age of social transformation will not come to an end with the year 2000 – it will not even have peaked by then.

In Chapter 1, the writing of Samuel P. Huntingdon was discussed and his geo-political proposition of the new world order – post-1990. It is against this background of social, political and economic change, that I would like to share with you the thoughts, views and opinions of leading professionals who have contributed to the theme of knowledge management. Although their contribution appears in this final chapter, it does not in any way suggest that their views are less valid than the case studies earlier. In Chapter 1, I also noted that learning about knowledge management was similar to putting together a complex jigsaw with various pieces that needed to fit in the right place. Some of the contributions in this final chapter might assist to clarify your thinking as you explore what will prove to be the most significant management challenge of the decade.

Knowledge management is a fusion of finance, information technology and human resource management. It is economics (both global and organizational), it is technology, both electronic and other forms and it is about people, which I believe is the most complex part to understand. After all, computers, buildings and money do not run companies, people do.

Chief Learning Officer, Steve Kerr, has responsibility for knowledge creation and sharing at General Electric. He says that the real success of General Electric and Jack Welch has been to create a 'boundaryless' organization.

> We have transferred knowledge from one part of the company that deals with aircraft engines, for example, to another that deals with lightbulbs. (telephone interview, 2000)

General Electric has been named by *Fortune* magazine as the 'Global Most Admired Company'. Also on this list, at number 8, is Nokia. This is a special company and one which, I believe, many European firms can learn from. In 1921, Nokia was one of 12 Finnish companies to inaugurate the Helsinki Stock Exchange. Today Nokia is the only survivor, having transformed itself from an old economy firm into one of the most successful new economy firms in the world. According to Lauri Kivinen at Nokia:

We are putting a lot of emphasis on people, this means that of 60,000 employees, 20,000 work in research and development. Putting people first is important when you are managing skilled specialists.

We have learned how to combine bureaucracy and discipline with creativity and agility. Discipline and speed are essential. (telephone interview, 2000)

With a $20 billion dollar turnover and 9000 employees in the USA, Nokia is a company that has not been standing still in the new economy.

Seija Kulkki, Director of the Centre for Knowledge and Innovation Research at the Helsinki School of Economics and Business and Mikko Kosonen, Senior Vice President, Strategy and Information Management at the Nokia Corporation, write of Nokia's success and discuss 'knowledge as a major source of renewal and growth of the firm'. They note that:

Multinational corporations, in general, are of special interest because they can create and exploit knowledge in a variety of culturally, socially and economically different environments. They have the worldwide opportunity to recombine and recompose knowledge-based assets through their international or global network, and they can deploy strategies that reflect variations in global knowledge intensity and extensity. (Hedlund, AIB Conference, 1996)

They argue that 'knowledge can in fact be an "engine" of renewal and growth provided that it is consciously and holistically managed' (2001, forthcoming). Although Kulkki and Kosonen recognize there may be limitations to what management can actually do, they do recognize that management can 'fuel and facilitate the intertwined co-existence of knowledge creation and exploitation'.

One key insight from Kulkki and Kosonen is of their interpretation of the 'future-oriented nature of tacit knowledge'. They mention Polanyi's discussion of learning, 'based on tacit latent knowledge, as a heuristic act of insight where the mind is in contact with a still hidden reality. In that condition, the mind may be anticipating an indeterminate range of yet unknown and unconceivable'. Kulkki 'discusses the multidimensional nature of tacit knowledge and the capacity of the individual mind to create the future'.

Nokia experienced a rapid transformation and globalization process in the early 1990s and sent hundreds of people overseas on various assignments. Nokia 'had to take big risks and place its trust especially in its front line people. People learned to take responsibility for the whole business, not only the present task at hand, as there were simply no senior people around to lean on'.

Kulkki and Kosonen note (2001, forthcoming) the following qualities that are still strongly affecting its knowledge-based renewal and growth capacity:

■ Management learned to trust the problem-solving capabilities and foresight of their front line people

■ Management also learned to trust intuition and rapid decision-making. The whole organization learned to act and prioritize, based on intuitive anticipation of the future

■ The whole organization also learned to trust and like the opportunity to learn new things and stretch its competence

■ Nokia Telecommunications (NTC) learned to build new global markets, and consequently the managerial and organizational ways and means to operate globally in deep cooperation with their customers

■ Nokia Mobile Phones (NMP) learned to build globally brand-based market positions that benefited from inter-linked R&D centres and from a cost-efficient network of high quality manufacturing and logistics.

The authors write that these lessons did not come easily. 'People made many small mistakes, but usually learned before making bigger mistakes'. This strengthened Nokia's corporate culture. It, 'accepted failure and saw it as a learning opportunity'.

For Kosonen: 'Knowledge is anchored in the beliefs and commitments of its holder. Trust and similar values are important to our success. People are straightforward with each other and we have a unifying culture.' I suggested to Mikko Kosonen that there are generally four levels of management.

1. Punishment and reward
2. Assertive persuasion
3. Trust and participation
4. Common vision.

I then suggested to Kosonen that Nokia had achieved common vision, which I prefer to call organizational telepathy. He agreed.

At Tata Consultancy Services (TCS), knowledge management is integral to their competitive advantage. According to Kesav V. Nori, Chief Information Officer at TCS:

> Knowledge management in TCS is organised, but managed and maintained informally, without recourse to using technology that is available today. TCS's competitive advantage comes from operational knowledge of information in service of business in the different vertical market sectors it is active in. Strategically, TCS is poised to spread its spectrum of services towards consulting in business systems on the one side and into facility management, operations and outsourcing services of the IT function for its clients. However, the principal source of strength comes from its ability to engineer IT solutions – based on intimate understanding of the information needs of businesses as well as the strengths and weaknesses of contemporary technologies which need to be combined in integrated and well-engineered IT solutions.

For TCS, 'experiential knowledge is of the essence'.

Georg Von Krogh, Kazuo Ichijo and Ikujiro Nonaka are clear about their philosophy in their book, *Enabling Knowledge Creation* (2000). They write (Preface, p. vii), 'It is our strong conviction that knowledge cannot be managed, only enabled.' They also introduce the concept of 'cyber ba', or, electronic knowledge space.

On the subject of the corporate university and virtual learning, I would have liked to have devoted more time and space. Debbie Carlton and Dick Davies, along with a number of other professionals, are developing 'online learning' products and services for the government and commercial firms.

Competition and innovation requires lifelong learning and according to Alan Gilbert, Chair Universitas21, 'education will become the biggest industry in the world'. There has been a growth in public/private partnerships and one example is the European Commission's elearning Summit Models for Public/Private Partnerships. According to Jeanne Meister of Corporate eXchange, 'by the year 2010 Corporate Universities will outnumber traditional Universities'.

Debbie Carlton's team are developing leading edge solutions in this area. 'There is evidence that universities both in the UK and overseas are forming consortia to address the opportunities of global e-learning. Some consortia involve partnerships between universities and companies. Such developments will have a significant impact on the way traditional universities conduct their business. Examples are the UK e-University project to which Online Courseware Factory has provided extensive consultancy. The Online Courseware Factory Limited, uses XML (Extended Mark-up Language) and understands the philosophy of the 'learners' right to their own development'. Carlton believes that in a knowledge-based economy it will be harder for her to know the needs of the learner. She believes that 'people will get smarter about what they need to know and when they need to know it'. Carlton also speaks of 'public learning object exchanges' where people can buy content.

The future of e-learning is of fundamental importance in the new economy. The one competitive advantage a company can possess in the new economy is to learn faster than its competitors. Dick Davies believes that there is a shift from 'event' training to 'process' within corporations. These changes are occurring for three reasons:

1. *Demographics.* Labour force growth is slowing. There is a demand for 'life-long learning' and there are 'free agent learners'.

2. *Enterprise.* There are shorter product cycles, with increasing product complexity. Outsourcing is increasingly creating the extended enterprise.

3. *Technology* – the Internet – the 'webification' of business processes.

Davies suggests there will be a standardization of learning management systems along with a standardization of content information for manipulation. There will be a move towards 'learning objects' and their assembly. The standards will be XML, XSL and DTD (Document Type Definition). This learning experience will be supported, collaborative, customized and personalized. It will be embedded, remotely managed and performance linked.

Davies also believes we will move from continuous information environments to continuous learning environments and notes the changes in technology and performance support between 2000 and 2004 (Figure 15.1). As Professor Joseph Kessels says:

> The knowledge economy is here to stay. It requires flexible, adaptable and creative organisations with employees who are innovators and creators. In turn this requires the organisations to develop corporate curricula which enable learning to happen continuously and at all levels within the workforce.

Kessels, of Twente and Leiden universities, adds: 'When in the 21st century knowledge productivity becomes the driving force the knowledge

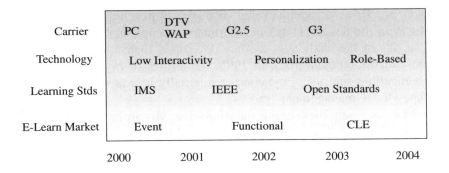

Figure 15.1 Futures: technology and performance support
Source: © Telecom Experience Ltd, 2000

workers will take charge. This may lead to the end of management as we understand it' (telephone conversation).

Another area that requires further investigation is intellectual property. I interviewed Edmund Fish, a Director at Intertrust in California. Intertrust's business is digital rights management in an information-based world. This area will become ever more complex for lawyers and the business community.

Dr Frank Kappe, Director at Hyperwave, has developed 'stable product search engines to facilitate e-learning integrated into one product. 300 man years of development means that Hyperwave's technology is not easily replicated.'

At Cisco, William Buller, Director, Internet Business Solutions Group, says that knowledge management is 'embedded in everything we do. We have secure fast networks, which are globally available. E-learning in virtual teams is assisted by our open architecture' (telephone interview).

Melinda Lockhart, director of thought leadership and innovation at EDS, provided many insightful comments. EDS has 120,000 employees in 43 countries worldwide and since its formation in 1960 has enjoyed continual growth. For Lockhart, knowledge management can be a simplifying process with clients. 'When you probe into their information and data, they often have information overload. Knowledge management is not a technology issue; it is a people and performance management issue. We don't make a product, we consult and create. One of our challenges is, how do we get people to share their knowledge? It is important to discover the golden nuggets of knowledge that are in every organization' (telephone interview).

There are firms of occupational or business psychologists that will benefit from the developments in information technology. Ron Davies at SHL speaks of the challenges as they developed their corporate intranet system called Grapevine back in 1995. 'One third of my job is internal communications and using cyberspace internally was an integral part of the "knowledge management" process.'

Dr Marcus Speh Birkenrähe mentions the Motorola executive who poses questions relating to business ethics and whether corporations have a social duty to citizens. The subject of business ethics has been widely debated and Charles Handy and other writers have made important contributions during the last century. As corporations become more powerful, many of them are much larger then the economies of numerous countries combined. Will their social and political role be redefined?

An essay written in 1994 by M.B. Athreya, 'The Brahman (Soul) in Training' is, in my opinion, really pertinent. He writes from an Eastern philosophical perspective, in particular, the Hindu-Buddhist ethos to 'draw some lessons for learners and trainers'.

The corporate soul (samuthana)

In this essay, Athreya recognizes 'artha' (wealth) as one of the four legitimate human life goals. Within the hierarchy, it came only second with 'dharma' (righteousness) at the top. For Athreya:

> Business was a legitimate human occupation. It was a respected component of society. Its role was to create wealth and promote internal and external trade. Philanthropy was demonstrated and expected. It brought the businessman social recognition and spiritual merit. Business shared the prosperity and sufferings of society. The name 'samuthana' (joint structure) came from the concept of it as a cooperative endeavour.

For the learner, Athreya makes the distinction between content (vidya):

> Every executive, worker, citizen will have access to more and more knowledge. The opportunities are immense – learning in formal institutions, at home, through advances in telecommunications and computers, e-mail, databases, and so on. Indian philosophy divides learning into two major categories:

- Vidya – knowledge of the external world

■ Brahma vidya – knowledge of the self and its relationship to Brahman, the cosmic soul, mediated through the team, organisation and society

and process (parampara):

In addition to self-learning through reading, audio and video, Indian philosophy lays stress on the 'guru-shishya parampara', the teacher-student tradition. A senior is more effective if he is seen as a guru. A junior learns more if he approaches his senior as a 'shishya'. The 'parampara' transmits learning through two basic processes.

■ Sruti – by hearing, through recitation and repetition
■ Smitri – by memory, recollection, accumulation.

Athreya also comments upon wisdom:

Indian philosophy has recognised the value of learning; as well as its limitations. Much of learning takes place in the 'manas', the mind. There is an important distinction to be made between 'manas' and 'buddhi', the intellect, discrimination, insight, wisdom. The 'manas' has many potential weaknesses, such as:

■ Chanchalam – restlessness
■ Vegam – fast, like the wind, flitting from one thing to the next
■ Ahankar – ego, preventing insight and giving rise to defensiveness
■ Tamasic – sluggish, dull, slothful
■ Rajasic – feverish, domineering.

'Buddhi' helps the learner to guide the manas in the right directions for effective learning

and the soul (atman):

Contemporary explorations, beyond communism and capitalism, are leading behavioural scientists to look for something beyond the logic of the head and the feelings of the heart. For that third dimension, some have started using the term soul. Indian tradition would support this.

The learner needs to understand his 'self' as not just his body, mind or even 'buddhi'. The crown, the core the source of his self is his 'atman', soul. It is unsullied by physical and psychological experiences, successes and traumas. It is linked to the cosmic soul. There is great strength and encouragement in each individual when we realise that we are all 'amritasya putrah' – children of the immortal, deathless 'Brahman'.

Athreya then provides advice for the trainer.

Confront chauvinism (vasudha)

> In an integrating global village, the trainer must prevent any kind of chauvinism, to the extent possible. If it sets in, he may counsel. If it persists, he must take the risk of confronting it. A heterogenous cultural human world is a human asset, if we can integrate the global economy, in a peaceful manner. [The] trainer should be vigilant to pick up signals of different forms of chauvinism, racial, national, religious, linguistic and any other manifestation. All mankind has to be seen as 'kutumbam' (family).

This message from one consultant in Delhi is, I believe, a message not just for trainers, but also for all professionals in the future.

Finally, I wonder if we eventually will need to redefine the new economy entrepreneur. Based on the recent problems with Boo.com and Breath.com, will we need to move towards a more socially responsible model, if this is possible? No doubt you will have ideas of your own, but in developing markets, for example expanding the EU, will we move away from the individual to a more collective enterprise model where people's expectations of social responsibility are higher than in the past? Will we be able to change the nature of human nature?

Charles Leadbeater writes, in *Living on Thin Air* (2000), that 'knowledge entrepreneurs will be vital in the future'. He writes (Preface, p. ix):

> Most of us make our money from thin air: we produce nothing that can be weighed, touched or easily measured. Our output is not stockpiled at harbours, stored in warehouses or shipped in railway cars. Most of us earn our livings providing service, judgement, information and analysis, whether in a telephone call centre, a lawyer's office, a government department or a scientific laboratory. We are all in the thin air business.

SUMMARY

- Knowledge Management is a fusion of finance, information technology and human resource management

- It is economics (both global and organizational) it is technology, both electronic and other forms, and it is about people

- Computers, walls, buildings and money do not run companies, people do

- Knowledge can be an engine of renewal and growth provided that it is consciously and holistically managed

- Although there may be limitations to what management can actually do, management can 'fuel and facilitate the intertwined co-existence of knowledge creation and exploitation'

- Management must learn to trust the problem-solving capabilities and foresight of their front line people

- An organization must also learn to trust and enjoy the opportunity to learn new things and stretch its competence

- Experiential knowledge is of the essence

- The future of e-learning is of fundamental importance in the new economy

- The one competitive advantage a company can possess in the new economy is to learn faster than its competitors

- There is a shift from 'event' training to 'process' within corporations

- Indian philosophy has recognized the value of learning; as well as its limitations

- There is an important distinction to be made between the intellect, discrimination, insight and wisdom

- Knowledge entrepreneurs will be vital in the future

- Many of us make our money from thin air: we produce nothing that can be weighed, touched or easily measured, providing service, judgement, information and analysis

Bibliography

Adair, J. (1993) *Effective Leadership – How to Develop Leadership Skills*, Macmillan, London – now Palgrave

Alexander, G. and Rushe, D. (2000) 'Sun goes down on the dotcom darlings', *Sunday Times*, 22 October

Amidon, D.M. and Skyrme, D.J. (1997) 'Creating the Knowledge-based Business', Business Intelligence, London

Andrewartha, L. (1999) 'Using business intelligence to achieve a sustainable competitive advantage', Dokumentation, *The Nordic Journal of Documentation*, Stockholm

'An Overview of The Knowledge Management Market', Central Computer and Telecommunications Agency, (June 1999)

Argyris, C. (1982) *Reasoning, Learning and Action – Individual and Organisational*, Jossey-Bass, San Francisco

Argyris, C. (1993) *Knowledge for Action: A Guide to Overcoming Barriers to Organisational Change*, Jossey-Bass Management, New York

Argyris, C. (1998) 'Teaching Smart People How to Learn' in *Harvard Business Review of Knowledge Management*, Harvard Business School Press, pp. 81–108

Ayers, C. (2000) 'Life after the crash', *The Times*, 14 June, p. 3

Ayres, C. and Jones, A. (2000) 'Net pioneer in world's biggest deal', *The Times*, 11 January

Bahra, N.S. (1997) '360 degree appraisal', *Financial Times Management*, Pitman, London

Barham, K. and Heimer, C. (1998) *ABB – The Dancing Giant*, Financial Times Management, London

Barron, T. (2000) 'A Smarter Frankenstein: The Merging of E-learning and Knowledge Management', American Society for Training and Development (ASTD), Alexandria, VA

Bassis, L. (ed.) (1999) 'The ASTD Trends Watch – The Forces That Shape Workplace Performance And Improvement'

Belbin, M. (1996) *Management Teams: Why They Succeed or Fail*, Butterworth Heinemann

Bell, D. (1973) *The Coming of Post-industrial Society*, Basic Books, New York

Birley, S. (1995) *The Failure of Owner Managed Businesses: The Diagnosis of Accountants and Bankers*

Bock, F. (1998) 'The Intelligent Organisation', *Prism*, Arthur D. Little, Cambridge, MA

Borghoff, U. (1998) *Technology for Knowledge Management*, Springer-Verlag, London

Botkin, J. (1999) *Smart Business: How Knowledge Communities Can Revolutionize Your Company*, Simon & Schuster, New York

Boyatzis, R.E. (1982) *The Competent Manager*, John Wiley & Sons, New York

Brand, A. (1998) 'Knowledge Management and Innovation at 3M', *Journal of Knowledge Management*, **2**(1), September

Breu, K. (2001) 'Europe's Competitive Future in the Knowledge Economy: The Need for a European Contribution to the Emerging Knowledge-based Theory of the Firm', European Academy of Management (EURAM), IESE, Barcelona, 20–21 April

Breu, K., Grimshaw, D. and Myers, A. (2000) 'Releasing the Value of Knowledge: A Survey of UK Industry', Cranfield School of Management

Breu, K. and Smith, G. (2001 forthcoming) *Selling Knowledge: Making Knowledge Management Mainstream in Today's Connected Enterprise*, *Financial Times*/Cranfield Management Research in Practice Series

Brown, A. and Weiner, E. (1997) *The Insiders Guide to the Future*, Boardroom, USA

Brown, H. and Hand, K. (2001) 'Staying Power', Kendall Tarrant, London

Burgess, P. (1993) (ed.) *Training and Development*, (European Management Guides), Institute of Personnel Management, London

Burgoyne, J.G. (2000) 'What are the implications of the virtualisation of organisations and the emergence of knowledge management for management development?', Lancaster University Management School

Burlison, D. (2000) Dotcoms, *Recovery Magazine*, London

Burton-Jones, A. (1999) *Knowledge Capitalism – Business, Work, and Learning in the New Economy*, Oxford University Press, Oxford

Campbell, A. (1996) 'Mission and Management Commitment', Ashridge Strategic Management Centre, London

Campbell, T. and Duperret, V. (eds) (1995) 'Learning Organisations', Innovations, Initiatives, Proceedings International Conference, La Hulpe (Belgium), European Consortium for the Learning Organisation, May 16–18

Cates, A. (2000) 'Global Economic and Strategy Research', *New Economy Perspectives*, 13 June

Chawla, S. and Murphy, K. (1995) 'Coaching Your Way to a Learning Organisation: A New Paradigm for Human Systems in Organisations' in Kohli, U. and Sinha, D.P. (eds) *Human Resource Development – Global Changes and Strategies in 2000 AD*, Indian Society for Training and Development, Allied Publishers, India

Coles, M. (2000) 'Sharing knowledge boosts efficiency', *Sunday Times*, 29 April

Davenport, T.H. and Prusak, L. (1997) *Information Ecology: Mastering the Information Knowledge Environment*, Open University Press, New York

Davis, S. and Meyer, C. (2000) *Future Wealth*, Harvard Business School Press, Boston, MA

Dickson, M. (2000) 'World Economy Report', *Financial Times*, 22 September

234   *Bibliography*

Dixon, N. (2000) 'The Insight Track', Knowledge Management Feature, *People Management*, 17 February

Dobbs-Higginson, M.S. (1994) *Asia Pacific – It's Role In The New World Disorder*, Heinemann, London

Drucker, P. (1994) 'The Age of Social Transformation', *Atlantic Monthly*, **274**(5): 53–80

Drucker, P. (1998) *The Coming of the New Organisation*, Harvard Business Review, Boston, MA

DTI (1998) 'Our Competitive Future – Building the Knowledge Driven Economy' (White Paper) Department of Trade and Industry, London

DTI (1999) *Small and Medium Enterprise (SME) Statistics for the UK, 1999*, available from Small Business Service, UK, www.businessadviceonline.org

Dulewicz, V. and Higgs, M. (1997) 'An Investigation into the Relationship between Divergent Thinking and Measures of Competence', Working Paper Series HWP 9709, Henley Management College, Henley

Empson, L. (1999) 'Knowledge Management', Mastering Management Series, *Financial Times*, 4 October

European Commission (1998) *Enterprises in Europe*, Fifth Report, SME Project, Eurostat. Available from the Stationery Office

European Industrial Training (1999) **23**(8): 387

Evans, C. (2000) 'Developing a Knowledge Creating Culture', Roffey Park Institute

Frank, E. (2001) *Competitive Advantage Through Knowledge Management*, Hindustan Publishing Corporation (India), New Delhi

Gibson, J. (1968) *Locke's Theory of Knowledge and its Historical Relations*, Cambridge University Press, Cambridge

Graef, J. (1997) *CEO's Guide to Intellectual Capital*, Montague Institute, Montague (MA)

Guptara, P. (1998) 'Relationship Marketing', paper presented at the Annual Conference of the Chartered Institute of Bankers, Cambridge, 14–15 September, and subsequently published on the website of the Wolfsberg Executive Development Centre, Switzerland, www.wolfsberg.com

Harvard Business Review on Knowledge Management (1998) President and Fellows of Harvard College, Harvard Business School Press, Boston, MA

Hoffman, E. (1996) *Future Visions – The Unpublished Papers of Abraham Maslow*, Sage, London

Huntingdon, S.P. (1997) *The Clash of Civilisations and the Remaking of World Order*, Simon & Schuster, London

Hyam, R. (1975) *Britain's Imperial Century – 1815–1914*, London

IOD (2000) 'Innovation is a never ending commitment' in *A Directors Guide*, IOD, Kogan Page

Islam, F. and Farrelly P. (2000) 'Boo.com sale hopes suffer early blow', *Observer*, 21 May

Kelleher, M. (1995) 'The Development of New Skills in a Japanese Manufacturing Company in Britain: The Case of Yamazaki Mazak', Centre for Research and Educational Development, Gwent

Kelly, K. (1998) *New Rules for the New Economy*, Viking, London

Kempton, J. (1995) *Human Resource Management and Development: Current Issues and Themes*, Macmillan Business, Basingstoke – now Palgrave

Knell, J. (2000) *Most Wanted – The Quiet Birth of the Free Worker*, Futures, The Industrial Society

Korac-Kakabadse, N., Kouzmin, A. and Korac-Kakabadse, A. (2001) 'From Tacit Knowledge to Knowledge Management: Leveraging Invisible Assets', *Knowledge and Process Management*, **8**(1), Jan, 2001

Kulkki, S. and Kosonen, M. (2001, forthcoming) 'How tacit knowledge explains organizational renewal and growth: the case of Nokia', in Nonaka, Ikujiro and Teece (eds) *Managing Industrial Knowledge: Creation, Transfer and Utilization*, Sage, London

Laskin, E. and Gardner, H. (1996) *Leading Minds*, Basic Books

Leadbeater, C. (2000) *Living on Thin Air*, Penguin, London

Masie, E. Knowledge Management: Training's New Umbrella, can be found on http:// www.masie.com/articles/knowl.htm

Margerison, C. and McCann, D. (1990) *Team Management – Practical New Approaches*, Management Books 2000, Oxfordshire

McFadzean, E. (1997) 'Enhancing Creative Productivity in Groups' Working Paper Series, HWP 9711, Henley Management College, Henley

Mohrman, S. and Finegold, D. (2000) 'Strategies for the Knowledge Economy: From Rhetoric to Reality', Korn Ferry International in Conjunction with The Center for Effective Organisations, Marshall School of Business, University of Southern California

Moss Kanter, R. (2001) *Evolve! – Succeeding in the Digital Culture of Tomorrow*, Harvard Business School Press, New York

Negroponte, N. (1995) *Being Digital*, Hodder & Stoughton, London

Nonaka, I. and Takeuchi, H. (1995) *The Knowledge-Creating Company: How Japanese Companies Create the Dynamics of Innovation*, Oxford University Press, London

Ohmae, K. (1995) *The End of the Nation State*, HarperCollins, London

Ohmae, K. (2000) *The Invisible Continent – Four Strategic Imperatives of the New Economy*, Nicholas Brearley, London

Oldfield, C. (2000) 'UK plans to lure skilled immigrants', *Sunday Times*, 30 April, p. 3

Orton, P.Z. (1995) 'Effects of Story Strength Elements and Interactivity on Audience Interest in and Liking of Story', Dissertation, Department of Communication, Stanford University

Porter, M. (1985) *Competitive Advantage – Creating and Sustaining Superior Performance*, Free Press, New York

Probst, G., Raub, S. and Romhardt, K. (1998) *Wissen Managen – Wie Unternehmen ihre wertvollste Ressource optimal nutzen* (2nd edn), Faz, Frankfurt

Rajan, A. and Eupen, P.V. (1994) *Winning People*, Create, Tunbridge Wells

Rajan, A. and Eupen, P.V. (1998) *Tomorrow's People*, Create, Tunbridge Wells

Rajan, A., Lank, E. and Chapple, K. (1999) *Good Practices in Knowledge Creation and Exchange*, Create, Tunbridge Wells

Reason, P. (1994) (ed.) *Participation in Human Enquiry*, Sage, London

Redlich, F., MD. (2000) *Hitler – Diagnosis of a Destructive Prophet*, Oxford University Press, Oxford.

Roll, E. (1992) *A History of Economic Thought*, 5th edn, Faber and Faber, London

Roos, J., Roos, G., Dragonetti, N.C. and Edvinsson, L. (1997) *Intellectual Capital – Navigating the New Business Landscape*, Macmillan Business, Basingstoke – now Palgrave

Rushe, D. (2000) 'Winners and losers in the drive to add value', *Sunday Times* 24 September, section 3, p. 10

Scarbrough, H. and Swan, J. (eds) (1999) 'Case Studies in Knowledge Management', Institute of Personnel and Development, London

Scarbrough, H., Swan, J. and Preston, J. (1999) 'Knowledge Management – A Literature Review', Institute of Personnel and Development, London

Schein, E.H. (1997) 'Empowerment, Coercive Persuasion and Organisational Learning: Do they connect?' Working Paper Series HWP 9718, Henley Management College, Henley

Schein, E.H. (1997a) *Organisational Culture and Leadership*, 2nd edn, Jossey-Bass Business and Management Series, New York

Sheina, M. (1999) *Knowledge Management: Building the Collaborative Enterprise*, Ovum, London

Silver, M.D.K. (1998) *e-shock 2000*, Macmillan Business, Basingstoke – now Palgrave

Skyrme, D. (1997) 'Measuring the Value of Knowledge – Metrics for the Knowledge Based Business', Business Intelligence, London

Smith, A. (1970) *The Wealth of Nations*, Penguin, Harmondsworth

Snowden, D.J. (2000a) 'Story telling: an old skill in a new context', *Business Information Review*

Snowden, D.J. (2000b) 'The ASHEN model: an enabler of action', *Knowledge Management*, **3**(7)

Stewart, A. (1998) 'The cunning plots of leadership', *Fortune*, 7 September

Stewart, T.A. (1997) *Intellectual Capital – The New Wealth of Organisations*, Doubleday, New York

Taylor, C. (2000) An EC Employment Conference Report, *People Management*, 23 November

The Journal of Brand Management', **7**(4), March 2000, Henry Stewart Publications, London

Thompson, K. and Bates, T. (1988) *Information Technology in Education and Training*, Open University Press, Milton Keynes

Touraine, A. (1969) *La Societé Post-industrielle*, Denoel, Paris

Trompenaars, F. and Hampden-Turner, C. (1993) *The Seven Cultures of Capitalism*, Doubleday, New York

Von Krogh, G., Ichijo, K. and Nonaka, I. (2000) *Enabling Knowledge Creation – How to Unlock the Mystery of Tacit Knowledge and Release the Power of Innovation*, Oxford University Press, Oxford

Ware, L. and Fern, B. (1997/2000) *The Challenge of Retaining Top Talent: The Workforce Attrition Crisis*, www.itsinc.net/retention-research.htm

Weiner, E. and Brown, A. (1997) *Insider's Guide to the Future*, Boardroom Inc.

World Bank (1998) World Development Report

Radio

Doole, C. (2000) BBC World Service, 3 May 0100 bst 'United Nations Report on Central and Eastern Europe', Geneva

Cassette Recordings

Greenes, K. (1999) 'Knowledge Management & Organisational Learning Conference' (Keynote Address), Chop em out, London

Snowden, D. (2000) 'Knowledge Management: Turning Your Intangible Assets To Business Advantage' MBA Speaker's Evening, University of Bath

Index